P9-DHK-063

SUSANNA FOO FRESH INSPIRATION

SUSANNA FOO FRESH INSPIRATION

New Approaches to Chinese Cuisine

————————( )————————

SUSANNA FOO

with

HERMIE KRANZDORF

PHOTOGRAPHS BY TINA RUPP

Houghton Mifflin Company
Boston   New York
2005

Copyright © 2005 by Susanna Foo
Photographs copyright © 2005 by Tina Rupp
All rights reserved

For information about permission to
reproduce selections from this book, write to
Permissions, Houghton Mifflin Company,
215 Park Avenue South,
New York, New York 10003.

Visit our Web site:
www.houghtonmifflinbooks.com.

LIBRARY OF CONGRESS
CATALOGING-IN-PUBLICATION DATA

Foo, Susanna.
  Susanna Foo fresh inspiration : new approaches
to Chinese cuisine / Susanna Foo with Hermie
Kranzdorf ; photographs by Tina Rupp.
      p. cm.
  Includes index.
  ISBN-13: 978-0-618-39330-5
  ISBN-10: 0-618-39330-7
  1. Cookery, Chinese. I. Title: Fresh inspiration.
II. Kranzdorf, Hermine. III. Title.
  TX724.5.C5F594 2005
  641.5951—dc22   2005009225

Book design by Anne Chalmers
Typefaces: Perpetua, Meta
Food styling by Toni Brogan
Prop styling by Gerri Williams

Printed in China

C&C 10 9 8 7 6 5 4 3 2 1

To my father,

Lieutenant General Yang Z. Su,

who taught me
honesty, drive, and
passion for food and life

Acknowledgments

Writing this second book seemed easier than writing the first, *Susanna Foo Chinese Cuisine,* because all the wonderful friends who worked on that one helped me with this one.

First and foremost, I would like to thank Hermie Kranzdorf, my dearest friend for over twenty years, for her devotion to this book, her passion for food and cooking, and her endless rewriting and testing of recipes.

Thank you to my editor, Rux Martin, who believed in me and helped make the first book successful, for her precise editing and her drive for perfection. She put her heart and soul into this book. Thanks also to my agent, Judith Weber, whose excellent guidance I can always count on and who comforts me whenever I have doubts.

Thanks to my loyal kitchen team for their support and for their help in developing recipes during the past twenty-six years. To my chefs, Joe Zhou and Anne Coll, thank you for helping to create and refine many of these dishes. Thanks to Marie Stecher for her help. And thanks to my husband, E-Hsin, and my two sons, Gabriel and Jimmy, who love to try new dishes.

Contents

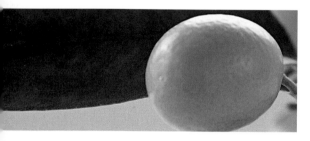

Introduction

When I finished my first cookbook nearly a decade ago, I was convinced I would never write another. That book was drawn from my experiences in China, where I grew up, and the United States, where I raised a family and later embarked on a career as a chef. My cooking then focused on faithfully re-creating the flavors I remembered from China, using ingredients available in America. I thought I'd said it all.

But with the recent explosion of fresh produce and the increased availability of ethnic ingredients, my culinary horizons suddenly expanded, and my style of cooking changed radically. After twenty-five years as a restaurateur and a lifetime as a home cook, I firmly believe that freshness is the single most important quality of any dish. Although being Chinese defines who I am and the way in which I think about food, I refuse to be limited by a single tradition: my primary goal is to preserve the natural flavor and integrity of the ingredients. Cooking this way has resulted in an unexpected bonus: my food is even simpler to prepare than before.

As a Chinese housewife, I used standard Chinese ingredients and cooking techniques. Although northern China, where I spent the first part of my life, has a cold climate and a brief growing season, I had never tasted canned or frozen food before I came to this country. Our meals featured lots of root vegetables, such as sweet potatoes, pumpkins, daikon, and turnips, along with a variety of onions, scallions, leeks, and cabbages. Later my family moved to Kaohsiung, a southern seaport city in Taiwan, where the climate is similar to that of Florida. It was a paradise of tropical fruits and vegetables, and fresh seafood was everywhere. Even our soy sauce was fresh, for it came from big covered urns in the back yard of my best friend's family's three-acre home. I spent many happy hours shopping in the open markets with my mother.

When I came to the United States, a little more than thirty years ago, I was surprised to find that Chinese food here was often made with such things as canned bamboo shoots, canned water chestnuts, and canned baby corn. Even traditional ingredients like black vinegar and Shaoxing wine tasted very different from the ones I remembered. Gradually I began to experiment, incorporating the fresh vegetables and herbs that were available here, many of which I had never tasted in China. Visitors to my kitchen often question my use of such "unconventional" vegetables as artichokes (they taste remarkably like fresh bamboo shoots when they're lightly cooked), rhubarb, Brussels sprouts, beets, parsnips, and celery root.

My daily trips to the local markets over the past twenty years have taught me much about the ever-increasing variety of produce. At the same time, more and more Asian supermarkets have opened, providing a larger range of products from which to choose. My travels have been an equally important influence on my cooking. Chinese cuisine continues to fascinate me, and I return often to China and Taiwan to cook alongside master chefs. I've visited other Asian countries to learn about local ingredients and cooking styles.

My recipes blend the techniques of both East and West. I use French methods of making sauces and stocks, for example, and roasting and baking, cooking methods that never developed in China. And all of my food has been deeply influenced by the simple cooking of Mediterranean countries, especially Spain and Italy.

This book, the result of all my travels and experiences, illustrates how the extraordinary produce in this country can be approached in a new and fresh way and how regional and ethnic ingredients can be combined in unique culinary interpretations. The result is not traditional Chinese cuisine but a style of cooking that is lighter, fresher, easier, and purely my own — and now yours.

Three of My Favorite Pieces of Equipment

Good food is about top-quality ingredients, not fancy equipment. Although all the recipes in this book can be made using ordinary kitchen tools, these three will make your cooking much easier.

A JAPANESE BENRINER — With a Benriner, which is similar to the slicer known as a mandoline, you'll be able to slice vegetables uniformly thin, much thinner than with a food processor or a chef's knife, and it's easier to use. Small, easily stored, and with razor-sharp blades, these sell for about $25. When you need to julienne hard root vegetables, such as potatoes or carrots, you can do it on the Benriner or thinly slice them and then cut them into julienne with a sharp knife. You can even use the Benriner to cut frozen meat into paper-thin slices for beef carpaccio (page 31) or soups.

A FLAT-BOTTOMED WOK — When I came to the United States in 1968, the woks being manufactured were not at all practical for American kitchens. Made of carbon steel and with rounded bottoms, they were designed for Chinese stoves, which are recessed so the wok sits directly in the fire. These woks were also hard to clean and had to be well seasoned before using and thoroughly dried afterward, or they would rust.

Now flat-bottomed woks are widely available. This kind of wok is really a multipurpose pan that can be used for stir-frying, sautéing, poaching, deep-frying, and pan-searing, just as you would use a skillet. The wok's flat bottom and high flared sides enable you to toss quantities of ingredients vigorously without splashing food or oil all over the stove. A 14-inch nonstick wok at least 3 inches deep is the most useful size. The wok should be made of a heavy stainless heat-conductive metal, such as anodized aluminum or cast iron. Having a nonstick wok means that you'll use less oil and food won't stick to the bottom of the pan. I prefer a wok that has one long handle and a small "helper" handle on the opposite side, which makes it easier to lift the pan. You can't go wrong with an excellent brand: All-Clad, Calphalon, and Le Creuset all make very good woks. (See page xv for tips on cooking with a wok.)

A MICROPLANE GRATER — Patterned after a woodworking tool called a rasp, the microplane grater is made of stainless steel and looks somewhat like a long metal ruler with a handle and rows of tiny sharp teeth. The microplane accomplishes the chore of removing the zest from citrus, shaving it away in seconds without taking any of the bitter white pith, and finely grating fresh ginger effortlessly, leaving the rough strands of fiber behind. It's also good for grating cheese. As sharp as the cutting edges are, they're angled in such a way that you're unlikely to grate yourself. This invaluable tool costs about $12 to $14.

Stir-Frying Principles

1. Always start with a clean wok or deep skillet and fresh oil: these are significant factors in making any dish properly. Prepare all your ingredients ahead of time and place them near the stove for easy access.

2. First add the aromatics, such as garlic, shallots, onions, and peppers. Traditional recipes instruct you to heat the oil until it is very hot, but this will almost invariably result in burning the aromatics, giving an acrid flavor to the dish. Instead, add the oil to a *cold* wok, not one that has been preheated, and heat just until the oil is hot but not smoking. Then add the aromatics and cook, stirring, until they are soft and fragrant, usually only about 30 seconds. Use your sense of smell to make sure they have cooked enough before you add other ingredients.

3. Because the bottom of a wok gets hotter than the sides, ingredients should be cooked in the bottom and tossed to the sides after they have been seared. Constant motion will ensure that the ingredients will be perfectly cooked.

4. When you are stir-frying skinned chicken, shelled shrimp, lobster meat, or fish, the oil should be warm (about 250 degrees), not extremely hot. Cooked at this low temperature, chicken will become tender, velvety, and juicy. Very hot oil is likely to overcook chicken and fish, making them dry and tough. High heat will also shrink shrimp and lobster.

5. Poultry with the skin on and shrimp in the shell should be cooked at a higher temperature, about 375 degrees. When searing fish or chicken or other poultry, first place it skin side down in the oil and cook until browned, then turn to sear the other side. The fatty skin helps protect the flesh and keep it moist — and the skin will become crisp, well browned, and flavorful. Leaving the shells on shrimp when stir-frying ensures that they will be tenderer and more flavorful.

6. To sear meat, heat the oil to 375 to 400 degrees. Sear the meat quickly, tossing, so it remains pink and juicy inside. Do not overcrowd the wok, or the meat will not brown properly; sear it in two or three batches if necessary.

Dim Sum and First Courses

Wild Mushroom Dumplings with Mushroom Sauce

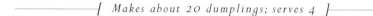

Cooked mushrooms combined with cellophane noodles and Parmesan cheese make a light and airy stuffing for these dumplings. In northern China, cooked noodles are often mixed into stuffings for dumplings or flatbreads or into meatballs. Here the noodles not only lighten the stuffing but also absorb any excess liquid, which could cause the dumplings to break open during cooking. I prefer chanterelle mushrooms for the sauce because they have a delicate nutty flavor and a beautiful golden yellow color, but you can substitute fresh shiitakes.

Chanterelles are in season from August through December. They come from the Pacific Northwest or are imported from France and can be found in specialty food stores and even some supermarkets. Choose mushrooms that are plump and spongy; avoid any with broken or shriveled caps. Don't wash them, since they will absorb too much water. Instead, use a soft brush to clean off the dirt. I cook these mushrooms briefly so they retain their color and texture.

[Makes about 20 dumplings; serves 4]

4	large portobello mushrooms, stemmed
8	ounces shiitake mushrooms, stemmed
3	tablespoons extra-virgin olive oil
4	large shallots, finely chopped
1	1.5- to 1.7-ounce package thin cellophane noodles or ½ cup fresh bread crumbs
2	tablespoons finely chopped fresh tarragon or cilantro
1	tablespoon toasted sesame oil
1	teaspoon truffle oil
¼	cup freshly grated Parmesan cheese
½	teaspoon kosher salt, or more to taste
	Freshly ground pepper
	Cornstarch for dusting
20	dumpling skins (gyoza)

MUSHROOM SAUCE

3	tablespoons extra-virgin olive oil
1	shallot, finely chopped
1	scallion, trimmed and chopped
8	ounces chanterelle or shiitake mushrooms, sliced
1	teaspoon soy sauce
¼	cup Mushroom Stock (page 56) or chicken stock Kosher salt and freshly ground pepper
1	teaspoon truffle oil (optional)
1	tablespoon aged balsamic vinegar (optional)

Using a teaspoon, gently scoop out the brownish black gills from the portobello mushrooms and discard. Using damp paper towels, wipe both kinds of mushrooms clean.

Cut the shiitakes and portobellos into 1-inch dice. In several batches, coarsely chop in a food processor, filling the processor only one-third full; be careful not to overprocess. Transfer to a large bowl.

Heat the olive oil in a large skillet over medium heat. Add the shallots and cook, stirring, until softened. Add the chopped mushrooms, stir, and reduce the heat to low. Cook until all the liquid from the mushrooms has evaporated and they are dry, about 30 minutes, stirring often to prevent them from sticking. Remove from the heat and cool.

Meanwhile, if using cellophane noodles, soak them in a

Dumpling Skins

Dumpling skins (*gyoza* is the Japanese name) are 3½-inch rounds of fresh flour-and-water dough; they are thicker than wonton wrappers. They are available fresh or frozen in Asian markets and large supermarkets. I like the Twin Dragon brand. They are sturdier than many other brands and don't break during cooking; they also retain some bite. They are good with the meaty-textured mushrooms in this filling or with meat fillings or with the mashed-potato filling on page 12, where the extra body they provide is welcome.

bowl of warm water for 10 minutes. Bring a pot of water to a boil. Drain the soaked noodles in a large sieve, then pour them, stirring, into the boiling water. Cook until the noodles turn transparent, about 2 minutes. Immediately drain and plunge into a bowl of cold water to stop the cooking; drain well. Finely chop enough of the noodles to measure ½ cup. (Reserve any remaining noodles for another use, if desired.)

Add the tarragon or cilantro, sesame oil, and truffle oil to the mushrooms and mix well. Add the chopped noodles or bread crumbs, Parmesan cheese, salt, and pepper to taste and stir to combine well. If not using immediately, cover tightly with a layer of wet paper towels, then plastic wrap, and set aside until ready to fill the dumplings. *The filling can be made 1 day ahead and refrigerated, well covered.*

Line a baking sheet with parchment or waxed paper and dust with cornstarch. Place about 1 tablespoon of the stuffing in the center of each dumpling skin. Moisten the edges with cold water, then fold over to form a half-moon shape. Pinch the edges together with your fingers, forcing out the air and sealing well. Then moisten the two ends with water and bring them together, curling them around your finger and pressing them together to form a ring. Transfer the dumplings to the baking sheet.

TO MAKE THE SAUCE: Heat the olive oil over medium heat in a medium saucepan. Add the shallot and scallion and cook for 1 to 2 minutes, or until soft. Turn the heat to high, add the mushrooms, and stir until they are just coated with oil. Add the soy sauce and stock and cook until the mushrooms soften, about 1 minute. Remove from the heat and add salt and pepper to taste. Cover to keep warm.

MEANWHILE, COOK THE DUMPLINGS: Line a baking sheet with paper towels. Bring a large pot of water to a boil and add the dumplings. When the water returns to a boil, add ½ cup cold water. Return to the boil and cook until the dumplings float to the surface. Remove with a slotted spoon, draining well, and place on the towel-lined baking sheet. *The dumplings can be cooked up to 2 hours in advance. Reheat in a microwave oven or lightly panfry before serving. (Do not boil again.)*

TO SERVE: Reheat the sauce if necessary. Place 5 dumplings on each of four warmed plates. Spoon the sauce around the dumplings. Sprinkle with the truffle oil and balsamic vinegar, if desired.

TO FREEZE THE DUMPLINGS: Spread them out on a flat tray or baking sheet lined with plastic wrap, cover loosely with plastic wrap, and freeze for 1 hour. Transfer them to a heavy-duty zipper-lock bag, seal the bag, pressing out any excess air, and return to the freezer. *The dumplings can be frozen for up to 3 months.* Remove as many as you want to cook, and thaw at room temperature before cooking.

Crispy Tuna Spring Rolls with Fresh Herb Salad

Creating contrasts in a dish — soft and crisp, hot and cold — is a classical Chinese technique. Here the hot, crisp wrappers envelop cold, soft tuna.

Choose sashimi-quality tuna for this recipe. It should be very fresh and deep red.

If you want to be really fancy, garnish the plates with any or all of the following: Pickled Baby Beets with Green Peppercorns (page 274), Cucumber Mint Relish (page 278), and/or Mango-Kumquat Relish (page 283).

Serves 6

1¼	pounds sashimi-quality tuna, about 1 inch thick
¼	teaspoon kosher salt
	Freshly ground pepper
1	large carrot
8	ounces spinach, stemmed and washed
1	cup fresh cilantro leaves
6	Shanghai-style spring roll wrappers
1	large egg yolk, lightly beaten

4	cups soybean oil or corn oil for deep-frying
	Wasabi Crème Fraîche (recipe follows)
½	cup pickled ginger (without added food coloring)
	Fresh mild herbs or baby greens (any or all of the following: basil, arugula, watercress, cilantro, chives)
	Honey Soy Glaze (recipe follows)

Cut the tuna into 6 strips, each about 3½ inches long and 1 inch thick. Mix the salt and pepper to taste in a small bowl. Rub the mixture evenly over the pieces of tuna.

Peel the carrot and cut into 3-inch lengths. Using a Japanese Benriner, mandoline, or sharp knife, cut the carrot into paper-thin slices; you need a total of 12 slices.

In a medium saucepan, cook the carrot in boiling salted water for 1 minute. Immediately remove from the water and transfer to a bowl of ice water to stop the cooking. Drain, dry with paper towels, cover, and refrigerate. Repeat with the spinach and then the cilantro, squeezing out any excess water. Refrigerate, covered.

Lay 1 spring roll wrapper on a flat surface with a point facing you. Place 2 slices of carrot and a little spinach crosswise on the wrapper, about one third of the way from the top. Top with 1 piece of tuna and some cilantro. Fold the point farthest from you down and over to cover the filling, then fold in the left and right sides tightly, brush the bottom edges with a little of the egg yolk, and roll up tightly to seal. Repeat with the remaining wrappers and filling ingredients.

Heat the oil to 375 degrees. Add the spring rolls and fry until the wrappers are firm, 1 to 2 minutes. Do not overcook. Drain on paper towels.

To serve, cut the spring rolls diagonally in half and place in the center of six plates. Spoon 2 tablespoons of the crème fraîche around the spring rolls, mound a little of the pickled ginger next to each one, and garnish with the herbs or baby greens. Drizzle some of the glaze around the rolls and serve.

Shanghai-Style Spring Roll Wrappers

Made from a flour and water batter, spring roll wrappers are nearly transparent 6- to 7-inch-square sheets that are much like very thin crepes. Don't confuse these with egg roll wrappers; they are much more delicate and crisp. The brand I prefer is TYJ Spring Roll Pastry from Singapore; the sheets are especially crisp and don't absorb much oil when fried. ⟳ The wrappers are sold frozen in Asian markets in plastic packages of about 25 . They break easily, so it's useful to keep an extra pack at hand as you work. Unused wrappers can be rewrapped tightly and kept in the freezer for 6 months; defrost at room temperature.

Wasabi Crème Fraîche

—————— [*Makes about ¾ cup*] ——————

I use crème fraîche for this recipe, but you can substitute sour cream. Feel free to tone down the wasabi to your taste.

- 2 tablespoons wasabi powder
- 2 tablespoons rice wine vinegar
- ½ teaspoon kosher salt
- ½ cup crème fraîche

In a small bowl, combine the wasabi powder with 2 tablespoons cold water and slowly mix until it becomes a smooth, thick paste. Add the vinegar and salt and mix well. Cover and set aside for about 10 minutes, until the flavors blend.

Add the crème fraîche and mix gently until well blended. *The sauce will keep, covered and refrigerated, for 1 week.*

Wasabi

Wasabi, the Japanese version of horseradish, is the rhizome of an Asian plant. Available as a light green paste or powder (fresh wasabi is hard to find in this country), it has a sharp, pungent flavor. Look for it in Asian markets and some large supermarkets. 🌀 I prefer the powdered kind, because it is the most potent. It comes in 1- to 4-ounce tins. Buy in small quantities; once the tin is opened, the wasabi's flavor will fade. When you are ready to use it, mix with water and let sit for 10 minutes or more to develop its flavor, as you would with dried mustard powder. 🌀 Wasabi paste is packaged in 1.2-ounce tubes and has the advantage of convenience. Refrigerate once opened. 🌀 Pure wasabi can be expensive, but it is worth the price. I buy only powdered wasabi made by Japanese companies.

Honey Soy Glaze

[Makes about ½ cup]

This glaze is also good drizzled over Cantonese Egg Foo Yung (page 234) or almost any plain grilled fish.

2	tablespoons soybean oil or corn oil
1	shallot, minced
1	garlic clove, minced
1	teaspoon crushed red pepper flakes
¼	cup sake or dry white wine
¼	cup soy sauce
2	tablespoons honey
2	tablespoons balsamic vinegar or fresh lemon juice
½	teaspoon cornstarch, mixed with 1 tablespoon water

Heat the oil in a small skillet over high heat. Add the shallot, garlic, and red pepper flakes and cook until soft, 1 to 2 minutes. Turn the heat to low, add the sake or wine, stir, and cook for 1 minute.

Add the soy sauce, honey, and vinegar or lemon juice. Stir in the cornstarch mixture and simmer until the sauce is thick, 8 to 10 minutes. Strain and discard the solids; cool.

Store in a squeeze bottle or covered container. *The sauce will keep for 1 to 2 weeks at room temperature or for up to 1 month refrigerated.*

Lobster Ravioli with Soybean Puree and Coconut Lobster Sauce

— (✿) —

Delicate in texture and color, these dumplings are filled with chopped shrimp and lobster bound together and lightened by beaten egg whites. Undercooking the lobster meat ensures that it will stay tender — it finishes cooking when the dumplings are panfried.

Thin wonton wrappers are essential (see page 9). I use a cookie cutter to make rounds and then sandwich the filling between them, so there are no tough, doughy edges. The soybean puree has a mild, fresh flavor, and the coconut lobster sauce adds richness.

Always buy live lobsters (still in the tank) and cook them the same day you bring them home. Hard-shelled lobsters are best because they are the meatiest. To test, press hard on the lobster's head with your fingers; the shell should be very firm. For a more lavish presentation, buy extra shelled lobster meat, and garnish each portion with a whole or half claw.

—[*Serves 6*]—

32–40	thin wonton wrappers
1	1½-pound live lobster
4	ounces large shrimp (15–20 count), peeled and deveined
1	tablespoon lightly beaten egg white
1	tablespoon heavy cream
1	tablespoon vodka
½	teaspoon toasted sesame oil
½	teaspoon kosher salt

½	teaspoon freshly ground white pepper
3	tablespoons minced scallions (white part only)
	Cornstarch for dusting
2	tablespoons soybean oil or corn oil, or more if needed
	Soybean Puree (recipe follows)
	Coconut Lobster Sauce (recipe follows)
	Fresh cilantro sprigs for garnish

Cut the wonton wrappers into rounds with a 3-inch round cookie cutter.

Fill a large deep pot with water and bring to a boil over high heat. Plunge the whole lobster into the boiling water, cover, and cook for 4 minutes. Remove, drain, and plunge into a bowl of ice water to stop the cooking. Drain and cool.

When cool, twist off the lobster claws and the tail; reserve the body for the sauce. Using kitchen shears, cut through the shell down the length of the tail, and remove the meat. Remove the vein on top of the tail and discard. Crack the knuckles and remove the meat. Thinly slice the meat from the tail and knuckles and place on a plate. Slice the claws and reserve for garnish, and place on the plate. Cover and refrigerate.

Wash the lobster body under cold water. Crush it, and reserve it for the sauce.

TO MAKE THE RAVIOLI: Place the shrimp in a food processor and coarsely chop. Transfer to a large bowl. Mix in the egg white and cream, and then fold in the vodka, sesame oil, salt, and white pepper. Add the scallions and mix well. Gently fold in the sliced lobster meat. *The filling can be made 3 to 4 hours ahead, covered, and refrigerated.*

Line a baking sheet with a piece of parchment or waxed paper and dust with cornstarch. Moisten the edges of a dumpling wrapper with a little water, then spoon a generous tablespoon of stuffing onto the middle. Place another wrapper on top and seal tightly by pressing the edges together

with your fingers, forcing out the excess air. Place the ravioli on the baking sheet, and repeat with the remaining wrappers and filling. *The ravioli can be made in advance and refrigerated, covered, overnight. They can also be frozen for up to 3 months; see page 3 for directions on freezing.*

TO COOK THE RAVIOLI: Preheat the oven to 325 degrees. Heat 1 tablespoon of the oil in a large nonstick skillet. Place only as many dumplings as will fit in a single layer in the pan and pour in ¼ cup cold water. Turn the heat to medium, cover, and cook for about 4 minutes, until the water has evaporated and the bottoms of the ravioli are crisp and golden. Transfer to a baking sheet and keep warm in the preheated oven while you cook the remaining ravioli. Wipe the skillet clean with paper towels and add another tablespoon of oil between batches.

TO SERVE: Spoon the soybean puree into the center of each of six serving plates. Place 3 ravioli on top and spoon the coconut lobster sauce around the puree. Top each with a piece of cold lobster claw and decorate with a sprig of cilantro. If you prefer, you can reheat the lobster claw in a little of the sauce before serving.

SIMPLE VARIATION

NOTE: You can also boil the ravioli. Add half of the dumplings and 1 tablespoon soybean or corn oil to a large pot of boiling water (the oil gives the ravioli a sheen and helps keep them from sticking together). Add ½ cup cold water. As soon as the water returns to a boil, remove the ravioli with a slotted spoon and place in a single layer on a tray or baking sheet lined with waxed or parchment paper to drain. Cook and drain the remaining ravioli. Transfer to a heated platter for serving.

Wonton Wrappers

Good Chinese wontons are made with very thin wrappers and are very delicate. To choose thin wrappers, go by the number in the package: there should be at least 75 and as many as 120 wrappers per pound. 🌸 Wonton wrappers come in 4- to 4½-inch squares. They can be made of simply flour and water or in the Cantonese style, with egg added, in which case they will be golden yellow. Either kind is fine to use. 🌸 Today many different brands of fresh Chinese, Korean, and Japanese wrappers are available. You can find them in Asian markets and the produce section of large supermarkets. The wrappers are also sold frozen; defrost them overnight in the refrigerator before using.

Fresh Green Soybeans (Edamame)

The Chinese call them "fuzz beans" because they have hairy seedpods. The Japanese call them edamame. When I called for soybeans in my first cookbook back in 1996, very few Americans had heard of them. Now, happily, soybeans have become quite popular, thanks to Japanese restaurants, which serve them as appetizers, still in the pod. While it's hard to find fresh soybeans in the market, they are well worth seeking out when they are in season (they are usually harvested in July and August), because they keep their firm texture without becoming mushy. ✿ Frozen soybeans are widely available in health food stores and, increasingly, supermarkets as well as Asian grocery stores. They normally come in 1-pound plastic bags, either in the pod or shelled. Shelled beans are most convenient for this recipe. ✿ Fresh or frozen soybeans must be peeled, because the tough outer skins will separate from the beans during cooking and are unpleasant to eat.

Soybean Puree

———{ *Makes about ¾ cup* }———

This silky bright green puree pairs perfectly with the lobster, and it lends beauty to the finished plate.

½	cup shelled fresh or frozen soybeans (edamame; peeled fava beans or peas can be substituted)
2	tablespoons extra-virgin olive oil
1	garlic clove, thinly sliced
2	shallots, thinly sliced
¼	cup dry white wine
1	cup chicken stock or Lobster Stock (page 57)
2	tablespoons coarsely chopped fresh cilantro
½	teaspoon kosher salt
¼	teaspoon freshly ground white pepper

If using fresh soybeans, plunge into a pot of boiling water and cook for 3 minutes over high heat to loosen the skins. Drain well and cool.

Squeeze the soybeans with your fingers and peel off and discard the skins. Place in a bowl. If using frozen soybeans, thaw, then place in a bowl of cold water and let stand for 10 minutes to loosen the skins, then drain and peel.

Heat the oil in a small saucepan over high heat. Add the garlic and shallots and cook until soft and fragrant, about 1 minute. Add the white wine, bring to a boil, and cook for 2 minutes. Add the stock and bring to a boil, then turn the heat to medium and cook until reduced by half, 6 to 8 minutes. Add the soybeans and cook for 2 minutes. Remove from the heat and cool.

Transfer the soybean mixture to a food processor or blender, add the cilantro, salt, and white pepper, and puree until smooth. *The sauce can be made ahead and frozen in a tightly sealed container for up to 1 month.*

Reheat the sauce in a microwave oven just until hot. Or reheat in a small saucepan over low heat.

Coconut Lobster Sauce

—[*Makes about ½ cup*]—

The coconut cream and ginger change the character of this sauce from French to Chinese. The cream, which is simply the solidified fat that forms at the bottom of coconut milk, contributes extra richness.

1   crushed lobster body (reserved from ravioli, page 8)

1   tablespoon soybean oil or corn oil

1   2-inch piece fresh ginger, peeled and sliced

¼   cup dry white wine

2   teaspoons tomato paste

1   cup Lobster Stock (page 57), chicken stock, or Vegetable Stock (page 56)

2   tablespoons unsweetened coconut cream (see page 77)

1   tablespoon butter
    Kosher salt and freshly ground white pepper

Place the lobster body, oil, and ginger in a medium saucepan and cook over high heat for 5 minutes, stirring frequently. Add the white wine and tomato paste and cook and stir for 3 minutes. Turn the heat to low, add the stock and coconut cream, and simmer, uncovered, for 30 minutes.

Stir in the butter and season to taste with salt and white pepper. Strain through a fine sieve. *This sauce can be made ahead and refrigerated for up to 3 days or frozen for up to 2 weeks; reheat gently before serving.*

Truffled Potato Dumplings

— (✦) —

When you bite into these piping-hot dumplings, the taste of truffles explodes in your mouth. Truffles and truffle oil give the dumplings added depth of flavor. Yukon Gold potatoes have a firm texture and a succulent, buttery taste, and they are preferable to russets for this recipe. The dumplings can be pan-fried, as for pot stickers, or deep-fried, or steamed; all three options are given below.

[Makes about 30 dumplings; serves 6]

1	pound (4–5) medium Yukon Gold potatoes, peeled and cut into quarters
2	tablespoons olive oil
4	shallots, minced (1 cup)
¼	cup dry white wine
⅓	cup milk
1	teaspoon kosher salt
2	tablespoons butter

2	teaspoons truffle oil
¼	cup minced black truffles (about 1½ ounces)
	Cornstarch for dusting
	About 30 dumpling skins (gyoza; see page 3)
2–3	tablespoons soybean oil or corn oil, if panfrying, or about 8 cups oil if deep-frying
	Blanched cabbage leaves if steaming
1	small fresh black or summer truffle, thinly shaved (optional)

Bring a large pot of water to a boil. Add the potatoes, turn the heat down to medium, and cook for 15 to 20 minutes, or until the potatoes are tender.

Meanwhile, heat the oil in a small skillet over medium heat. Add the shallots and cook for 1 minute. Pour in the white wine and cook until the shallots are soft, about 3 minutes. Add the milk and heat until warm. Stir in the salt.

Drain the hot potatoes and turn into a large bowl. Crush them gently with a fork; do not overmash — some small lumps should remain. Mix in the warm shallot-milk mixture, the butter, truffle oil, and minced truffles. Cover and cool.

Line a baking sheet with parchment or waxed paper and dust with cornstarch. Place 1 tablespoon of the potato stuffing in the center of each dumpling skin. Moisten the edges of the skin with cold water, and fold it into a half-moon shape, pressing the edges together well to seal and forcing out the excess air. Place the prepared dumplings on the baking sheet. Cover loosely and refrigerate if not using immediately. *The dumplings can be refrigerated for up to 1 day, or they can be frozen for up to 3 months; see page 3 for instructions on freezing. Let sit for 10 minutes at room temperature, just until partially thawed, before cooking; do not thaw completely.*

TO PANFRY: Heat 1 tablespoon oil in a large skillet with a tight-fitting lid over high heat until hot. Place only as many of the dumplings as will fit in the pan without touching, flat side down, add ¼ cup water, cover, lower the heat to medium, and cook for 5 minutes, or until the water is evaporated and the dumplings are golden brown and crisp on the bottom. With a slotted spoon, transfer the dumplings to a layer of paper towels to drain, then place on a baking sheet and keep warm in a 200-degree oven while you cook the remaining dumplings. Wipe the skillet clean with paper towels between batches, adding 1 tablespoon oil each time. *The dumplings can be cooked up to 2 hours in advance and kept at room temperature, loosely covered. Reheat in a 325-degree oven.*

TO DEEP-FRY: Fill a large deep saucepan with 8 cups of

Truffle Oil

Truffle oil is high-quality olive oil that has been infused with the flavor of white or black truffles. It is pungent and earthy; use it sparingly. Like any oil, it should be kept in a cool, dark place. Unopened, it will last for about 6 months; it lasts for about 3 months once it has been opened. Storing it in the refrigerator will extend its shelf life but cause it to become cloudy and partially solidify; leave it at room temperature until it liquefies. Truffle oil can be found in specialty food shops or ordered by mail (see sources, page 320).

oil and heat to 375 degrees. Add only as many dumplings as will fit without crowding and fry until the wrappers are golden brown and crisp, 1 to 2 minutes. Remove with a slotted spoon and place on a layer of paper towels to drain, then transfer to a baking sheet and keep warm in a 325-degree oven while you fry the remaining dumplings.

TO STEAM: Place the dumplings in a single layer on a steamer rack lined with blanched cabbage leaves to keep them from sticking to the rack. Several baskets can be stacked in the steamer at one time. Line each with a single layer of blanched cabbage leaves. Make sure the dumplings do not touch each other, or they will stick together. Fill the bottom of the steamer with water and bring to a boil. Add steamer rack of dumplings, cover, and cook over high heat for 7 to 8 minutes, until the filling is thoroughly cooked.

TO SERVE: Place 4 or 5 dumplings on each plate and top with the shaved truffle, if desired.

Citrus-Cured Salmon

You can serve slices of this cured salmon as an hors d'oeuvre in any number of ways. Curl thin slices into flowerlike whorls and serve them on their own. Or moisten them with vinaigrette, add a dab of Wasabi Crème Fraîche, and serve with toast points. Or top them with crème fraîche and osetra or beluga caviar or with red onions and chives, or serve them with Korean Pancakes (page 19) or Chinese Chive Pancakes (page 16). I also like the salmon for lunch or breakfast.

In the summertime, when wild salmon is in season, I use king or sockeye salmon for this recipe. Pacific salmon is richer, fattier, and more flavorful than the more common farmed Atlantic salmon, and the flesh has a beautiful deep orange color.

Because this dish takes time to make and is so versatile, the quantities here are generous.

[Serves 16 to 24]

3	pounds center-cut salmon fillet, skin left on, pinbones removed
½	cup sugar
½	cup kosher salt
	Grated zest of 3 lemons
	Grated zest of 3 limes
	Grated zest of 3 oranges
1	tablespoon grated peeled fresh ginger
2	tablespoons finely chopped fresh cilantro stems
2	tablespoons Pernod or vodka

FOR SERVING

Citrus Vinaigrette (page 68) or juice of 1 lime

Chopped fresh chives

Curly cress, mâche, or watercress for garnish (optional)

Wasabi Crème Fraîche (page 6)

Toast points

Rinse and dry the salmon. Make shallow diagonal slashes in the skin of the salmon, being careful not to cut into the flesh.

Combine the sugar and salt in a small bowl and mix well. Spread half the salt-sugar mixture evenly over the bottom of a platter with a deep rim, just large enough to hold the salmon. Lay the salmon skin side down on the mixture.

Put the zests in a small bowl. Rinse the grated ginger in a strainer under cold water, and drain well. Mix the ginger and cilantro into the zests.

Spoon the Pernod or vodka over the salmon and spread the remaining salt-sugar mixture evenly over it. Spread the zest mixture on top and press down so the zest adheres to the salmon. Cover tightly with plastic wrap and refrigerate for 48 hours.

Using a small spoon, scrape off the citrus topping and discard. Using a very sharp knife, thinly slice the salmon across the grain and on a sharp diagonal, cutting the flesh away from the skin.

Curl the slices of salmon into flower shapes and place 2 to 4 on each serving plate. Spoon over the vinaigrette or lime juice, sprinkle with chopped chives, and decorate with a few leaves of greens, if using. Top with a dab of the crème fraîche. Serve with toast points. *Leftover salmon will keep in the refrigerator for up to 1 week. Do not slice it until ready to serve.*

Salmon Tartare

The first few slices from the cured salmon are usually too small and uneven to serve attractively. Rather than waste them (and any other slices that don't look right), finely chop them, using a cleaver or a chef's knife, and use them for salmon tartare.

Pile a tablespoon or so of the minced salmon on top of toasted bread rounds or Melba toast, garnish each with a dollop of crème fraîche, and add a small sprig of fresh cilantro or parsley. Pass them on a platter as an appetizer.

Chinese Chive Pancakes

Cooked cellophane noodles give these pancakes a delicate texture. The noodles must be both soaked and boiled to soften them properly for this recipe. Serve with Watercress Salad (page 65) or with sliced smoked salmon or Citrus-Cured Salmon (page 14), a dollop of crème fraîche, and perhaps caviar.

Makes 30 pancakes; serves 10

1 skein (1–2 ounces) thin cellophane noodles	½ cup chopped Chinese flowering chives or scallion greens
3 large eggs	⅓ cup all-purpose flour
1 cup finely chopped fresh corn, preferably white (about 2 ears)	½ teaspoon kosher salt
	3 tablespoons soybean oil or corn oil, or more as needed

Soak the noodles in a medium bowl of cold water for 10 minutes. Drain the noodles in a large sieve, then pour them, stirring, into a medium saucepan of boiling water. Immediately drain the noodles in the sieve and plunge into a bowl of ice water to stop the cooking. Drain well. Finely chop enough of the noodles to measure ½ cup. (Reserve any leftover noodles for another use, if desired.)

Beat the eggs in a medium bowl. Add the corn, chives or scallions, and noodles and mix well. Add the flour and salt and mix thoroughly.

Heat 1 tablespoon of the oil in a large nonstick skillet over medium-high heat. Using a tablespoon per pancake, drop the batter into the skillet; do not crowd the pan. Cook the pancakes until the bottoms are golden brown, 3 to 4 minutes. Turn the pancakes and cook until the second side is golden, 3 to 4 minutes. Drain on paper towels, then transfer to a baking sheet. Keep warm in a low oven. Repeat, adding another tablespoon of oil for each batch, until all the batter is used.

The pancakes can be made up to 1 day in advance. Arrange in a single layer on a baking sheet, cover tightly, and refrigerate. Warm the pancakes on the baking sheet in a preheated 325-degree oven for 5 to 10 minutes before serving. They can also be frozen for up to 2 months. Reheat frozen pancakes for 10 to 15 minutes.

Chinese Flowering Chives

Beginning in the spring and lasting through late fall, Chinese flowering chives make their appearance in Asian markets. Graceful and long-stemmed, thicker than regular chives, they are tipped with tight whitish buds. Once opened, the flowers are too tough and fibrous to eat. Sweeter and milder than regular chives, with a faint garlic flavor, they become very tender when cooked. If you can't find flowering chives, substitute scallion greens or finely julienned leeks, which are closest to them in flavor.

Korean Pancakes

───────────────── (✿) ─────────────────

These pancakes are not to be missed. They are a standard at Korean tables, where they are served as a first course, but they're similar to the scallion crepes I enjoyed as a child. A generous amount of cooked diced onion gives them a sensational texture: they are very moist inside. I like them spicy and don't seed the hot peppers; those with timid palates will want to.

Serve with Citrus-Cured Salmon (page 14), gravlax, or plain smoked salmon and Wasabi Crème Fraîche (page 6). Spread a thin layer of crème fraîche over each pancake, cover with about an ounce of sliced salmon, and garnish with thinly sliced red onion, chopped chives, and watercress. Serve with lemon wedges. Watercress Salad with Lime Vinaigrette (page 65) is another accompaniment.

─────────────── [*Serves 4*] ───────────────

½   cup all-purpose flour

½   cup rice flour (not sweet rice flour)

¼   teaspoon baking powder

3   large eggs, lightly beaten

¼   cup soybean oil or corn oil

3   Italian long hot peppers, stemmed, seeds removed if desired, and sliced ⅛ inch thick

1   cup diced red onion

3–4 large scallions, trimmed, thinly sliced lengthwise, then cut into 1-inch lengths (about 1 cup)

1   teaspoon kosher salt

Freshly ground pepper

Sift the flour, rice flour, and baking powder together in a large bowl. Slowly blend in ¾ cup water and the eggs, mixing until smooth. The batter will be thick. Cover and refrigerate.

Heat 2 tablespoons of the oil over medium-low heat in a large skillet. Add the hot peppers and the onion and cook until the onion is soft but not browned, 3 to 5 minutes.

Add the scallions and cook, stirring, for 1 minute. Turn off the heat and sprinkle with the salt and some pepper to taste. Cool.

Mix the pepper-onion mixture into the batter. Add a scant teaspoon of the oil to a 6-inch nonstick skillet and heat over medium heat. Using a dry measure, scoop out ½ cup of the batter and drop into the skillet, spreading it out with a spatula if necessary. Turn the heat to medium-low and cook until the pancake is golden brown and crisp on the bottom, about 2 minutes. Turn and cook until the second side is gold- en brown, about 2 minutes. Remove from the pan and keep warm in a low oven. Repeat with the remaining batter. *The pancakes can be made ahead of time, layered between sheets of plastic wrap, and refrigerated for 2 to 3 days. Remove from the plastic, place on a baking sheet, and reheat in a 350-degree oven until hot, about 10 minutes.*

Serve warm.

Rice Flour

There are two varieties of Chinese rice flour: ordinary rice flour and sweet (glutinous) rice flour. For this recipe you need the ordinary kind, which is milled from long-grain rice. Sweet rice flour is made from short-grain sweet rice and is stickier, or more glutinous, and much sweeter. Rice flour is sold in Asian markets, health food stores, and large grocery stores, usually in 1-pound bags.

Wok-Shaking Shrimp with Pink Peppercorns

This is my interpretation of one of the most popular Chinese dishes. The shrimp are fried in their shells, which keeps them tender and juicy. In the original version, they're coated with a spicy mixture of sea salt, white pepper, chopped scallions, and ginger. I prefer to use pink peppercorns, which I like because of their subtle spiciness. If pink peppercorns are unavailable, substitute green ones. At the table, peel off the shells with your fingers and pop the shrimp into your mouth.

[Serves 4]

12	jumbo shrimp (11–15 count) in their shells
½	small head romaine, tough outer leaves removed
½	cup all-purpose flour
½	cup soybean oil or corn oil
1	tablespoon pink peppercorns
1	teaspoon finely chopped garlic

1	teaspoon kosher salt or sea salt, or more to taste
3	tablespoons chopped scallions (white part only)
1	tablespoon butter
1	tablespoon citrus-flavored vodka
1	lemon, thinly sliced
1	tablespoon minced fresh flat-leaf parsley

Using a sharp knife or kitchen shears, slit the top shell of each shrimp down the back. Remove and discard the veins. Cut off the legs and discard, but leave the shells intact. Rinse the shrimp well under cold water and dry with paper towels.

Cut the romaine leaves into julienne (you should have about 1 cup) and plunge into a bowl of ice water. Lift out and dry in a salad spinner. Wrap and refrigerate until needed.

Place the flour on a large plate. Coat each shrimp well with the flour, shaking to remove any excess.

Heat the oil in a large skillet or flat-bottomed wok until it reaches 375 degrees. Add half the shrimp and fry, turning once, until they turn pink, about 2 minutes (the shrimp should still be slightly undercooked). Remove and drain on a paper towel–lined plate. Repeat with the remaining shrimp. Pour the oil into a small bowl.

Wipe out the pan with a paper towel. Spoon 1 tablespoon of the oil back into the pan; discard the rest. Add the peppercorns, garlic, and salt and cook for about 1 minute, or until the garlic is lightly golden. Add the shrimp and scallions and swirl so that the shrimp are well coated with the seasonings. Add the butter and vodka and mix well until the butter melts. Remove from the heat.

Place the romaine in the center of four serving plates. Place 3 shrimp on top of the lettuce on each plate and decorate with the sliced lemon and parsley. Place bowls on the table for the shrimp shells.

Grilled Shrimp with Avocado and Spicy Papaya Vinaigrette

Just about every house in southern Taiwan, where I grew up, had at least one papaya plant growing nearby. It grew so quickly that if you dropped some seeds into the ground, the very next year you could harvest fruit. My brothers and I always picked the ripe papayas from our own back yard — they were so sweet and mellow that they melted in our mouths. I ate them greedily until I became a teenager, when my girlfriends were convinced that papaya would make our skin turn yellow. I never touched the fruit again until I came to the United States, though I continued to dream about picking up the ripe papayas from the yard.

I hadn't thought of using papaya in a vinaigrette until I vacationed in Jamaica. The papaya-habanero dressing I had there was unbelievably spicy, but I loved its complexity and the natural sweetness the papaya brought to it. After lots of research and testing, I created a spicy papaya vinaigrette for grilled shrimp marinated in coconut milk and fresh cilantro, which makes a spectacular and colorful first course.

[Serves 4]

1	small ripe but firm papaya (about 1 pound)
2	tablespoons orange juice
12	jumbo shrimp (about 1 pound), peeled and deveined
1	teaspoon kosher salt
1	shallot, chopped
1	garlic clove, finely chopped
1	teaspoon minced peeled fresh ginger

1	tablespoon coarsely chopped fresh cilantro
¼	cup whisked unsweetened coconut milk
1	teaspoon honey
2	tablespoons soybean oil or corn oil, plus more for the grill
1	avocado (preferably a Hass avocado)
	Spicy Papaya Vinaigrette (recipe follows)
1	cup mâche, baby spinach, or arugula, washed and dried

Peel the papaya and cut in half lengthwise. Spoon out and discard all the seeds. Cut each half crosswise in half, then cut each half lengthwise into ¼-inch-thick slices. Rinse under cold running water and drain on paper towels.

In a large bowl, mix half of the papaya slices with the orange juice, and reserve for the garnish. Coarsely chop the remaining papaya slices and set aside for the vinaigrette.

Lightly rub the shrimp with ½ teaspoon of the salt, then rinse under cold running water until the water runs clear. Dry well with paper towels.

To make the marinade, put the shallot, garlic, ginger, cilantro, coconut milk, honey, and remaining ½ teaspoon salt in a blender or food processor and puree until a smooth paste is formed. Transfer to a large bowl. Add the shrimp to the marinade, turning to coat. Cover and refrigerate for 2 hours.

Meanwhile, soak 12 wooden skewers in water for 30 minutes; drain and dry. Lightly brush the grill rack with oil, then heat the grill until hot.

Quarter the avocado and remove the peel. Cut each quarter into 5 or 6 thin slices, keeping them attached at the top. Fan out the avocado on four large plates.

Remove the shrimp from the marinade and thread 1 shrimp onto each skewer so it lies flat. Reserve the marinade. Brush the shrimp with the oil. Grill, turning once, until lightly browned, about 2 minutes on each side, brushing with the reserved marinade while they cook. Remove the shrimp from the skewers before serving.

Place 3 shrimp on the avocado slices, decorate with the reserved sliced papaya, and pour the vinaigrette over all. Garnish with the greens and serve.

Spicy Papaya Vinaigrette

Makes about 1⅓ cups

½   papaya (reserved from previous recipe), chopped

3   tablespoons olive oil

3   serrano peppers, stemmed, seeded, and sliced (about
       1 tablespoon)

1   small shallot, thinly sliced

¼   cup plus 1 tablespoon orange juice

¼   cup fresh lime juice

1   tablespoon sugar

1   teaspoon kosher salt

Place the papaya, olive oil, peppers, shallot, orange juice, lime juice, sugar, and salt in a food processor and puree. Strain through a fine sieve; discard the solids. *The vinaigrette will keep, covered and refrigerated, for 2 days. If it solidifies, warm in a microwave oven just until it becomes liquid. Or let stand at room temperature until it liquefies.*

Papaya

Papayas grow in semitropical zones throughout the world. There are many varieties, and the fruit ranges from 6 inches to about a foot in length and weighs between 1 and 5 pounds. When ripe, the skin is a vivid golden yellow; depending on the variety, the flesh may be yellow, orange, or pink. All types are very juicy and silky smooth, with an exotic tart-sweet flavor. The large center cavity is filled with shiny blackish seeds, which are edible but are usually discarded. ✿ Choose papayas with golden yellow skin, firm but ripe, without any bruising. I buy papayas from Asian markets or markets that get fresh supplies often and care about their produce, such as Whole Foods. Many of the papayas available in this country have been picked while too green and therefore never ripen properly. To test for ripeness, press the stem end of the papaya with your finger; if it yields, it is fully ripe. Refrigerate completely ripe fruit and use as soon as possible.

Warm Asparagus, Scallop, and Arugula Salad

Make this in the spring, when fresh asparagus is plentiful. The slightly bitter arugula is a perfect foil for the mild scallops and asparagus. Walnut oil dressing brings them all together.

[Serves 4]

16	spears large white asparagus or jumbo green asparagus
8	large sea scallops (about 12 ounces), preferably dry-packed (see page 128)
2	tablespoons olive oil
1	shallot, thinly sliced
1	garlic clove, thinly sliced
1	small red bell pepper (about 6 ounces), roasted (see page 110), peeled, and cut into ½-inch dice
¼	cup chicken stock or fish stock
1	tablespoon unsalted butter
	Kosher salt and freshly ground pepper
2	cups arugula leaves, washed and dried
2	tablespoons walnut oil
2	tablespoons fresh lemon juice
4	sprigs fresh chervil or cilantro

Using a vegetable peeler, carefully peel the asparagus so as to remove just a thin outer layer of skin; be careful not to peel away the flesh. Cut off and discard the tough bottom ends. Rinse well.

Fill the bottom of a steamer with water and bring to a boil. Place the asparagus on the rack, cover, and steam for about 3 minutes, or until tender. Drain and dry. *The asparagus can be steamed 1 to 2 days ahead; cover and refrigerate. Serve at room temperature, or warm in a microwave oven until hot before serving.*

Dry the scallops well with paper towels. Heat 1 tablespoon of the olive oil in a large skillet over high heat. Add the scallops and sear for about 1 minute on each side, until lightly golden. Transfer to a plate.

Heat the remaining tablespoon olive oil in the same skillet. Add the shallot and garlic and cook just until soft, about 1 minute. Add the red pepper and stock, bring to a boil, and cook for about 2 minutes to reduce slightly.

Add the scallops and butter and cook until the scallops are hot, about 30 seconds. Season to taste with salt and pepper. Remove from the heat.

Divide the arugula among four serving plates, top each with 4 spears of asparagus, and place 2 scallops on top of the asparagus. Whisk the walnut oil and lemon juice into the hot pan juices and spoon this vinaigrette over the salads. Garnish with the chervil or cilantro and serve.

White Asparagus

I used to avoid white asparagus, believing that it was too expensive to be worth the cost. But that was before one of my regular customers presented me with two bunches of large white asparagus that had just been flown in from Germany. I peeled the stalks, steamed them, and dressed them with a little butter and salt. They were the best I had ever tasted — juicy and tender, and much better than ordinary asparagus. I suddenly understood why the Germans and French get so excited at the first harvest in the spring, and I have been using white asparagus ever since. ❀ White asparagus is grown entirely underground, with soil mounded on top of it to keep out the light and prevent it from turning green. Although it is now available almost year-round in specialty markets, the best time to buy it is still the spring. ❀ White asparagus has a tough outer skin that must be removed; this is best done with a vegetable peeler. Buy only the freshest and thickest spears, with tight pinkish tips. Older asparagus will be dry and will have lost its sweetness. Cook it as soon as possible, just as you would fresh corn, before its natural sugars turn to starch.

Panko-Crusted Goat Cheese with Tomato and Asparagus Salad

Panko, or Japanese bread crumbs, are much coarser than ordinary bread crumbs and create a deliciously crunchy crust — a startling contrast to the hot, creamy cheese.

This recipe was inspired by my mother, who often told me about the goat cheese she used to eat while growing up in Inner Mongolia. Most people can't imagine cheese in Chinese cuisine, but in that cold region, goat's milk and goat cheese provide essential nutrition. When she tasted my version, it brought back happy memories of the panfried goat cheese she had enjoyed as a young girl.

[Serves 4]

1 log (about 11 ounces) fresh mild goat cheese, preferably French Chevrion	½ cup soybean oil or corn oil
½ cup all-purpose flour	2 small vine-ripened tomatoes, peeled (see page 123) and cored, each cut into 8 wedges or slices
2 large eggs, lightly beaten	1 cup baby greens, such as arugula or watercress, any tough stems removed, washed and dried
1 cup panko (Japanese bread crumbs; see page 28)	Balsamic Vinaigrette (recipe follows)
8 spears jumbo asparagus	

Using a sharp knife dipped into hot water and wiped dry, a cheese wire, or a piece of (unflavored) thick dental floss, slice the goat cheese log into 8 pieces slightly less than 1 inch thick. Place on a large plate.

Line a baking sheet with parchment or waxed paper. Place the flour, eggs, and panko in three separate shallow bowls. Coat each slice of goat cheese with flour, shaking to remove any excess. Dip into the eggs and turn to coat well, then dip into the panko, turning and pressing lightly to coat well. Place on the lined baking sheet. Refrigerate until ready to fry.

Trim off the tough bottom ends of the asparagus spears. Peel the stems, then cut into diagonal pieces about 2 inches in length. Cook the asparagus in a medium saucepan of boiling salted water for about 1 minute after the water returns to a boil. Immediately plunge the cooked asparagus into a bowl of ice water to stop the cooking. Drain well and refrigerate until ready to use.

Heat the oil in a large nonstick skillet over medium heat. Add the cheese slices and cook until lightly browned on the first side, about 2 minutes. Turn and cook until golden on the second side. Remove and place on a baking sheet lined with several layers of paper towels to drain. *The cheese can be kept warm on a baking sheet in a 200-degree oven for up to 30 minutes.*

To serve, place 4 pieces of tomato in the center of each of four large chilled plates. Top with 2 spears of the asparagus. Place the greens on top of the vegetables, and spoon the vinaigrette over all. Place 2 slices of the hot goat cheese on one side of each salad and serve.

Balsamic Vinaigrette

——————[*Makes about ¾ cup*]——————

Briefly cooking the garlic along with the oil subdues its harshness and gives it a nutty, sweet flavor. For convenience, make the vinaigrette in a micro-waveable glass jar. Spoon the garlic over the salad, along with the dressing.

2	garlic cloves, thinly sliced
½	cup extra-virgin olive oil
3	tablespoons balsamic vinegar
1	teaspoon kosher salt
	Freshly ground pepper

Put the garlic slices and oil in a small glass bowl and microwave on high power for 1 minute. Or heat in a small saucepan over medium heat for 1 to 2 minutes, until the garlic softens. Remove from the heat and stir in the balsamic vinegar, salt, and pepper to taste. *The dressing will keep for 1 to 2 weeks in the refrigerator, tightly covered. Shake well before using.*

Panko

Panko are Japanese-style bread crumbs. Commonly used as breading for foods, they are coarse and irregular in shape and become exceptionally crisp when fried, with a pleasing toasty flavor. They also have the advantage of absorbing less oil than plain bread crumbs, and they will remain crisp even after sitting for a while after frying. Because they are so crisp, I use them for toppings as well as for frying. Panko can be found in Japanese or Asian markets, specialty food stores, and some supermarkets. They keep for several months in a well-sealed container at room temperature.

**GRILLED SQUID
WITH ENDIVE AND MANGO SALAD
PAGE 30**

Grilled Squid with Endive and Mango Salad

My husband taught school at Tsin Hwa University at Shin Chu from 1972 to 1976. Some Sundays we would take my sons to a seafood restaurant there. Squid was their favorite dish, whether fried, sautéed, or grilled. We always ordered a plate of grilled squid "Japanese style." The squid were small, about 2½ inches in length, and each one was cut into three pieces. They were tender, with just a slightly chewy bite, and we ate them along with a bowl of white rice. To this day, I have never forgotten the taste of this dish.

Fresh squid are best for this recipe, for when cooked, they are tender and will not shrink. Cleaning them takes a little time, but it's worth the effort. Most of the already cleaned squid sold in this country have been frozen, but if you're lucky, you will be able to find cleaned fresh squid in some fish markets. Fresh squid should be very firm and smooth.

[Serves 4]

8	small to medium squid		1	small firm mango
2	tablespoons soy sauce		½	small red bell pepper, julienned
2	tablespoons olive oil or soybean oil		½	teaspoon kosher salt
3	tablespoons sake or vodka		3	tablespoons fresh lime juice
1	teaspoon grated peeled fresh ginger		4	sprigs fresh cilantro, flat-leaf parsley, or other herb (optional)
1	tablespoon sugar			
1	Belgian endive			

Clean the squid and rinse well; dry with paper towels. Cut off the tentacles and reserve for another use. Mix the soy sauce, oil, sake or vodka, ginger, and sugar in a medium bowl. Add the squid and stir to coat.

Cut off the core end of the Belgian endive, separate the leaves, and slice into julienne strips. Peel the mango. Using a Japanese Benriner, mandoline, or sharp knife, cut the flesh into ⅛-inch-thick slices, then julienne the slices.

Place the endive, mango, and red pepper in a bowl of ice water and soak for 3 to 5 minutes. Drain well, return to the bowl, and mix in the salt. Refrigerate until needed.

Lightly oil a grill rack or grill pan, then heat to medium. Meanwhile, using tongs, remove the squid from the marinade and place them on a plate. Pour the marinade into a small saucepan, bring to a boil, and cook for 1 minute; set aside.

Grill the squid for about 4 minutes, turning frequently to cook on all sides, just until they are firm but not tough. Brush the reserved marinade over the squid and grill just until the bottom surfaces begin to blister, then turn and repeat on the other side. Remove and let cool.

Slice each squid lengthwise into 4 sections.

Drain any excess liquid from the endive mixture and discard. Stir in the lime juice. Mound the salad in the center of four plates. Arrange the squid on top of the salad, and drizzle with any remaining marinade. Garnish with the herb sprigs, if using, and serve.

Beef Carpaccio with Vietnamese Vinaigrette

———————————————— (✿) ————————————————

Dressed with crushed peanuts and a light lime dressing, these paper-thin slices of raw beef are tender, light, and full of flavor. Kobe beef, an expensive cut that contains even more fat than prime, makes the best carpaccio. (See sources, page 320.) I learned to make this dish from John Vhon, a talented cook who used to own a Vietnamese restaurant where we often went for a late dinner. A few years ago, John sold the restaurant and came to work with me.

———————————————— [*Serves 4*] ————————————————

2	6-ounce Kobe steaks or boneless top sirloin steaks, preferably prime (2 inches thick)
1	teaspoon kosher salt
1	tablespoon coarsely cracked black pepper
¼	cup Vegetable Stock (page 56)
2	tablespoons strained fresh lime juice
1	tablespoon fish sauce (preferably Three Crabs brand)
1	teaspoon sugar

1	shallot, minced
1	tablespoon minced fresh cilantro stems (see page 145)
1	small fresh hot red pepper, stemmed and thinly sliced
2	tablespoons extra-virgin olive oil
¼	cup julienned red onion
¼	cup julienned carrot
2	tablespoons crushed unsalted roasted peanuts
2	fresh basil leaves, julienned

Completely trim the beef, removing any fat or sinew. Season with a little of the salt and cracked pepper. Tightly wrap the steak in plastic wrap and freeze so it will be easy to slice paper-thin. *The beef can be frozen for 24 hours.*

In a medium bowl, mix the stock, lime juice, fish sauce, sugar, shallot, cilantro, and hot pepper. Cover and refrigerate. *The lime juice mixture will keep, refrigerated, for up to 3 days.*

Remove the steak from the freezer and let sit at room temperature for about 10 minutes; it should still be partially frozen. Brush four large plates with a little of the olive oil, using 1 tablespoon in all.

With a Japanese Benriner, mandoline, or sharp knife, thinly slice the steak. Cover each plate with slices of meat. Drizzle the remaining 1 tablespoon olive oil over the meat. *The meat can be covered with plastic wrap and refrigerated for up to 6 hours.*

Just before serving, sprinkle the beef with the remaining salt and pepper. Scatter the red onion, carrot, and crushed peanuts evenly over the beef, and sprinkle the basil on top. Spoon the dressing over the carpaccio and serve. Serve chilled.

Jellied Lamb Terrine with Cucumber Mint Relish

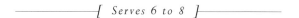

This is a classic northern Chinese dish from Inner Mongolia, where I was born. My mother always served it at the beginning of a special meal with seven other small dishes, especially during the Chinese New Year. Our cook made a stock using pork skin, chicken feet, and lean pork, which she used to braise the lamb; I simplify things by using lamb stock. When chilled, the liquid becomes gelatinous, and the cubes of meat scattered throughout the terrine shine in the amber-colored jelly. Homemade stock prepared with plenty of bones or a good stock purchased from a specialty market will jell, but if you use canned broth or weak stock, you'll need to stiffen it by adding gelatin.

Serve the terrine with a simple balsamic or black vinegar and ginger dipping sauce.

[*Serves 6 to 8*]

1½	pounds boneless lamb shoulder or leg, trimmed of visible fat and cut into 1-inch cubes
2	tablespoons soybean oil or corn oil
4	large garlic cloves, peeled but left whole
¼	cup brandy, whiskey, or dry sherry
1	tablespoon soy sauce
3–4	pieces star anise
1	1-inch piece fresh ginger, crushed
¼	teaspoon cayenne pepper
6	cups lamb stock (page 59), beef stock, or veal stock
	Kosher salt and freshly ground pepper
3	envelopes gelatin (if needed)
½	cup balsamic vinegar or Chinese black vinegar (see page 183)
¼	cup julienned fresh young ginger or julienned peeled regular ginger, soaked in ice water to crisp
	Cucumber Mint Relish (page 278)

Place the lamb in a large pot of boiling water, return the water to a boil, and cook for 1 minute. Drain well.

Heat the oil in a large heavy skillet or Dutch oven over medium heat. Add the garlic and cook, stirring, for 1 minute. Add the lamb, liquor, soy sauce, star anise, crushed ginger, and cayenne pepper, cover, and cook over low heat for 5 minutes.

Add the stock and bring to a boil. Reduce the heat to low and simmer for 30 minutes, skimming off any scum.

Cover and continue to cook for 45 minutes to 1 hour, or until the meat is very tender. Remove from the heat and discard the garlic cloves, star anise, and ginger. Season to taste with salt and pepper.

To test the stock to see if it will jell, place 1 teaspoon of the hot liquid on a small plate and refrigerate until cool. In 10 minutes, it should have solidified. If it is still liquid or if you used canned broth, mix the gelatin with ¾ cup stock in a small bowl and let sit for 3 minutes to soften. Reheat the lamb mixture, stir in the gelatin mixture, and cook until dissolved.

Line an 8-by-4-inch loaf pan (6-cup capacity) with plastic wrap. Pour the lamb mixture into the pan and let cool, then refrigerate for at least 4 hours, or until completely set.

Bring the vinegar to a boil in a small saucepan. Turn the heat to low and reduce the vinegar to about 2 tablespoons. Pour into a small bowl and reserve.

To serve, dip the bottom of the loaf pan into hot water for a few seconds to loosen the terrine, and invert it onto a plate. Peel off the plastic wrap. Using a sharp knife, cut into ½-inch-thick slices and arrange on a platter. Drizzle with the reduced vinegar, top with the drained julienned ginger and the relish, and serve.

Soups and Stocks

Ten-Vegetable Vegetarian Hot-and-Sour Soup

Prepare to sweat, sneeze, and warm your body: this is a favorite comfort soup in northern China, especially in winter. My version contains many different vegetables to enrich the flavor of the broth. You can substitute any other vegetables you like (such as turnips and daikon) if you don't have the ones listed here. Use fewer vegetables but keep the proportions the same.

The balance of hot and sour is perfect in this soup, and it's hard to believe something so rich and delicious is vegetarian. But if it's too spicy for you, seed the jalapeño peppers or cut down on the amount of white pepper.

[Serves 8 as a first course]

4	ounces firm tofu
3	tablespoons soy sauce
3	tablespoons rice wine vinegar or white wine vinegar
2	teaspoons kosher salt
1½–2	teaspoons freshly ground white pepper
2	tablespoons cornstarch, mixed with ¼ cup water
8	cups Vegetable Stock (page 56) or Mushroom Stock (page 56)
2	tablespoons soybean oil or corn oil
¼	cup thinly sliced shallots
2	jalapeño peppers, stemmed and chopped
½	cup diced (¼-inch) peeled celery root

½	cup diced (¼-inch) peeled parsnips
½	cup diced (¼-inch) peeled carrots (1 large)
10–12	(½ cup) dried shiitake mushrooms, soaked in warm water for 20 minutes, drained, stemmed, and diced
½	cup diced (¼-inch) Yukon Gold potatoes
½	cup diced (¼-inch) zucchini
½	cup diced (¼-inch) tomatoes
½	cup chopped scallions (about 4)
1	teaspoon sesame oil
2	tablespoons finely chopped fresh cilantro or flat-leaf parsley

Rinse the tofu under cold water, then place on several layers of paper towels and drain for 10 minutes. With a sharp knife, cut the tofu into ½-inch dice.

Combine the soy sauce, vinegar, salt, white pepper, and cornstarch mixture in a large bowl and mix well. Stir in the stock.

Heat the oil in a large stockpot over high heat. Add the shallots and jalapeño peppers and cook, stirring, until the shallots are soft, 1 to 2 minutes. Add the celery root, parsnips, carrots, shiitakes, and potatoes, stir, and cook for 2 minutes to sear and coat the vegetables. Add the stock mixture and bring to a boil. Turn the heat to low and simmer, uncovered, for 20 minutes, or just until the vegetables are soft.

Add the tofu and zucchini and simmer for another 10 minutes, or until the zucchini is soft. Add the tomatoes and scallions, stir, and cook for 1 minute.

Ladle the soup into bowls, drizzle with the sesame oil, sprinkle with the cilantro or parsley, and serve.

Celery Root

Also known as celeriac, celery knob, or turnip-rooted celery, celery root has the flavor of celery without its stringy texture. It resembles a rough brown turnip with creamy white flesh. A winter vegetable, celery root is available from late September until April. ✿ Raw celery root can be grated or cut into thin strips or sticks and added to salads, or it can be cut into slices or chunks and boiled, steamed, or braised. Mash cooked celery root with an equal quantity of potatoes, or puree it and enjoy it by itself. It's also delicious in soups, stews, and braised dishes. ✿ To prepare it, peel it with a sharp knife and trim off the long, scraggly brown roots. Since the cut pieces turn brown quickly, place them in a bowl of cold acidulated (lemon) water until ready to use. ✿ Choose fresh, firm celery root, preferably with the green stems still attached; avoid any with soft spots, as they will decay rapidly. Discard any leaves; they're inedible. Stored in a plastic bag in the refrigerator, celery root will keep for a month or longer.

White Corn Soup

In July and August, my husband and I buy white corn from a small New Jersey farmers' market near us, where the owners pick the corn each morning. It's the best I have ever eaten anywhere. When making this soup, I simmer the cobs in the broth for added flavor. I like this soup served chilled with a sprinkling of fresh herbs or herb oil to start a summer dinner or barbecue. For special occasions, I serve it hot with either jumbo lump crabmeat or chunks of lobster meat. It is also great sprinkled with pieces of hot fried rice cakes; the pieces crackle when they hit the hot soup.

Serves 6 to 8 as a first course

8	ears white corn
2	tablespoons soybean oil or corn oil
1	small onion, chopped
½	cup chopped celery
3	quarts Vegetable Stock (page 56) or chicken stock
1	Idaho (russet) potato (about 8 ounces), peeled and cut into 8 pieces
½	cup heavy cream

3	tablespoons butter
	Kosher salt and freshly ground white pepper
1	tablespoon minced fresh chives
8	ounces jumbo lump crabmeat, picked over to remove any shells or cartilage, or diced cooked lobster (optional)
	Crispy rice cakes, deep-fried, or croutons (optional)

Husk the corn and remove any strands of silk. Cut the kernels off the cobs and reserve both the kernels and cobs.

Heat the oil in a large stockpot over high heat. Add the onion and celery and sauté until soft, about 3 minutes. Add the stock and cobs and bring to a boil. Turn the heat to low and simmer, uncovered, for 1 hour.

Using tongs, remove the cobs and discard. (You should have about 6 cups of stock.) Add the corn kernels and potato. Bring to a boil, cover, and gently simmer for 30 minutes, or until the potato is very tender.

Add the cream and cook for about 5 minutes. Add the butter, turn off the heat, and cool a little.

Puree the soup in a blender, in batches if necessary, until very smooth. Strain through a fine sieve. Season to taste with salt and white pepper. *The soup can be made up to 3 days ahead, covered, and refrigerated.*

Serve hot or chilled. Garnish with the chives and with crabmeat or lobster and/or pieces of crispy rice cakes or croutons, if you like.

Crispy Rice Cakes

Rice cakes are made by drying steamed sweet rice (also called sticky rice) until it has hardened. You can buy them in Chinese grocery stores. Two kinds are available. The best is Instant Sizzling Rice, which comes in 1½-inch squares. Although it has already been cooked, it must be deep-fried in hot (400-degree) oil for a few seconds until it puffs. The second kind has already been deep-fried and needs to be heated in the oven; unfortunately, these are not very good, so I avoid them.

Roasted Butternut Squash Soup

(⟳)

Roasting the butternut squash and parsnips before cooking them in the stock gives a deep, rich taste to this velvety soup. The recipe comes from my former chef Anne Coll. Serve it during the fall and winter, when both vegetables are at their peak of flavor. It is a great way to begin Thanksgiving dinner.

─┤ *Serves 6 to 8 as a first course* ├─

1	2- to 2½-pound butternut squash		½	cup heavy cream
2	medium parsnips (about 8 ounces)		2	tablespoons butter
3	tablespoons extra-virgin olive oil		1	tablespoon honey
3	shallots, sliced		6	cups chicken stock or Vegetable Stock (page 56)
2	garlic cloves, minced			Kosher salt and freshly ground pepper
1	tablespoon grated peeled fresh ginger		1	tablespoon Basil Oil (recipe follows)
½	cup dry white wine			Croutons (optional)
½	teaspoon ground cinnamon			

Preheat the oven to 300 degrees. Peel the butternut squash using a very sharp knife or vegetable peeler. Cut it crosswise in half, then cut each half lengthwise into 4 pieces. Remove the seeds with a spoon, then cut each section into approximately 1-inch slices. Cut off the tops of the parsnips, peel them, and cut into 1-inch pieces.

Place the butternut squash and parsnips on a large non-stick baking sheet. Spoon 2 tablespoons of the olive oil over them and turn to coat well with the oil. Bake for 45 minutes to 1 hour, until the vegetables are soft. Set aside.

Combine the remaining tablespoon of oil, the shallots, and garlic in a small stockpot, turn the heat to medium, stir, and cook until the garlic and shallots are soft, 2 to 3 minutes. Add the ginger and white wine and simmer for 2 minutes.

Stir in the cinnamon, cream, and butter and cook until reduced by almost half.

Add the butternut squash and parsnips, honey, and stock and bring to a boil. Reduce the heat to low, cover, and simmer for 20 minutes. Turn off the heat and allow the soup to cool a little.

Puree the soup in a blender or food processor, in batches if necessary. Strain the soup through a fine sieve, pushing with a wooden spoon to extract all the liquid. Season to taste with salt and pepper. *The soup can be made up to 3 days in advance and stored, tightly covered, in the refrigerator, or it can be frozen for up to 3 months. Reheat before serving.* Drizzle a little of the basil oil over each serving and top with croutons, if desired.

Basil Oil and Puree

—[*Makes about 1 ¼ cups basil oil and 1 ½ cups puree*]—

I make basil oil in the summer, when there is plenty of fresh basil in my garden. The fresher the basil, the brighter green the oil. It's a waste of time to use old, wilted leaves in this recipe.

Use the oil to flavor salads, such as Warm Asparagus, Scallop, and Arugula Salad (page 24), and vegetables. A few drops make a colorful garnish for White Corn Soup (page 38) or Roasted Butternut Squash Soup. A spoonful of basil puree perks up salad dressings and pasta dishes.

2   pounds very fresh basil

2   garlic cloves, sliced

2   cups extra-virgin olive oil

1   teaspoon kosher salt

Pick through the basil leaves, choosing only the unblemished ones; discard the stems (you will need 1 pound leaves). Bring a large pot of water to a boil over high heat. Blanch the basil for just 1 second, then drain and plunge into a bowl of ice water to keep the color bright green. Drain and squeeze out the excess water.

Combine the garlic and 2 tablespoons of the oil in a small glass bowl and microwave on high power for 1 minute. Or cook in a small saucepan over medium heat for 1 to 2 minutes, until the garlic is softened. Cool.

Place the garlic oil and the basil in a food processor or blender. With the motor running, slowly add the remaining oil. Add the salt and process to mix.

Place coffee filter in a fine sieve, set it over a deep bowl, and pour in the basil mixture. Allow the oil to slowly drip through the filter, then press down on the residue with a spoon until you have extracted most of the oil.

Pour the oil into a glass jar or bottle and refrigerate. *The oil will keep for up to 1 month.* Spoon the solids into small covered containers (3 or more) and freeze. The puree can also be frozen in ice cube trays until solid, then individually wrapped and stored in the freezer in a zipper-lock bag. *The frozen puree will keep for up to 1 year.*

Coconut Soup with Leeks and Mushrooms

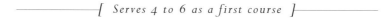

Fresh ginger, jalapeño peppers, and lime juice give the slightly sweet and nutty coconut milk–based soup a spicy kick. Usually this Southeast Asian soup is made with chicken or shrimp, but I like this version with leeks and fresh mushrooms, and a flavorful mushroom stock. It's a good first course before a noodle dish, such as Soba Noodles with Ginger, Scallions, and Shrimp (page 193) or Pasta with Cilantro Pesto, Zucchini, and Tomatoes (page 194).

———[Serves 4 to 6 as a first course]———

1	large leek, white and tender green part only
1	tablespoon soybean oil or corn oil
2	shallots, minced
4	ounces small white button mushrooms, trimmed and thinly sliced
1	jalapeño pepper, stemmed, seeded, and diced
1	tablespoon minced fresh lemongrass (tender inner part only; see page 150)
1	tablespoon grated peeled fresh ginger
4	cups Mushroom Stock (page 56), Vegetable Stock (page 56), or chicken stock

½	cup whisked unsweetened coconut milk
2	tablespoons fish sauce (preferably Three Crabs brand)
1	teaspoon cornstarch, mixed with 1 tablespoon water
	Grated zest and juice of 1 small lime
2	tablespoons butter
	Kosher salt and freshly ground pepper
	Chopped fresh chives, cilantro, chervil, or basil
	Basil Oil (page 41) for drizzling (optional)

Cut the leek lengthwise in half, then cut crosswise into thin shreds. Wash well in cold water to remove any grit, then drain well.

In a large stockpot, heat the oil over medium heat. Add the shallots and cook until lightly browned, about 1 minute. Add the mushrooms, jalapeño, lemongrass, and ginger and cook, stirring, for 1 minute. Add the stock, coconut milk, fish sauce, and leek. Stir in the cornstarch mixture and bring to a boil. Reduce the heat to low and simmer, uncovered, for 30 minutes.

Add the lime zest and juice and the butter to the soup and season to taste with salt and pepper. *The soup can be made up to 1 day ahead. Cool and refrigerate, covered. Reheat before serving.*

Ladle the soup into soup bowls and garnish with fresh herbs. Drizzle with the basil oil, if using.

Fish Sauce

Called *nam pla* in Thailand and most of the rest of Southeast Asia and *nuoc nam* in Vietnam, fish sauce is used as a condiment or flavoring or as a substitute for salt, much as the Chinese use soy sauce. A thin pale brown liquid, fish sauce is made from salted, fermented fish (usually anchovies) or squid and crab. It is extremely pungent and has a strong salty flavor. Don't be afraid to try it, though — the smell will dissipate once it is cooked. ✿ I prefer Three Crabs Fish Sauce, manufactured by the Viet Huong Fishsauce Company. It has a strong, rich flavor that is better than that of most other brands. It is more expensive, but it's worth it. It keeps well and can be stored for up to 2 years at room temperature. It is readily available in Asian markets and by mail order (see sources, page 320).

Spicy Seafood Rice Soup

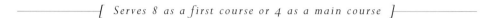

Rice soup, or congee, a rather plain broth made with rice and water, is Chinese comfort food. It is usually served for breakfast, but my grandmother liked it for dinner with steamed bread and several small dishes. My mother made pumpkin congee when we were sick.

I never realized that rice soup could be anything more than that until I visited Thailand in 1989 and had a spicy rice soup for breakfast one morning. It was made with lots of fresh herbs, spices, and seafood.

I serve this for lunch with bread or for dinner as a first course. Long-grain sweet rice gives the soup a smooth consistency. Sweet rice can be found in short- and long-grain varieties. Long-grain sweet, or glutinous, rice is less sticky than the short-grain variety. If you can't find it, substitute long-grain jasmine rice.

The soup is best served the day it is made; if it sits too long, the rice will absorb most of the liquid.

[Serves 8 as a first course or 4 as a main course]

⅓	cup long-grain sweet rice (see above)
4	ounces medium shrimp (31–35 count), peeled, deveined, and cut into ¼-inch dice
2	tablespoons vodka, gin, or dry vermouth
2	tablespoons soybean oil or corn oil
1	piece fresh lemongrass (see page 150), tender inner part only, very thinly sliced
3	garlic cloves, minced
2	shallots, minced
1	tablespoon grated peeled fresh ginger
1	jalapeño pepper, stemmed and coarsely chopped

2	tablespoons Thai red curry paste (see page 107)
2	tablespoons fish sauce (preferably Three Crabs brand) Grated zest and juice of 1 large lime
1	large vine-ripened tomato, peeled (see page 123), cored, and diced
6	cups fish stock, chicken stock, or Vegetable Stock (page 56), or more if needed
4	ounces jumbo lump crabmeat, picked over to remove any shells and cartilage
1	fresh kaffir lime leaf, julienned (optional)
6	fresh basil leaves, julienned

Wash the rice well in cold water, changing the water 2 or 3 times, or until the water remains clear. Drain and set aside.

Combine the shrimp and liquor in a small bowl and set aside to marinate.

Heat the oil in a medium pot over medium heat. Add half the lemongrass, all of the garlic, the shallots, and ginger and cook, stirring, until soft, about 2 minutes. Add the rice, jalapeño, and red curry paste and cook, stirring, for 30 seconds.

Add the fish sauce, lime zest and juice, tomato, and stock. Bring to a boil, then turn the heat to low and simmer, covered, for 20 to 25 minutes, until the rice is soft but not broken or mushy. If the soup seems too thick, dilute it with a little more stock or water.

Add the shrimp to the soup and cook, stirring, until the shrimp turns white, about 1 minute. Add the crabmeat and heat just until hot. Stir in the remaining lemongrass and the kaffir lime leaf, if using.

Spoon into a soup tureen or individual soup bowls, sprinkle with the basil, and serve.

Kaffir Lime Leaves

Kaffir lime leaves, which have an intensely fragrant citrus aroma, are widely used in Thai cuisine. The leaves are sold fresh or frozen in Asian markets in this country; they are usually packed in 1-ounce plastic bags. However, kaffir lime is now being grown in Florida and California, and the fresh leaves are becoming more available. They freeze well and will keep for 6 months. (I don't use dried kaffir lime leaves, which have infinitely less flavor.) ✻ When used whole for flavoring, the leaves should be removed after cooking. If you are going to include them in the finished dish, remove the tough center vein and finely shred the leaves. ✻ If you can't get kaffir lime leaves, you can substitute lime zest, although it won't be as flavorful or pungent.

Velvety Chicken Pumpkin Soup

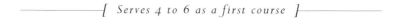

Velveting is a classic Chinese technique used for making soups and other traditional dishes. In this recipe, the chicken is finely ground, then marinated in a mixture of cornstarch, egg white, vodka, and ice water. When it is slowly added to the well-flavored stock, the pureed chicken forms small, soft, velvety lumps and the soup becomes thick and beautiful. Kabocha squash gives the soup an intense flavor. The squash can be found in many supermarkets in the fall, but if you can't get it, substitute delicata or butternut squash.

Serves 4 to 6 as a first course

4	ounces boneless, skinless chicken breast
1	large egg white
1	tablespoon vodka
1	tablespoon cornstarch
1	tablespoon soybean oil or corn oil
2	shallots, minced
2	tablespoons grated peeled fresh ginger

½	kabocha squash (about 1 pound), peeled, seeded, and cut into small chunks (see page 48)
6	cups Vegetable Stock (page 56) or chicken stock
1	teaspoon cornstarch, mixed with 1 tablespoon water
2	tablespoons butter
	Kosher salt and freshly ground white pepper
	Chopped fresh chives, cilantro, or chervil

Cut the chicken into 1-inch chunks. Finely grind using a meat grinder or a food processor, and place in a medium bowl. Mix the egg white, vodka, 2 tablespoons ice water, and the cornstarch in a small bowl, then add to the chicken and stir until thoroughly combined. Cover and refrigerate.

Heat the oil in a large pot over medium heat. Add the shallots and cook, stirring, until lightly browned, about 2 minutes. Add the ginger and squash and cook, stirring, for 1 minute. Pour in the stock, then stir in the 1 teaspoon cornstarch mixed with water. Bring to a boil, reduce the heat to low, and simmer, uncovered, for 30 minutes, or until the squash is very tender.

Add the butter to the soup and season to taste with salt and pepper. Remove from the heat and cool.

When it has cooled, puree the soup using a blender or food processor, in batches if necessary. *The chicken mixture and the soup can be made up to 1 day ahead and kept covered and refrigerated.*

Just before serving, bring the soup to a boil, then turn the heat to very low. Slowly add the chicken mixture and stir until all the pieces are separated, then return the soup to a boil. Ladle into soup bowls, garnish with fresh herbs, and serve.

Kabocha Squash

We ate a lot of pumpkin when we were young, cooked into the rice porridge called congee or stir-fried. My grandmother always complained that the pumpkins in Taiwan were not as sweet as the orange-red variety with sweet red flesh found in her hometown in the province of Shanxi. ✿ After I came to the United States, I found a type of winter squash called kabocha in a Japanese market and immediately knew that this was what my grandmother had been talking about. Unfortunately, I wasn't able to tell her how right she was, because she passed away in 1969, just one year after I came to this country. ✿ Kabocha is shaped like a pumpkin but is usually no more than about 8 inches in diameter, with dark green, rough-looking skin. The flesh is a bright orange or deep yellow with a firm, fine, dense texture. When cooked, it becomes sweet, with a mild chestnut flavor reminiscent of a cross between a sweet potato and a pumpkin. Steaming and dry-roasting are best for this squash, since they highlight its flavor. ✿ The easiest way to peel the thick, hard skin is to parboil the whole squash first. Place the squash in a medium pot, cover with water, and bring to a boil. (You may need to weight it down with another pot to keep it submerged.) Cook for about 5 minutes, then remove and let cool. Cut the squash in half, and with a small spoon scoop out the seeds from the center. (You can dry the seeds, salt them, and then roast for a snack.) ✿ Place the kabocha on a cutting board and trim away all of the skin using a paring knife or a vegetable peeler. Cut the flesh into strips or slices as the recipe directs. Cover tightly and refrigerate if not using right away.

Silken Tofu and Bay Scallop Soup

This is a beautifully simple soup, with the creamy texture of silken tofu, tiny scallops, and fresh tomatoes. It's also very quick to prepare. To preserve its bright character, be careful not to cook it too long once you add the tomatoes, scallions, and scallops. Bay scallops are best because of their natural sweetness, but quartered sea scallops can be substituted.

Serves 4 as a first course

4	ounces silken tofu
1	teaspoon cornstarch
1/2	teaspoon freshly ground white pepper
4	cups bottled clam juice or chicken stock
1/2	cup diced (1/4-inch) celery root
1/2	cup diced (1/4-inch) carrot
1/2	cup fresh regular peas or frozen peas, preferably petite peas

2	scallions, white part only, thinly sliced
1/2	cup grape tomatoes, peeled (see page 123) and halved
4	ounces bay scallops
1/4	cup chopped fresh cilantro
1/2	teaspoon toasted sesame oil
	Kosher salt

Place the tofu on several layers of paper towels, cover with another layer of towels, and drain for 10 minutes. Using a thin-bladed knife, carefully slice the tofu into 1/2-inch dice.

In a small bowl, mix the cornstarch and white pepper. Stir in 2 tablespoons water.

Pour the clam juice or stock into a 4-quart saucepan, stir in the cornstarch mixture, and bring to a boil over high heat. Stir in the celery root and carrot, turn the heat down to medium, and cook, uncovered, for about 15 minutes, or until the celery root is tender.

Slowly and carefully add the tofu to the pan, trying not to break it up. Stir gently, add the peas, and cook for another 5 minutes.

Add the scallions and tomatoes and bring to a boil. Mix in the scallops. When they have turned white, about 30 seconds to 1 minute, remove from the heat (the scallops will continue to cook in the hot soup). Add the cilantro and sesame oil, season to taste with salt, and serve immediately.

Duck Wonton Soup

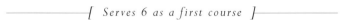

In Kaohsiung in southern Taiwan, where I went to high school, long lines would form at a cart run by two old street vendors near the school. The couple sold only one thing — duck wonton soup. On one side of their cart sat a pot of boiling water for the wontons, and on the other simmered a pot of clear duck stock. The wontons were boiled, then floated in a bowl of the aromatic broth. The soup was topped with fried shallots, wild mountain celery, and duck cracklings. The dumpling filling was made with dried shiitakes; I use fresh.

This recipe makes twice as many wontons as you need for the soup, but they're handy to have on hand in the freezer. They can be panfried or deep-fried in 350-degree oil and passed as an appetizer, with or without Mango-Kumquat Relish (page 283), or topped with sautéed shiitake mushrooms and baby arugula and served as a first course.

I cut the wonton wrappers into 3-inch squares because I prefer smaller wontons, but you can skip that step if you like. Any unused wrappers can be rewrapped and refrozen for later use.

[Serves 6 as a first course]

DUCK WONTONS

8	large shiitake mushrooms, stemmed
1	12- to 14-ounce whole boneless duck breast
1	tablespoon toasted sesame oil
3	tablespoons soy sauce
3	tablespoons brandy
3	tablespoons chicken stock, Duck Stock (page 58), or water
2	tablespoons grated peeled fresh ginger
¼	cup finely chopped fresh tarragon

4	scallions, finely chopped (about 1 cup)
	Cornstarch for dusting
50–60	thin wonton wrappers (see page 9), cut into 3-inch squares

SOUP

5	cups Duck Stock (page 58) or chicken stock
	Kosher salt and freshly ground pepper
2	large shiitake mushrooms, cut into thin strips
½	cup pea shoots (see page 52) or fresh cilantro leaves

TO MAKE THE WONTONS: Coarsely chop the mushrooms. Add the chopped mushrooms to a food processor and pulse until coarsely ground. Place the ground mushrooms in a medium bowl and set aside.

Remove the skin (with the fat layer still attached) from the duck breast (save for duck cracklings; see page 53). Cut the meat into 1-inch cubes, and coarsely grind in a meat grinder or the food processor. Place in a large bowl.

Add the sesame oil, soy sauce, brandy, stock or water, and ginger to the duck and mix until well incorporated. Add the tarragon, scallions, and ground mushrooms and mix until thoroughly combined. *The filling can be covered and refrigerated overnight.*

Cover a baking sheet with a sheet of parchment or waxed paper and dust with a little cornstarch. Place a wonton wrapper on a flat work surface and put 1 heaping teaspoon of the duck mixture in the center. (Keep the remaining wontons covered as you work.) Moisten the edges of the wrapper with a little water and fold over the filling to form a triangle. Pinch the edges together with your fingers to make a tight seal. Moisten the two ends of the wonton with a little water, and bring them together to form a ring, overlapping them slightly

Pea Shoots

Long used in Chinese cooking, pea shoots are a spring and early summer delicacy. Called *dau miu* in Cantonese, they are the delicate young leaves and tendrils of the plant. They are usually harvested from snow peas, but they can come from other pea varieties as well. ✿ Pea shoots can be eaten raw or lightly cooked. They have a light pea flavor with a hint of sweetness. Use them soon after purchasing or harvesting, as they wilt quickly. Choose shoots that have fresh-looking green leaves. Remove any stems that appear tough; rinse and dry the shoots. They will last for a day or two if wrapped in paper towels and refrigerated. ✿ If you are adding them to soups or stir-fries, put them in at the very last minute so they will stay crisp and green.

and pinching together to seal. The wonton will resemble a little hat. Stand the wonton on the prepared baking sheet, and repeat until all of the filling is used. *The wontons can be refrigerated overnight; cover tightly with a sheet of plastic wrap. Or they can be frozen: place them in a single layer on a baking sheet in the freezer until they are frozen hard. Transfer to a zipper-lock bag; they will keep frozen for up to 3 months.*

TO PREPARE THE SOUP: Bring the stock to a boil in a medium saucepan and season to taste with salt and pepper. Keep warm over very low heat.

Bring a large pot of water to a boil. Add 24 of the wontons. Using a Chinese strainer or a slotted spoon, stir to prevent the wontons from sticking together, and return the water to a boil. The wontons will rise to the top, but the filling will not yet be completely cooked. Add ½ cup cold water and bring to the boil again to cook through. Using a slotted spoon, place 4 wontons in each of six soup bowls.

TO SERVE: Top the wontons with the sliced shiitake mushrooms and the pea shoots or cilantro. Ladle the hot broth into the bowls and serve.

TO STORE WONTONS: The remaining wontons can be frozen, uncooked, as directed, or cooked and refrigerated for up to 2 days. (Do not freeze cooked wontons; the wrappers will become too soft and will disintegrate when you cook them again.) Place the cooked wontons on a large baking sheet covered with a sheet of parchment or waxed paper. Pat dry with paper towels, then cool. Transfer the wontons to a second baking sheet lined with a clean piece of waxed paper or plastic wrap, cover tightly with plastic wrap, and refrigerate. They can be reheated in a microwave oven or in a steamer.

Duck Cracklings

I don't like to waste anything, and duck cracklings are a great way to use the skin from the duck when you need the meat for other dishes. They make wonderful nibbles — they'll be gone before you know it! ✿ To make cracklings, cut the skin into 2-inch pieces. Place in a heavy saucepan and add 1 tablespoon water. Cook over very low heat until the fat is completely melted and the pieces of skin are crisp and browned. Strain the fat into a jar and drain the cracklings on paper towels. Enjoy as a snack or garnish salads or soups with them. Refrigerate the duck fat and use for cooking; it will keep for several weeks. Or freeze, tightly covered, for up to 6 months.

Beef Soup with Somen Noodles

———————— (✿) ————————

For this hearty soup, I slowly braise the meat at a very low temperature. I prefer to leave the bones in, but when I have guests, I remove them. The pea shoots and cilantro, added at the last minute, lend freshness.

Oxtails used to come from oxen, but today they are simply the tails of beef cattle. The collagen released from the bones and marrow makes a thick, rich beef stock; the meat is also very tasty.

————————— [*Serves 6 as a main course*] —————————

6   pounds oxtails, excess fat trimmed, or beef shanks, cut into 2-inch pieces

2   large carrots, peeled and cut into large pieces

2   leeks, white and tender green parts only, well rinsed, cut into 2-inch pieces

2   large celery stalks, cut into 2-inch pieces

2   medium tomatoes, cut into quarters

3–5   star anise

1   tablespoon Sichuan peppercorns (see page 93) or black peppercorns

1   3-inch piece fresh ginger, thinly sliced
    Kosher salt and freshly ground pepper

4   ounces somen noodles

8   ounces pea shoots (see page 52)

½   cup fresh cilantro sprigs

Cook the oxtails or beef shanks in a large stockpot of boiling water for 2 minutes. Carefully drain in a large colander. Rinse the pot out well.

Return the meat to the pot and add the carrots, leeks, celery, tomatoes, star anise, peppercorns, ginger, and 1 teaspoon salt. Add cold water to cover by 4 inches and bring to a boil. Reduce the heat to low and simmer, covered, until the meat is very tender and almost falling off the bone, about 3 hours. As the soup cooks, remove the lid and skim the surface from time to time, discarding any scum.

Strain the stock; set aside. Let the oxtails or beef shanks cool slightly, and discard the vegetables and seasonings. When cool enough to handle, remove the meat from the bones, trim excess fat, and cut into ½-inch pieces. Refrigerate the stock and meat separately, well covered, overnight.

Remove the fat from the surface of the chilled stock and discard. Bring the stock to a boil in a large saucepan and boil to reduce by half; you should have about 6 cups. Season to taste with salt and pepper.

Meanwhile, bring a large pot of water to a boil over high heat. Add the noodles and boil for about 2 minutes, just until cooked through; do not overcook. Pour into a colander and drain well.

Reheat the meat in a microwave oven just until hot. Or reheat in a preheated 350-degree oven for about 10 minutes.

Divide the noodles among six soup bowls. Top each with a portion of the meat and the pea shoots, then spoon the hot broth over all. Garnish with the cilantro sprigs and serve.

Somen Noodles

Many people think somen noodles are Japanese, but they originally came from China. The name translates as long-life noodles (*so* means long life and *mein* means noodles in Mandarin), and the noodles are often served at the end of a birthday meal to symbolize a long and happy life. Very thin noodles made from hard wheat flour, which is high in gluten, they are similar to vermicelli. Although in Japan somen noodles are often served cold during the summer months, the Chinese reserve them for hot soups.

Vegetable Stock

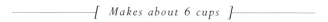

This flavorful stock is better than anything you can buy in a can, and it's easy to prepare, since a food processor does most of the work. I process each vegetable separately, so they are chopped evenly. If you are in a hurry, you can process them all together in one batch.

Makes about 2 quarts

2	celery stalks, cut into 1-inch pieces
1	medium carrot, peeled and cut into 1-inch pieces
1	2-inch piece fresh ginger, peeled and cut into ¼-inch slices
3	scallions, trimmed and cut into 1-inch pieces
1	small onion, cut into 1-inch pieces
½	cup firmly packed coarsely chopped fresh cilantro stems and leaves
	Kosher salt

Coarsely chop the celery in a food processor. Transfer to a large bowl. Add the carrot to the processor and coarsely chop. Transfer to the bowl with the celery. Repeat with the ginger, scallions, onion, and cilantro.

Pour 3 quarts of water into a stockpot. Add the vegetables and cilantro and bring to a boil. Turn the heat to very low and simmer for about 45 minutes.

Strain the stock through a fine sieve, pressing well to extract all the liquid, and season to taste with salt. *The cooled stock can be refrigerated, covered, for 3 days or frozen for up to 6 months. Freeze in 1- or 2-cup containers for easy use.*

Mushroom Stock

I save mushroom stems — shiitakes, portobellos, or even the bottoms of button mushroom stems — in a plastic container in the freezer. When I have about 2 pounds, I make a pot of stock. It is a flavorful foundation for almost any soup. Reduced to ½ cup, it can be used as a base for sauces. For an instant mushroom soup, heat the stock, then stir in ¼ to ½ cup heavy cream and a few thinly sliced button mushrooms and garnish with a sprinkling of chopped fresh flat-leaf parsley or chives.

Makes about 6 cups

2	pounds mushroom stems, plus any broken pieces
2	tablespoons olive oil
3	shallots, sliced
3	garlic cloves, sliced
8	cups Vegetable Stock or chicken stock
1	tablespoon butter

Coarsely grind the mushroom stems and pieces in a food processor.

Heat the oil in a medium stockpot over high heat. Add the shallots and garlic and cook for 2 to 3 minutes, or until soft. Add the ground mushrooms, turn the heat to low, and simmer for about 15 minutes, until the mushrooms release their flavor.

Add the stock and bring to a boil, then lower the heat, and simmer, uncovered, for about 45 minutes. Stir in the butter.

Strain the stock, pressing well to extract all of the liquid; discard the solids. *The stock can be refrigerated, covered, for several days or frozen for up to 6 months.*

Lobster Stock

———— (✿) ————

This stock is a good base for seafood soups or stews. It's used in Lobster
Ravioli (page 8) and Shrimp with Lobster Sauce (page 122).

———————{ *Makes about 1 ½ cups* }———————

Shells from 1 pound shrimp

Body from a 1½-pound lobster

2   tablespoons soybean oil or corn oil

1   small onion, coarsely chopped

1   garlic clove, sliced

1   tablespoon grated peeled fresh ginger

½   cup dry white wine

1   large tomato, cored and cut into pieces

6   cups chicken stock

Rinse the shrimp shells (this will prevent the stock from turning dark). Rinse the lobster body and crush it with the side of a heavy knife.

Pour the oil into a medium stockpot, turn the heat to high, and add the onion, garlic, and ginger. Cook until soft, 2 to 3 minutes. Add the shrimp shells and lobster body and cook, stirring, until the shells turn color, 3 to 4 minutes.

Add the wine, tomato, and chicken stock. Bring to a boil, then turn the heat to low and simmer for about 45 minutes.

Strain the stock through a fine sieve and pour into a medium saucepan. Simmer until reduced to about 1½ cups, about 20 minutes. *The stock can be refrigerated, covered, for 2 days or frozen for 1 month.*

Duck Stock

———————————— (✿) ————————————

Don't throw out the carcass from a duck — save it to make this intensely flavorful stock, which can be used in place of chicken stock in soups or sauces. Chop up the carcass and freeze it for a month or two if you like, then make the stock when you have the time. The stock is best made 1 to 2 days ahead and refrigerated so all the fat can rise to the surface and be skimmed off. Add leftover diced chicken or duck, diced vegetables, diced tofu, or cooked noodles for a quick soup.

————————— { *Makes 5 to 6 cups* } —————————

1	tablespoon soybean oil or corn oil
	Carcass from a 4- to 5-pound duck, chopped
1	small onion, halved
½	teaspoon Sichuan peppercorns (see page 93)

2	star anise
¼	cup thinly sliced peeled fresh ginger
2	tablespoons whiskey or brandy
	Kosher salt and freshly ground pepper

Add the oil and the duck carcass to a large stockpot and cook, stirring occasionally, over high heat until the duck pieces turn brown, about 10 minutes.

Add the onion to the pot and cook for another minute. Add the Sichuan peppercorns, star anise, ginger, and whiskey or brandy and cook, stirring, for 30 seconds. Add 8 cups water and bring to a simmer. Stir well, cover, and simmer gently over medium-low heat for about 1 hour.

Strain the stock and season to taste with salt and pepper. Cool to room temperature, then refrigerate for at least 6 hours. Skim off the layer of fat that forms on top (refrigerate or freeze the fat in a covered container and use for sautéing). *The stock can be frozen in a tightly covered container for up to 2 months or refrigerated for up to 3 days.*

Lamb Stock

(⟡)

Once you have this stock on hand, you'll find all kinds of uses for it: as a base
for sauces for lamb roasts or chops, as a flavorful addition to lamb stews or
braised dishes, or for lamb and barley soup.

[Makes 3 quarts]

5   pounds lamb bones

1   large onion, coarsely chopped

2   large carrots, coarsely chopped

1   2-inch piece fresh ginger, peeled and sliced

1   tablespoon Sichuan peppercorns (see page 93)

3–5   star anise

Preheat the oven to 425 degrees. Place the lamb bones in a roasting pan and roast for about 45 minutes, or until browned, turning once.

Transfer the bones to a stockpot. Carefully pour off and discard any fat from the roasting pan. Place the roasting pan over a burner, turn the heat to high, and pour in 1 to 2 cups water. Deglaze the pan by scraping it well to dislodge the brown bits sticking to the bottom. Add the liquid, along with the brown bits, to the stockpot.

Add the remaining ingredients, along with 5 quarts water, to the pot and bring to a boil over high heat. Reduce the heat to a simmer, and cook, uncovered, for 6 hours. Skim off and discard any foam that rises to the top of the pot during cooking, and add water as needed to keep the bones covered.

Strain the stock, cool to room temperature, then refrigerate. After it has chilled, remove the congealed fat from the surface and discard. *The stock can be refrigerated, covered, for up to 3 days or frozen for up to 6 months. Freeze in 1- or 2-cup containers for easy use.*

Salads and Cold Vegetable Dishes

Preparing
Salad Greens

The secret to a great salad is to be particular (almost obsessive) about how you wash the greens, so as to remove even the minutest traces of grit and keep them crisp. Start with the best and freshest greens available. I prefer baby greens, especially micro-greens, which are very small and young — only 1 to 1½ inches long. They're tender and flavorful and the prettiest for garnishes. If you can't find micro-greens, buy the smallest greens available. If you are using head lettuces, remove and discard the outer leaves and the core or stem bottoms, then separate the leaves and wash individually. ✿ The sink or large bowl you use to wash the greens must be very clean. Fill it with lots of cold water. Then add ice cubes to the water until it is so cold that they stop melting — you should still have some cubes floating around. Now your water is chilled enough for the greens. Scoop out the floating cubes before proceeding, for they can "burn" the tender greens, just as frost would, if they come into contact with them. ✿ Place the greens in the water and let soak for about 1 minute. Lift out, transfer to a salad spinner, and spin off all the excess water. Place them in a tightly sealed container and refrigerate until ready to use. Delicate greens such as cress will remain fresh for 3 days; heartier greens will keep for up to 1 week.

Toasting
Nuts and Seeds

Toasting brings out the flavor of nuts and seeds. Nuts can be
toasted in the oven or on top of the stove. ⟳ To toast nuts in
the oven, preheat the oven to 325 degrees. Spread out the nuts
on a baking sheet in a single layer and toast, stirring occasionally, just until lightly browned, about 10 minutes. Watch carefully to make sure they don't burn. Or toast nuts or seeds, such as
sesame seeds, in a skillet over low heat, shaking the pan and
stirring, until lightly golden, 3 to 4 minutes. Remove from
the heat and pour into a bowl to cool. Toasted nuts and
seeds can be stored in a tightly covered glass jar
in the refrigerator for up to a month.

Watercress Salad with Lime Vinaigrette

The peppery taste of young cress is a good match for the lime dressing and crunchy toasted almonds. Serve as a first course or alongside Citrus-Cured Salmon (page 14), Wild Mushroom Dumplings (page 2), or Truffled Potato Dumplings (page 12).

[Serves 4]

2   tablespoons extra-virgin olive oil

1   garlic clove, minced

1   teaspoon grated lime zest

2   tablespoons fresh lime juice

1   teaspoon sugar

Kosher salt and freshly ground pepper

2   bunches watercress, tough stems removed, washed and dried as described on page 63

¼   cup sliced almonds, toasted (see page 64)

Mix the oil and garlic in a small bowl or jar and microwave for 1 minute on high power; remove and immediately add the lime zest, lime juice, and sugar. Mix well to blend, then season to taste with salt and pepper. Or heat the oil and garlic in a small saucepan over medium heat for 1 to 2 minutes, until the garlic softens; remove from the heat and stir in the lime zest, lime juice, sugar, and salt and pepper to taste. *The dressing can be made up to 2 days ahead. Cover tightly and refrigerate.*

To serve, toss the watercress with just enough of the dressing to coat well. Divide among four salad plates, sprinkle with the sliced almonds, and serve.

Arugula and Golden Beet Salad with Citrus Vinaigrette

The sweet beets are set off by the slightly bitter arugula and tangy citrus dressing. If you can't find baby arugula, substitute mesclun or watercress. Disks of Panko-Crusted Goat Cheese (page 27) on top of the arugula are a nice addition. Serve with Salmon Braised with Soy and Ginger (page 98) or Roasted Squab with Port Wine Sauce (page 151).

[Serves 4]

1 pound (3 large) golden beets	¼ cup Citrus Vinaigrette (recipe follows), plus a few spoonfuls
3 cups baby arugula, washed and dried	for drizzling

Trim the beet tops to about 1 inch and leave the roots attached. Rinse well.

Fill the bottom of a steamer with water and bring to a boil. Place the beets in the steamer basket, cover tightly, and steam for 15 to 20 minutes, or until the beets are barely tender. Test by inserting the tip of a knife into them; they should give just a little. Remove the steamer basket and cool. When they are cool enough to handle, peel off the skins.

Using a Japanese Benriner, mandoline, or sharp knife, slice the beets into thin rounds. Arrange them, slightly overlapping, on four large chilled plates, covering the plates completely.

Place the arugula in a medium bowl and toss with the dressing. Mound in the center of each plate. Drizzle a little more dressing over the beets and serve.

SIMPLE VARIATION

The beets can also be roasted. Wrap in aluminum foil and place in a baking pan. Bake in a preheated 350-degree oven until they are firm-tender, 45 minutes to 1 hour.

Citus Vinaigrette

———[*Makes about 1 ¼ cups*]———

This is my favorite salad dressing. The base is fresh orange and lime juice. Cooking the vinaigrette to reduce it not only concentrates the flavor but also means the dressing can be stored for much longer in the refrigerator. Adding a little dissolved cornstarch helps prevent the separation of oil and vinegar that often occurs in homemade salad dressings.

This dressing goes well with other bitter-greens or fruit salads, as well as with Arugula and Golden Beet Salad.

	Grated zest of ½ orange
	Grated zest of ½ lime
2	cups orange juice
¼	cup fresh lime juice
¼	teaspoon cornstarch, mixed with 1 teaspoon water
1	tablespoon minced shallots
1½	teaspoons finely chopped fresh rosemary
¼	cup extra-virgin olive oil
1½	teaspoons kosher salt
	Freshly ground white pepper

Combine the zests, orange juice, lime juice, and cornstarch mixture in a medium saucepan and bring to a boil, then lower the heat to a simmer and cook, uncovered, until the liquid is reduced to about 1 cup, about 20 minutes. Remove from the heat and cool.

Pour the cooled liquid into a blender or food processor and add the shallots and rosemary. With the motor running, slowly drizzle in the olive oil, mixing until the vinaigrette is emulsified. Season with the salt and pepper to taste.

Store in a glass jar with a tight-fitting lid. *The dressing can be refrigerated for about 2 weeks.*

Belgian Endive and Orange Salad

————(✿)————

From December to late spring, when blood oranges are in season, make this salad with them instead of navel oranges — it will look even more striking. You can prepare the components for the salad in advance and refrigerate them separately, but wait until the last moment to mix in the orange pieces so the dressing doesn't become watery. The salad goes well with grilled fish or chicken.

——————[*Serves 4*]——————

2   Belgian endives

3   navel oranges

6   tablespoons sour cream

2   tablespoons Citrus Vinaigrette

1   teaspoon sugar

Slice the endives lengthwise in half. Remove the hard inner cores and discard. Cut the endives crosswise into half-circles about ¼ inch thick. Place in a bowl, cover with cold water, and soak for 20 minutes.

Drain the endives well, pat dry with paper towels, and refrigerate.

Remove the orange segments from the oranges. Cut the segments from 1 orange into ½-inch pieces; leave the rest of the segments whole.

Mix the sour cream, vinaigrette, and sugar in a medium bowl. Mix in the endives and diced orange segments.

Mound the salad in the center of four chilled salad plates. Place the whole orange segments decoratively around it and serve.

Removing Orange or Grapefruit Segments from Their Membranes

Cut a small slice from the top and bottom of the fruit. Stand the fruit on one end on a cutting board. With a sharp knife, remove the peel and pith by slicing downward from top to bottom, working your way around the fruit. Turn over and cut away any remaining pith at the base of the fruit. ✿ Holding the fruit over a bowl, carefully slice down either side of each segment, staying as close to the membranes as possible and letting the segments drop into the bowl. Then squeeze the membranes over the segments to extract all the remaining juices.

Frisée and Peach Salad with Honey Mustard Vinaigrette

Frisée, a member of the chicory family, is a variety of curly endive. It has slender curly green outer leaves and a delicate pale yellow to white center, with a mildly bitter flavor. It's one of my favorite greens because of its beautiful color and crisp bitterness. Here it's the perfect foil for the sweet peach. The slight licorice edge of the fennel and the cilantro leaves play off against the two. The salad is a stunning summer first course. When choosing frisée, select heads with lots of yellow-white center leaves that show no sign of wilting. Use only the tender white inner leaves for this salad.

When peaches are not in season, substitute a Gala or Fuji apple or an Anjou pear.

[Serves 4]

1 small head frisée	¼ cup fresh cilantro leaves, chopped
1 small fennel bulb	¼ cup Honey Mustard Vinaigrette (recipe follows)
1 medium peach, preferably a white peach, peeled	

Pull off and discard the tough outer green leaves of the frisée (reserve for another use, if desired). Using kitchen shears, trim away any tough green tips. Cut off and discard the root end, separating the individual leaves. Plunge into ice water to crisp, then drain and spin-dry in a salad spinner. Refrigerate, wrapped in a damp towel to keep the frisée very crisp.

Trim off the root end of the fennel bulb, cut off the stalks, and discard any tough outer layers. Using a Japanese Benriner, mandoline, or sharp knife, cut the fennel into paper-thin slices. Soak in a bowl of ice water for about 10 minutes (this will crisp the fennel and prevent the cut edges from turning brown). Drain and dry using a salad spinner. Place the fennel in a container, cover with a wet towel and then a lid or plastic wrap, and refrigerate.

Halve, then quarter the peach; discard the pit. With a very sharp knife, slice the peach into ⅛-inch-thick slices. *The peach can be sliced up to 2 hours ahead and placed in a bowl of cold water, to keep it from discoloring. Drain well before serving.*

Place the frisée, fennel, peach, and cilantro in a large bowl. Add the vinaigrette and mix well. Serve.

Honey Mustard Vinaigrette

——[*Makes about ¾ cup*]——

This thick, creamy dressing is perfect over chilled blanched vegetables. It is also especially good with fresh fruit, as in the Frisée and Peach Salad, or as a dressing for baby spinach, Belgian endive, radicchio, or any green salad.

1	tablespoon olive oil
1	garlic clove, minced
1	tablespoon minced peeled fresh ginger
½	cup Vegetable Stock (page 56) or water
1	teaspoon cornstarch, mixed with 1 tablespoon cold water
1	tablespoon soy sauce
1	tablespoon toasted sesame oil
1	tablespoon balsamic vinegar
1	tablespoon honey
½	teaspoon kosher salt
1	tablespoon grainy mustard (preferably Dijon)
2	tablespoons extra-virgin olive oil

Heat the tablespoon olive oil in a medium saucepan over high heat. Add the garlic and ginger and cook, stirring, until soft, about 30 seconds. Add the stock or water and the cornstarch mixture, mix well, and bring to a boil. Turn the heat to low and simmer, stirring, for 5 minutes. Add the soy sauce, sesame oil, vinegar, honey, and salt and return to a boil, then remove from the heat. Cool.

Place the stock mixture, mustard, and extra-virgin olive oil in a blender or food processor and process until creamy. Pour into a glass jar. *The dressing will keep, tightly covered, in the refrigerator for up to 2 weeks.*

Sesame Oil

Cold-pressed, unrefined sesame oil is used as a seasoning rather than for cooking. Made from toasted sesame seeds, it has a strong, nutty flavor and fragrance, but it has a low smoking point and burns easily. It is sold as 100 percent pure sesame oil or in a variety of other strengths, diluted with vegetable oil. I use 100 percent toasted sesame oil made in Japan, and I prefer the Kadoya brand. Japanese sesame oils have cleaner, purer flavors than Chinese oils, which tend to be cloudier and heavier-tasting.

Napa Cabbage and Sun-Dried Tomato Salad

———————————— (✦) ————————————

Think of this as a lively Asian interpretation of coleslaw, with the crunch of cabbage, the heat of fresh hot peppers, and the sweet tang of sun-dried toma- toes. Serve with Roasted Five-Spice Pork Tenderloin (page 175) or fish dishes, or add to sandwiches to spice them up.

—————[*Serves 8 to 10*]—————

1	head napa cabbage (about 2 pounds)		2	fresh hot red peppers, stemmed and chopped
2	teaspoons kosher salt		1	tablespoon white vinegar
2	tablespoons extra-virgin olive oil		2	teaspoons sugar
2	shallots, thinly sliced		½	cup minced scallions
4	sun-dried tomato halves, julienned		½	cup fresh basil leaves

Discard the tough outer green leaves of the cabbage. Slice off the base and cut the cabbage in half. Slice it into approxi- mately ⅛-inch-wide strips. Put the cabbage in a large bowl, sprinkle with the salt, and mix well. Let sit for 20 minutes.

Meanwhile, heat the oil in a small skillet over medium- high heat. Add the shallots and cook, stirring, until fragrant, about 30 seconds. Add the sun-dried tomatoes and red pep- pers and cook, stirring, for 1 minute. Remove from the heat, add the vinegar and sugar, and mix well. Cool.

Put the cabbage in a colander and gently press to drain the excess liquid. Transfer to a medium bowl and mix in the scallions. Add the shallot mixture and mix well. Refrigerate, covered, until ready to serve or serve immediately. *The salad will keep, refrigerated, in a sealed container for 3 days.*

Just before serving, cut the basil into julienne and sprin- kle over the salad (do not slice the basil leaves ahead of time, or they will turn black).

Sun-Dried Tomatoes

I always keep plenty of sun-dried tomatoes in a tightly sealed plastic container in my refrigerator for making salads and chutney or for braising and stir-frying. Choose sun-dried tomato halves with a soft texture and bright red color. I don't like the kind that are packed in olive oil, for the oil over- powers the flavor of the tomatoes and gives them an "off," greasy taste. Avoid chopped or juli- enned sun-dried tomatoes, which are too dry and often have less flavor than the tomato halves.

Red Cabbage and Jicama Salad with Spicy Dried Shrimp Vinaigrette

This colorful, slightly sweet-and-sour side dish is a crisp pick-me-up, especially in winter, when good lettuces are not in season. The Vietnamese-style dressing, which is made with shallots, fresh hot peppers, lime juice, and very little oil, makes a sprightly topping for the crisp vegetables and mint. The dried shrimp functions here much as anchovies do in a Caesar salad, contributing a subtle, fuller dimension and bringing the taste of the vegetables to new heights. Serve with Roasted Five-Spice Pork Tenderloin (page 175) or salmon.

[Serves 6]

2	cups julienned red cabbage (about ¼ head)
4	ounces jicama, peeled and julienned (about 1 cup)
1	very small carrot, peeled and julienned
¼	cup fresh mint leaves, julienned
1	tablespoon soybean oil or corn oil
1½	teaspoons minced soaked dried shrimp
1	shallot, thinly sliced

1–2	jalapeño peppers, stemmed, seeded, and finely chopped
2	tablespoons fish sauce (preferably Three Crabs brand)
	Grated zest and juice of 1 lime
1½	teaspoons sugar
2	tablespoons sliced almonds, toasted (see page 64), or unsalted roasted peanuts

Fill a large bowl with ice cubes and water. Add the cabbage, jicama, carrot, and mint and soak for about 10 minutes. Drain well; the vegetables should be very crisp. Transfer to a bowl and refrigerate, covered with a damp paper towel, until ready to serve.

Heat the oil in a small saucepan over medium heat and add the dried shrimp. Turn the heat to low and cook for about 1 minute, or until the shrimp are fragrant.

Transfer the shrimp and oil to a blender or food processor, add the shallot, jalapeño, fish sauce, lime zest and juice, and sugar, and puree. *The dressing can be made up to 2 weeks ahead and refrigerated in a tightly sealed container.*

Just before serving, toss the vegetables with enough of the dressing to coat well. Sprinkle with the toasted almonds or peanuts and serve. *Leftover salad will keep for up to a week in the refrigerator.*

Dried Shrimp

Dried shrimp lend depth rather than a pronounced flavor to a variety of dishes. Look for them in Asian markets. Packed in cellophane bags, they come in different sizes, the largest usually being the most expensive and best. They should be pinkish orange; avoid brown shrimp, which are old. ❧ Traditionally the shrimp are used whole, but that way their flavor is overpowering and their texture too firm. ❧ TO SOAK DRIED SHRIMP: Cover the shrimp with hot water and soak them for 10 to 15 minutes to soften them, then drain and mince them to a paste in a food processor or by hand. ❧ Prepared in this manner, the shrimp have a delicate, subtle, only faintly shrimpy flavor. Soaked and minced dried shrimp can be refrigerated in a tightly sealed jar, covered with a layer of olive oil, for up to 2 weeks, or they can be frozen for up to 3 months.

Sautéed Haricots Verts and Artichokes

(☉)

The idea for this came from an intriguing dish a friend's mother made when she was visiting from Singapore several years ago. She cooked green beans, bamboo shoots, and carrots in a spicy coconut-turmeric sauce and served the dish at room temperature. To duplicate it, I had to find a stand-in for the fresh bamboo shoots; quickly cooked sliced artichoke is a close approximation.

Haricots verts (French beans) are usually tenderer and have more flavor than regular beans. If they're not available, get the youngest, thinnest string beans possible. If you can't find fresh turmeric, powdered turmeric will give the same color, but it will not have the delicate taste of the fresh.

[Serves 4 to 6]

¼ cup raw peanuts, skins removed

8 ounces haricots verts (thin young green beans can be substituted)

1 small carrot, peeled

Juice of 1 lemon

1 large artichoke

3 tablespoons corn oil or olive oil

2 medium shallots, quartered

¼ cup dry white wine

1 jalapeño pepper, stemmed and sliced

1 tablespoon crushed peeled fresh turmeric (see page 101) or ½ teaspoon ground turmeric

½ cup unsweetened coconut cream

2 teaspoons sugar

Kosher salt and freshly ground pepper

Preheat the oven to 325 degrees. Place the peanuts in a shallow pan and bake for about 10 minutes, stirring occasionally, or until the nuts are lightly browned. Cool.

Chop the peanuts with a knife until finely crushed, or grind in a spice grinder or a small food processor; be careful not to overgrind them — you want very small pieces, not peanut butter.

Trim off the ends of the beans and cut each bean in half. Cut the carrot into 2-inch chunks. Using a Japanese Benriner or mandoline, cut the chunks into julienne. Or using a sharp knife, cut into slices about ¼ inch thick, then cut the slices into 2-inch lengths (about the same size as the beans).

Put the lemon juice in a medium bowl. Fill the bowl with cold water. Trim the artichoke as described on page 239

and cut into 16 pieces; place in the lemon water to keep it from discoloring.

Cook the beans and carrot in a medium pot of salted boiling water for 3 to 5 minutes, or until barely tender. Drain and plunge into a bowl of ice water to stop the cooking. Drain well.

Drain the artichoke. Heat 1 tablespoon of the oil in a large skillet or flat-bottomed wok over medium heat and stir-fry the shallots until softened, about 1 minute. Add the artichoke and wine and cook for about 3 minutes, until the artichoke is cooked through but not soft. Spoon the artichoke and shallots, along with all of the liquid, into a bowl.

Wipe the skillet or wok clean and return to the heat. Add the remaining 2 tablespoons oil, the jalapeño, turmeric, and coconut cream and cook, stirring, for 2 minutes. Add the

Unsweetened Coconut Milk and Cream

Though I ordinarily insist on fresh ingredients whenever possible, in the case of coconut milk, I always buy canned, since fresh coconut milk is a lot of work to prepare and not worth the effort. Many brands are available, but the one I like best is Chaokoh, imported from Thailand, which is very flavorful. Don't substitute sweetened coconut cream (such as Coco Lopez), which is overpoweringly sweet; it is intended for mixed drinks and desserts. ✿ Canned coconut milk separates into a layer of thin watery milk that rises to the top and a thick layer of solidified fat, called the cream. To blend the cream back into the milk, dump the contents of the can into a bowl and whisk until smooth. ✿ TO PREPARE UNSWEETENED COCONUT CREAM: Pour the thin coconut milk on top into a container, then spoon out the coconut cream layer. Discard the milk or reserve for another purpose. Store any leftovers in separate sealed plastic containers.

beans and carrot, the artichoke mixture, and the sugar. Cook, stirring often, until the coconut cream has thoroughly coated the vegetables, about 3 minutes. Add the crushed peanuts and season to taste with salt and pepper. Remove from the heat and cool.

Serve at room temperature or chilled. *The salad can be made ahead, covered, and refrigerated overnight.*

Beet, Rhubarb, and Grapefruit Salad

(✿)

Guaranteed to make people sit up and take notice, this brilliantly colored salad features garnet-hued silky beets in citrus vinaigrette, tender segments of ruby grapefruit, and crisp, sweet, rosy rhubarb on a bed of watercress. To keep the rhubarb from getting stringy or mushy, I flash-cook it by pouring boiling water over it, then let it sit in a little sugar to draw out its juices and moderate its sour bite.

Serve with Quick-Seared Sichuan Beef Tenderloin Stew (page 178) or Crisp Roasted Poussin with Leeks and Potatoes (page 149).

―――――――――[*Serves 4*]―――――――――

1	large red beet (6 ounces)
2	tablespoons olive oil
2	shallots, thinly sliced
1	fresh hot red pepper, stemmed and thinly sliced
1	teaspoon dry white wine or rice wine vinegar
½	teaspoon kosher salt
	Freshly ground pepper

1	small rhubarb stalk (about 1 cup sliced)
1	tablespoon sugar
1	small grapefruit, preferably ruby red
1	bunch watercress
¼	cup chopped fresh herbs, such as cilantro, mint, or basil
¼	cup Citrus Vinaigrette (page 68)

Wash the beet and cut off the greens. Trim away the top and bottom portion of the beet until just 2 inches remain. Peel the beet and cut into quarters, then cut each quarter into 3 wedges.

Bring a small saucepan of water to a boil. Add the beets, return to a boil, and cook until just tender, about 5 minutes. Drain well and dry on paper towels.

Put the oil in a small skillet, add the shallots and hot pepper, and cook over high heat for 1 minute to release their flavor. Add the wine or vinegar, salt, and pepper to taste, remove from the heat, and cool.

Put the cooked beets in a medium bowl, add the shallot mixture, and mix well.

Trim both ends of the rhubarb, peel away the tough outer part, and slice on the diagonal into ¼-inch-thick slices.

Place in a medium bowl and pour over boiling water to cover, then drain. Return the rhubarb to the bowl and mix in the sugar.

Remove the grapefruit segments from their membranes according to the directions on page 69 (you should have 1 cup). Place in a small bowl.

Pinch off the tough bottom stems of the watercress and discard. Wash the watercress in ice water, lift out, and spin-dry in a salad spinner.

Mix the rhubarb into the beets and add the chopped herbs. Place the watercress in the center of a large plate, spoon the beet mixture over the cress, and top with the grapefruit segments. Spoon the vinaigrette over and serve.

Pickled Daikon Salad with Oranges

— (✿) —

Sprinkling daikon with salt draws out some of its liquid, mellowing its mustardy edge and crisping it.

—[*Makes 2 cups; serves 4*]—

1   firm medium daikon (about 1 pound), with fresh green tops

1   teaspoon kosher salt

1   navel orange

1   tablespoon olive oil

1   shallot, thinly sliced

½   teaspoon ground turmeric

3   tablespoons dry white wine

1   teaspoon sugar

2   tablespoons chopped fresh cilantro

Peel the daikon, then cut it crosswise in half. Using a Japanese Benriner or mandoline, cut into julienne. Or using a sharp knife, slice into ¼-inch-thick slices, then cut the slices into julienne. Place the daikon in a medium bowl and sprinkle with the salt. Refrigerate for 1 hour.

Grate the zest from the orange and place in a small bowl. Trim away and discard the white pith, then cut the orange into segments, separating them from the membranes as described on page 69.

Heat the oil in a small skillet over low heat. Add the shallot, orange zest, turmeric, white wine, and sugar and cook for about 3 minutes, stirring often, until the shallot is softened. Remove from the heat and cool.

Drain any liquid from the daikon. Place the daikon in a large serving bowl, pour over the dressing, and mix well. Stir in the orange segments and cilantro.

Cover and refrigerate for 2 to 8 hours, to develop the flavors. *The salad will keep, tightly covered and refrigerated, for up to 3 days.*

Daikon

A member of the radish family, daikon is an important vegetable in the cuisines of
China, Japan, Korea, and Southeast Asia, where it is prized for its flavor and its crisp texture. Daikon is extremely versatile. Used raw in salads or pickles, it has a spicy crunchiness
and freshness. Braising brings out its natural sweetness and gives a rich, subtle depth to a
sauce or soup. Julienned daikon is an excellent garnish for grilled fish or meat. ✿ Two varieties of daikon are available in the market. The most common kind is snowy white and about a
foot in length, weighs anything from a pound up, and is mild in flavor. The second variety,
Japanese daikon, is 6 to 8 inches long, with a pale green top; it is firmer and crisper. If you
have a choice, use the larger kind for braising and the Japanese kind for salads. ✿
Daikon is available all year long, but it is sweetest and most flavorful in the winter. Buy firm, compact daikon; if the tops are still attached, they should
be bright green. Daikon will keep in the refrigerator in a
plastic bag for about a week.

Chinese Long Beans with Toasted Almonds

Whenever I see tender long beans in Asian markets, I buy them to make this dish, which is popular in Taiwanese restaurants. My mother-in-law used to make a similar version, serving it in the morning along with many small dishes, such as sautéed eggs with tomatoes, cold smoked fish or chicken, and roasted peanuts. I was in college then, and she would sit at the dining room table and demand that all of us sit down and have a proper breakfast. Her younger children stood by the table impatiently, barely finishing bowls of thin rice congee in their rush to leave for school. After the children left, the two of us would linger, eating and talking.

I've stayed close to her original salad, but I add toasted almonds and fresh tarragon. If you can't get long beans, substitute ordinary string beans. This makes a good side dish for grilled meat or poultry.

Serves 6 to 8

1   pound Chinese long beans (see page 243)
2   tablespoons extra-virgin olive oil
1   teaspoon toasted sesame oil
1   garlic clove, thinly sliced
2   scallions, white part only, chopped
1   tablespoon soy sauce

1   tablespoon rice wine vinegar or sherry wine vinegar
1   cup grape tomatoes, cored and peeled (see page 123)
1/4   cup fresh tarragon leaves, chopped
    Kosher salt and freshly ground pepper
1/2   cup slivered almonds, toasted (see page 64)

Cut off both ends of the beans, then cut the beans into pieces about 2 inches long.

Fill a medium bowl with ice and water. Cook the beans in a medium saucepan of boiling lightly salted water for 3 to 5 minutes, or until tender. Drain, then plunge into the ice water to stop the cooking and preserve the color. When the beans are cool, drain them again.

Place the olive oil, sesame oil, garlic, and scallions in a small bowl and heat in a microwave oven for 1 minute on high power. Or place in a small saucepan and heat over medium heat just until the garlic softens, about 2 minutes; remove from the heat. Add the soy sauce and vinegar and mix well. Set aside.

Mix together the beans, tomatoes, olive oil mixture, and tarragon in a large bowl. Season to taste with salt and pepper. Serve chilled or at room temperature.

Just before serving, mix in the toasted almonds.

Chinese Eggplant

Long and thin, Chinese eggplant looks more like a brilliant purple English cucumber than an Italian eggplant. It has thin skin and very few seeds, and the flesh is tender, white, and mild. Even raw, it has none of the bitterness of the more familiar Western variety, and it's much juicier. Soaking the cut slices in salted water will stop the white flesh from discoloring.

You'll find Chinese eggplant in Asian and specialty produce markets. Choose those with firm, unwrinkled skins without any nicks. They will keep in the refrigerator, unwrapped, for 1 week. Only white eggplant and the tiny round Sicilian variety are close to the Chinese kind in character.

Cold Chinese Eggplant Salad with Sesame Soy Vinaigrette

This was one of our family's favorite cold vegetable salads when I was growing up. It was always served ice-cold, topped with a simple dressing made with ginger, garlic, soy sauce, and black vinegar and garnished with a little chopped fresh cilantro. To this day I make it often. Soaking the eggplant in salted water sets the bright purple color of the skin and keeps the white flesh from discoloring. Steaming brings out all the natural flavor and makes it silky. If you can't find Chinese eggplant, substitute small white or baby Sicilian eggplant; Japanese eggplant is too bitter.

[Serves 8]

- 1 pound (about 4) Chinese eggplants
- 1 tablespoon kosher salt
- 2 tablespoons Aromatic Scallion Oil (page 86)
- 1 tablespoon soy sauce
- 2 teaspoons balsamic vinegar or Chinese black vinegar (see page 183)
- 1/2 teaspoon toasted sesame oil
- 1 teaspoon sugar
- 2 sprigs fresh cilantro

Cut off the stems of the eggplants and slice each eggplant crosswise into 2-inch pieces (about 3 pieces per eggplant). Cut each piece lengthwise into quarters.

Fill a shallow bowl with 4 cups cold water and mix in the salt. Add the eggplant, making sure each piece is covered, and soak for about 20 minutes. Drain well.

Place the eggplant in a heatproof dish that will fit into a steamer basket. Fill the bottom of the steamer with water and bring to a boil (the water should be rapidly boiling before you add the eggplant so it keeps its bright purple color). Add the eggplant, cover tightly, and steam for 6 to 8 minutes, or until the eggplant is soft.

Cool the eggplant in the dish with its juices. When the eggplant is cool, cover and refrigerate until chilled. Allow the eggplant to soak in its juices, turning the pieces over occasionally as it cools and again as it chills; this soaking process is important to the flavor of the finished dish and will keep the eggplant moist and sweet.

Mix the scallion oil, soy sauce, vinegar, sesame oil, and sugar in a small bowl.

Transfer the cold eggplant to a serving plate, arranging the sections so that the purple skin faces up. Spoon a small amount of the soy-vinegar mixture over the eggplant, garnish with the cilantro, and serve. Serve the remaining dressing on the side.

Aromatic Scallion Oil

[*Makes about 2 cups*]

This is a very old recipe that exemplifies how bits and pieces of everything —
tops and ends of scallions and garlic, the skin peeled from ginger — are used
in a traditional Chinese kitchen. They are slowly fried to produce an aromatic
oil for salad dressings, braising, or grilling. Lacking these odds and ends, you
can make this oil using fresh ingredients, as described here.

2   cups soybean oil, corn oil, or olive oil

1   bunch scallions, trimmed and cut into 2-inch lengths

5   garlic cloves, sliced

1   2-inch piece fresh ginger, crushed and sliced

1   teaspoon Sichuan peppercorns (see page 93), rinsed and
     dried

Combine the oil, scallions, garlic, ginger, and Sichuan peppercorns in a medium saucepan and cook over medium heat
until the scallions turn light brown, about 15 minutes.
Remove from the heat and strain into a bowl.

   When the oil is cool, pour into a sealed plastic or glass
container and store in the refrigerator. *The oil can be refriger-*
ated for up to 2 months.

Braised Dried Shiitake Mushrooms

———————————(✿)———————————

Dried shitake mushrooms are preferable to fresh in a dish like this, where you want an intense mushroom taste, because drying concentrates the flavor. But simply stir-frying or cooking the mushrooms after soaking, as most recipes suggest, doesn't make them satisfyingly tender. For that reason, I steam them for at least 20 minutes after soaking before adding them to a dish. (The plain steamed mushrooms will keep in the refrigerator for a few weeks and are handy for adding to stir-fries or braised dishes.)

Serve these braised shiitakes cold as part of a first course or thinly slice and add them to salads.

——————————[*Serves 6*]——————————

20	dried shiitake mushrooms, soaked in cold water for 20 minutes, drained, and stemmed
2	tablespoons olive oil or soybean oil
2	garlic cloves, thinly sliced
1/4	cup julienned red bell pepper

1	tablespoon soy sauce
2	teaspoons toasted sesame oil
1	teaspoon balsamic vinegar
1	teaspoon sugar
1	cup chicken stock or Vegetable Stock (page 56)

Fill the bottom of a steamer with water and bring to a boil over high heat. Place the soaked mushrooms in a shallow heatproof bowl or on a plate, set it in the steamer basket, place in the steamer, cover, and turn the heat to low. Steam for 20 minutes.

Heat the olive or soybean oil in a large skillet or flat-bottomed wok over high heat. Add the garlic and red pepper and cook for 30 seconds, or until the garlic turns golden. Add the steamed mushrooms, along with all of their liquid, the soy sauce, sesame oil, balsamic vinegar, sugar, and stock and bring to a boil. Turn the heat to medium and simmer gently until the stock is completely absorbed by the mushrooms, about 20 minutes.

Serve at room temperature or cold. *The mushrooms will keep well for a week, covered tightly and refrigerated.*

Mandarin Potato Salad with Cellophane Noodles

Still popular in northern China, this salad is nothing like heavy American potato salad: there's no mayonnaise, for one thing. The potatoes are lightly blanched so they keep their crispy texture. When mixed with the airy cellophane noodles, sesame oil, and vinegar, they make a light and tasty salad — a great companion to grilled meat or poultry. I like it at room temperature, but it's also good cold.

Note that you could cook the potatoes and carrot in the same pot of boiling water you use for the noodles, but not the other way around; the potatoes give off starch, so the water would be too gluey for the noodles.

Serves 6 to 8

- 2 ounces (1 skein) thin cellophane noodles, prepared and cooked as described on page 90
- 1 pound Yukon Gold potatoes, peeled and cut into 2-inch-long julienne
- 1 medium carrot, peeled and cut into 2-inch-long julienne
- 1 tablespoon corn oil or olive oil
- 1 teaspoon minced garlic

- 1 jalapeño pepper, stemmed and chopped (optional)
- 1 tablespoon toasted sesame oil
- 2 tablespoons rice wine vinegar
- 1 teaspoon sugar
- 1 teaspoon kosher salt, or more to taste
- 2 tablespoons coarsely chopped fresh cilantro

Cut the cooked cellophane noodles into 2-inch lengths.

Bring a medium pot of water to a boil. Fill a medium bowl with ice and water. Cook the potatoes and carrot in the boiling water until barely tender, 1 to 2 minutes. Drain well and plunge into the ice water. Drain again, place in a bowl, and mix in the cellophane noodles.

Mix the corn or olive oil with the garlic and jalapeño in a small glass bowl and microwave on high power for 1 minute. Or cook in a small saucepan over medium heat for 1 to 2 minutes, until the garlic softens. Stir in the sesame oil, vinegar, sugar, and salt.

Mix the dressing and cilantro into the potato salad. Serve at room temperature, cold, or warm. *The salad will keep, covered, in the refrigerator for 3 days. It can be warmed in a microwave oven or in a skillet for a few minutes to take off the chill.*

Cellophane Noodles

Popular throughout China, Korea, Japan, and Southeast Asia, cellophane noodles are known by many names, including glass noodles, bean thread vermicelli, and mung bean threads. They are made from dried mung beans that are ground into flour. Their texture is very different from that of traditional Western noodles, for they become translucent, slippery, and pleasantly gummy when cooked. Neutral in taste, they readily absorb the flavors of the ingredients they are cooked with, adapting themselves perfectly to soups, stir-fries, salads, and stuffings. ❧ Cellophane noodles come in a variety of thicknesses and are usually sold in 7- to 8-ounce packages that contain small skeins of the threads, about 2 ounces each. Since they are dried, they keep well for a long time. The most famous brand and the one that I prefer is Long Kon (with a Red Dragon label), which has been around for generations. When cooked properly, these noodles never break or get mushy. ❧ TO PREPARE CELLOPHANE NOODLES: Uncooked cellophane noodles are sharp, tough, and almost impossible to break or cut. They need both soaking and cooking to become tender. Soak them for about 10 minutes in cold water, until they are slightly softened, then drain. Bring a pot of water to a boil and cook the noodles for about 1 minute, just until their color changes from pale white to translucent. Don't cook them too long, because they will absorb too much water. Drain, and rinse them in cold water to stop the cooking and separate the noodles. Drain again and cut into 4- to 6-inch lengths, or as directed in the recipe. ❧ The wider noodles are best for stir-fries, the very thin noodles for soups and stuffing and some stir-fries. For salads, use the freshly cooked noodles immediately, so they absorb the flavor of the dressing. If you will be using them for soups or stir-fries, you can keep the cooked noodles in a zipper-lock bag in the refrigerator for up to a week. When adding them to a soup, be careful to use only a very small amount, as they will otherwise absorb all the broth and you will end up with a pot of just noodles. The later in the cooking process you add them, the less liquid they will absorb.

Sichuan Pickled Brussels Sprouts

The Brussels sprouts lend a mild bittersweet flavor to this crisp, cold salad. The inspiration for the dish was a Sichuan pickled cabbage my grandmother used to make.

1	pound Brussels sprouts
½	small red bell pepper, sliced
2	fresh hot red peppers, thinly sliced
1	teaspoon kosher salt
1	tablespoon Sichuan Peppercorn Oil (page 93)
1	garlic clove, sliced
2	tablespoons white vinegar
1	tablespoon sugar

Discard the tough outer leaves of the Brussels sprouts and cut the sprouts lengthwise into quarters.

Bring a medium saucepan of water to a boil. Add the Brussels sprouts, return to a boil, and cook for 1 to 2 minutes, or until they are slightly softened but still bright green. Drain the sprouts and immediately plunge them into a large bowl of ice water so they retain their color and texture.

Drain the sprouts, press out as much water as possible, and then transfer to a large bowl. Stir in the red bell and hot peppers, along with the salt.

Combine the peppercorn oil and garlic in a medium glass bowl and microwave on high power for about 1 minute, just until the garlic is cooked. Or cook in a small saucepan over medium heat for 1 to 2 minutes, just until the garlic is softened, then transfer to a medium bowl. Add the vinegar and sugar and cool.

Add the Brussels sprouts and peppers to the vinegar mixture and toss well to coat. Serve chilled or at room temperature. *The pickled sprouts will keep for up to 1 week, covered and refrigerated.* Although it can be eaten right away, the relish is better the next day.

Brussels Sprouts

I first tasted Brussels sprouts when I lived in a dormitory at the University of Pittsburgh in 1968. I hated them — they were bitter, mushy, and horrible! I didn't touch Brussels sprouts again until thirty years later, when I bought a pint from the local farmers' market. I reasoned that since they are part of the cabbage family, I could treat them like Chinese cabbage and stir-fry them quickly. I trimmed off the stems, peeled off the tough outer leaves, and stir-fried them with a little garlic in some olive oil. Much to my delight, they were beautifully sweet and crisp. Brussels sprouts are especially good in the fall and winter, once the ground is frosty, when they are less bitter. When choosing Brussels sprouts at the market, look for tight green heads with no hint of yellowing or drooping leaves. I select large sprouts with leaves that are slightly loose; they are easier to work with. Trim off the bottom of the sprouts and discard the very tough outer leaves (2 to 4 leaves). Sometimes I remove the remaining large outer leaves individually until I reach the inner tender heart of the sprout. I cook these hearts first, then add the outer leaves until they are just cooked. Other times, I quarter the sprouts or slice them crosswise into two or three pieces so they cook quickly.

Sichuan Peppercorn Oil

[Makes about 2 cups]

Sichuan peppercorns are widely used throughout China. Toasting them brings out their pungency.

¹/₂   cup Sichuan peppercorns

2   cups soybean oil or corn oil

2   garlic cloves, crushed

Place the peppercorns in a sieve and rinse them well under cold running water. Drain and let dry.

Heat the oil in a small saucepan over medium heat and add the peppercorns and garlic. Cook for about 5 minutes, until the peppercorns turn very dark. Remove from the heat and cool.

Strain the oil through a fine sieve; discard the solids. Pour the oil into a jar with a tight-fitting lid. *The oil can be refrigerated for up to 3 months.*

Sichuan Peppercorns

Sichuan peppercorns look like exploded tiny reddish brown flower buds with hairlike stems. Their flavor is far more complex and elusive than that of black peppercorns. Their peppery fragrance is overlaid with citrusy, warm, exotically spicy notes reminiscent of allspice. ✿ The Sichuan peppercorns in Asian markets in the United States are pale imitations of the fresh ones in China, which are so pungent you can smell their powerful aroma right through a sealed plastic bag. Their flavor is intense and mentholated, literally numbing the tongue. Unfortunately, the USDA has banned the import of Sichuan peppercorns, for the moment at least, because it is believed that they may carry a canker that poses a threat to American citrus trees. Nevertheless, they can still sometimes be found in Asian markets. (A close relative, the Japanese peppercorn called sansho, is a good substitute, though it has also been banned.) ✿ Sichuan peppercorns should be toasted to bring out their flavor. Place them in a small dry skillet over medium heat and toast for about 5 minutes, or until fragrant. Cool, then grind and store in a tightly covered container. ✿ If you can't find them, substitute black peppercorns, toasting them as described above before using.

Fish and Shellfish

How to
Buy, Store, and
Cook Fresh Fish

I was raised in Kaohsiung, a southern seaport city in Taiwan, where fresh seafood was available every day all year long. Growing up there has made me very picky about fish. If a fish is not fresh, it is a waste of time cooking it; its texture changes and the flesh loses its sweetness. ✹ Buying fish is a hands-on experience; you must touch it, smell it, and examine it closely. Buy whole fish if possible; have the market fillet and clean it for you — this is the best way to be certain that the fish is fresh. Learn to choose the best fish your market has to offer. The eyes should be bright, clear, vibrant, and bulging, not cloudy, dull, or sunken. Gills should be a healthy-looking red color, and the flesh should be firm and elastic. And of course fresh fish should not have any odor at all. ✹ When you buy fillets, such as salmon, halibut, or swordfish, the flesh should have a certain pearliness to the color. If the skin is still attached, it should have a sheen. When you press down gently with your hand, the fillets should feel springy, not flabby. ✹ Try to cook the fish the day you buy it. If you have to store fish overnight, first rinse it under cold water and dry it well with paper towels, then wrap tightly in plastic wrap. Place in a deep tray filled with ice cubes — the fish should be laid gently on top, not buried beneath the ice. Store in the coldest part of your refrigerator and replenish the ice cubes from time to time, pouring off the water. Store no longer than overnight before cooking. Before cooking any fish, rinse it well under cold water and dry with paper towels. ✹ Marinades help fish retain its moisture. I use three basic ingredients in my marinades: oil, soy sauce, and liquor. The oil keeps the fish moist, the soy sauce replaces salt to give flavor and tenderize the flesh, and the liquor, such as gin, vermouth, vodka, or sake, helps sweeten the flesh. ✹ Cooking fillets such as bass, red snapper, or pompano with the skin on gives them an extra layer of protection. When pan-searing marinated fish, I sprinkle a thin coating of cornstarch on the skin side and use a nonstick pan to keep it crisp. ✹ Overcooked fish will become dry. The best way to check for doneness is to poke the fish near the center with the point of a sharp knife and see what it looks like. When it is done, the flesh will be opaque or white. Immediately remove it from the heat.

Salmon Braised with Soy and Ginger

———— (✿) ————

Braised in a cornstarch-thickened, sweet sake-soy mixture that is thoroughly absorbed into its flesh, the salmon emerges plump, moist, and soft, with a mahogany sheen and none of the dry crusty edges that can result from roast-ing. Though this recipe is really simple, the results are excellent. Serve it with Herbed Mashed Potatoes (page 264).

———— [*Serves 4*] ————

4	6-ounce center-cut salmon fillets, skin removed
1/4	cup sake or dry vermouth
3	tablespoons soy sauce
1	tablespoon rice wine vinegar or sherry wine vinegar
1	tablespoon grated peeled fresh ginger

1	tablespoon sugar
1/2	teaspoon cornstarch, mixed with 1 teaspoon water
3	tablespoons soybean oil or corn oil
2	garlic cloves, minced
1	shallot, minced

Rinse the salmon fillets under cold water and pat dry. Mix the sake or vermouth, soy sauce, vinegar, ginger, and sugar in a small bowl. Stir in the cornstarch mixture.

Heat the oil in a large nonstick skillet or flat-bottomed wok over high heat. Add 2 of the salmon fillets and sear on both sides until lightly browned, about 1 minute per side. Remove the fish with a spatula and carefully place on a plate. Sear and remove the remaining fillets in the same way. Add the garlic and shallot to the skillet and stir-fry for 30 seconds. Return the seared salmon pieces to the skillet.

Pour in the soy sauce mixture and bring to a boil over high heat. Reduce the heat to low, cover, and simmer, turning the salmon every few minutes, until the sauce has been reduced to a glaze, 8 to 9 minutes. Place on four serving plates and serve.

SLOW-ROASTED SALMON
AND ISRAELI COUSCOUS
PAGE 100

Slow-Roasted Salmon and Israeli Couscous

———————————————— (✿) ————————————————

Forty minutes sounds like a long time to cook salmon, but primed by a long bath in a sake ginger brine, which both flavors and draws moisture into it, and then baked in a low oven, this fish will be perfection itself. It is served on a bed of Israeli couscous in a golden sauce spiked with turmeric, jalapeños, and fresh basil and topped with crisp slivers of fresh fennel.

Try to find wild salmon at your local fish store, since it has much more flavor and the flesh has a deeper red color than that of farm-raised salmon. Wild Alaskan salmon is usually available in the late spring through the fall. King salmon is best, if you can get it.

——————————— [*Serves 4*] ———————————

4	6- to 8-ounce center-cut salmon fillets, skin on
	Sake Ginger Brine (recipe follows)
2	tablespoons olive oil
½	cup Israeli couscous
2	tablespoons soybean oil or corn oil
1	shallot, thinly sliced
1	garlic clove, thinly sliced
1	tablespoon grated peeled fresh turmeric
	or ½ teaspoon ground turmeric
2	jalapeño peppers, stemmed, seeded, and chopped,
	or 1 teaspoon crushed red pepper flakes

2	tablespoons butter
2	cups chicken stock or fish stock
1	large tomato, peeled (see page 123), seeded, and diced
½	cup fresh or frozen peas or shelled soybeans (edamame), peeled
1	cup coarsely chopped fresh basil
½	cup paper-thin slices fennel, soaked in ice water and refrigerated, plus a few fronds for garnish

Place the salmon fillets skin side up in a container just large enough to hold them in a single layer. Pour the brine over the fish, cover, and marinate in the refrigerator for at least 4 hours.

Preheat the oven to 250 degrees. Drain the salmon, reserving the brine. Pour the olive oil into a shallow bowl or onto a rimmed plate. Roll the fillets in the oil, coating on all sides, and place them in a baking pan large enough to hold them in a single layer. *The salmon can be prepared ahead up to this point and refrigerated, covered, for a few hours.*

Bake the salmon, spooning some of the reserved brine over it from time to time, for 30 to 40 minutes, or until it just begins to flake. (Increase the time by 5 minutes if you refrigerated the fish.)

Soak the couscous in 2 cups cold water for 10 minutes. Drain in a sieve and rinse under cold water to separate the grains. Drain well.

Heat the soybean oil in a medium saucepan over high heat. Add the shallot, garlic, turmeric, and jalapeño peppers, turn the heat to low, and cook, stirring, until all the vegetables are softened and the raw taste of the turmeric is gone, about 5 minutes. Add the couscous and butter and cook, stirring, until the couscous is coated with the butter and the aromatics, about 1 minute.

Add the stock, tomato, and peas or soybeans, stir, and bring to a boil. Turn the heat to low and simmer for about 10 minutes, uncovered; the couscous should be soft but still have a little bite to it. Remove from the heat. *The couscous can be made up to 1 day in advance and refrigerated, covered. When ready to serve, bring the couscous to a boil.*

Add the fresh basil to the couscous and mix well. Drain the fennel slices.

Transfer the salmon to a platter. (If you made the couscous ahead of time, it may have absorbed most of the liquid from the sauce. You can strain out any liquid left in the baking pan in which you cooked the salmon and add this to the couscous, if you like.)

Spoon the couscous and vegetable mixture onto four large shallow plates and top each with a piece of salmon. Garnish with the fennel slices and fronds.

SIMPLE VARIATIONS

When fresh corn is in season, add ½ cup to the couscous, along with the peas or soybeans and tomato.

You can also serve the salmon on its own without the couscous.

Fresh Turmeric

Turmeric is one of the major ingredients used in curry powder; it also gives American-style mustard its bright yellow color. It has an earthy, almost musty smell, with a slightly bitter, peppery, pungent flavor. ❧ Fresh turmeric has a rich, clean flavor and gives a deeper yellow color to food than dried turmeric does. ❧ Like ginger, turmeric is a rhizome. The tuber has thin brownish skin covering bright orange-yellow flesh. It's smaller than ginger, usually 1 to 3 inches in length and ½ to ¾ inch in diameter. Fresh turmeric, like ginger, is peeled before it is used. ❧ You can find the fresh rhizomes in Asian and Indian grocery stores. If you can't get them, though, substitute ground turmeric, found in the spice section of any supermarket.

Sake Ginger Brine

[Makes about 1 cup]

This brine lends just the right amount of flavor and moistness to the salmon. I prefer the mellow flavor of rock sugar, but honey can be substituted.

½	cup sake
1	1- to 2-inch piece fresh ginger, peeled and thinly sliced
2	tablespoons chopped fresh cilantro
1	tablespoon soy sauce
1	tablespoon rock sugar or honey
1½	teaspoons kosher salt
2	fresh thyme sprigs, preferably lemon thyme

Combine all the ingredients in a large saucepan, add ½ cup water, and bring to a boil over high heat, stirring until the sugar is dissolved. Turn heat to low and simmer for 10 minutes. Cool before using. *The brine can be refrigerated in a covered jar for up to 2 weeks.*

Rock Sugar

These yellow or amber-colored sugar crystals are made from a mixture of unrefined sugar and honey and are not as sweet as granulated sugar. In cooking, they impart a subtle flavor and lustrous sheen to braised dishes. Relatively expensive, rock sugar can be found in Asian markets in 1-pound boxes or plastic bags. Many of the crystals are large and very hard. Don't bother trying to crush them to measure them for a recipe — just estimate and choose a lump of the approximate size; the results won't be thrown off. An equal amount of honey can be substituted.

**SESAME-CRUSTED HALIBUT
WITH MIXED BEANS AND THAI LEMONGRASS SAUCE
PAGE 104**

Sesame-Crusted Halibut with Mixed Beans and Thai Lemongrass Sauce

Whenever fresh halibut from either coast is in season, usually from March to November, I prepare this dish. Sesame seeds form a crisp coating for the fish. Don't substitute frozen halibut, which would be too dry; any fresh, thick, firm-fleshed white fish, such as grouper or catfish, is a better alternative.

Serve with Creamy Coconut Polenta (page 216) or Rice Noodle Flan (page 202).

[Serves 4]

1	cup sesame seeds
½	cup fresh or frozen soybeans (edamame)
½	cup shelled fresh or frozen fava beans, peeled, or peas
1	cup Chinese long beans (see page 243) or French beans, cut into 1-inch lengths
3	tablespoons soy sauce
2	tablespoons vodka
3	tablespoons olive oil

4	6-ounce halibut fillets
1	cup cornstarch
	Kosher salt and freshly ground white pepper
½	cup plus 1 tablespoon soybean oil or corn oil
1	cup Thai Lemongrass Sauce (recipe follows)
1	cup grape tomatoes, peeled (see page 123)
½	cup fresh cilantro leaves or small basil leaves, julienned (optional)

Place the sesame seeds in a dry large nonstick skillet and toast over medium heat, tossing and stirring constantly, until light brown. Watch carefully, as the seeds can burn very easily. Remove from the heat and pour into a small bowl to cool.

Cook the soybeans, fava beans, and long or French beans separately in a medium pot of boiling water over high heat, cooking the soybeans and fava beans for 1 minute each and the long or French beans for 3 minutes. Remove from the water with a slotted spoon and plunge into ice water to cool. When all the vegetables are cooked, drain well and set aside.

Mix the soy sauce, vodka, and olive oil together in a small bowl. Place the halibut fillets on a large shallow platter. Pour the soy sauce mixture over them and turn the fish until all sides are coated with the marinade.

Put the cornstarch in a large bowl, pour in ½ cup cold water, and mix until well incorporated; the mixture will be very thick. Stir in ½ teaspoon each salt and white pepper. Place the toasted sesame seeds on a large plate.

Remove the fish fillets from the marinade and place in a shallow baking pan or on a large platter. Spoon the cornstarch mixture over the fillets, then turn to coat the other side (only a very thin coating will stick to the fish). Press 1 fillet at a time into the sesame seeds, turning to coat both sides.

Preheat the broiler until hot, and lightly oil the broiler pan. Heat ½ cup of the soybean or corn oil in a large nonstick skillet over medium-high heat. When it is hot, place 2 fillets in the pan and cook for 2 minutes. Turn to sear the other side for about 2 minutes; the sesame coating will be only lightly colored. Place the seared fish on the broiler pan. Repeat with the remaining fillets.

Broil the fish for 4 to 5 minutes, turning once, just until

Fava Beans

Fava beans are one of the oldest cultivated plants known to man, dating back to prehistoric times. They have been used in Chinese cooking for at least five thousand years. In the eastern coastal region of China around Shanghai, fresh favas are considered a delicacy and are used in classic dishes with spring bamboo shoots, fresh shrimp, or julienned meat or chicken. ✿ In early spring, fava beans are small and tender. As the season turns to summer, the beans mature and become much bigger, about the size of a lima bean. When shopping for fresh favas, choose those with crisp-looking green pods, avoiding any that look wilted; the pods should be well filled with plump beans. ✿ To prepare favas, remove the beans from the pods and blanch them in a pot of boiling water for 3 minutes, or until the skins have softened. Drain, and pop the tender beans out of their tough whitish outer skins. Store the beans in a tightly closed container layered with paper towels. They will keep well this way in the refrigerator for about 3 days. You can also use frozen favas — defrost, then peel off the tough skins.

the fillets are cooked through. Watch closely, as the seeds burn easily.

Meanwhile, heat the remaining 1 tablespoon oil in a medium skillet over medium heat. Add all the beans and ¼ cup of the lemongrass sauce and cook only until heated through. Add the tomatoes. Taste and correct the seasonings with salt and pepper if needed. Remove from the heat.

Heat the remaining lemongrass sauce.

Place one quarter of the bean mixture in the center of each of four plates. Place the fish fillets on top of the vegetables, then spoon over the remaining sauce. Garnish with the herbs, if using.

SIMPLE VARIATION

I love the tang and spice of the lemongrass sauce and the contrast of the three-bean mixture, but with its flavorful coating, the fish can stand on its own.

Thai Lemongrass Sauce

I tasted a sauce similar to this when I was in Thailand and thoroughly enjoyed its spiciness and aromatic flavors. Serve with the Sesame-Crusted Halibut or with any broiled or sautéed fish.

1	tablespoon soybean oil or corn oil
1	stalk fresh lemongrass (see page 150), tender inner part only, very thinly sliced
1	tablespoon minced shallots
1	tablespoon minced garlic
½	tablespoon grated peeled fresh ginger
½	jalapeño pepper, stemmed and coarsely chopped
1	tablespoon Thai red curry paste
2	tablespoons fish sauce (preferably Three Crabs brand)
1	tablespoon rice wine vinegar
1	small vine-ripened tomato, peeled (see page 123), seeded, and diced
2	cups fish stock or Vegetable Stock (page 56)
1	small fresh kaffir lime leaf (see page 45), julienned, or 1 teaspoon grated lime zest

Heat the oil in a medium saucepan over medium heat until warm. Add the lemongrass, shallots, garlic, and ginger and cook, stirring, until soft, about 2 minutes. Mix in the jalapeño and red curry paste. Add the fish sauce, rice wine vinegar, tomato, stock, and lime leaf (if using lime zest, do not add it now). Turn the heat down to a simmer and cook, uncovered, for about 45 minutes.

Stir in the lime zest, if using, remove from the heat, and cool. *The sauce can be made in advance and refrigerated in a tightly covered container for up to 3 days or frozen for up to 2 months.*

Thai Curry Paste

Thai curry paste is very different from Indian curry powder, which is more familiar to many American cooks. While Indian curry powders are made from a mixture of dried spices and are predominantly yellow, Thai curry pastes are made from fresh green or red bird's-eye chiles, lemongrass, shallots, garlic, galangal (Thai ginger), coriander, shrimp paste, palm sugar, tamarind, and many other fresh herbs pounded together. Red curry paste takes its color from red chiles, green curry paste from green ones, and yellow curry paste from fresh turmeric. ✿ Since making your own fresh curry paste is a lot of work and good brands are available in Asian food markets, I buy mine. Many brands claim to be family secrets, made from recipes handed down by mothers or aunts. I usually buy a 4-ounce can, then doctor it up by adding some fresh ingredients to give it a little extra zing.

Poached Striped Bass with Balsamic Vinegar Sauce

Maintaining the temperature of the poaching liquid just shy of boiling keeps the fish exquisitely tender. The juices from the striped bass and the vegetables — daikon, carrot, celery root, and scallions — make their way into the gingery poaching liquid, which is then used to flavor the balsamic sauce.

If striped bass is not available, use freshwater trout, black sea bass, red snapper, or branzino (European sea bass).

[Serves 4]

FISH AND MARINADE

4	6-ounce striped bass fillets, skin on
2	tablespoons vodka
2	tablespoons olive oil
1	tablespoon kosher salt

POACHING LIQUID AND VEGETABLES

8	cups chicken stock or fish stock
1	tablespoon grated peeled fresh ginger
1	shallot, thinly sliced
1	tablespoon kosher salt
1	small daikon (about 1 pound), peeled and julienned
1	medium carrot, peeled and julienned
1	small celery root, peeled and julienned
2	scallions, white part only, cut into ½-inch lengths

BALSAMIC VINEGAR SAUCE

2	tablespoons balsamic vinegar
1	tablespoon soy sauce
¼	medium tomato, chopped
1	tablespoon julienned peeled fresh ginger, soaked in ice water
	Freshly ground pepper
2	tablespoons butter
8	fresh basil leaves, julienned

TO MARINATE THE FISH: Rinse the fish under cold water and dry well with paper towels. Place on a shallow platter. Mix the vodka, olive oil, and salt in a small bowl. Pour over the fish and turn to coat. Marinate for about 10 minutes. (Refrigerate for up to 2 hours if not cooking the fish within 10 minutes.)

MEANWHILE, MAKE THE POACHING LIQUID: Add the stock, ginger, shallot, and salt to a fish poacher or a roasting pan just large enough to hold the fish in a single layer. Cover, bring to a boil, turn the heat to low, and simmer for 10 to 15 minutes to infuse the stock with the aromatics.

TO POACH THE FISH: Place the julienned vegetables and scallions on the poaching rack or a wire rack. Place the striped bass in a single layer on top of the vegetables, and carefully lower into the pan. Pour any remaining marinade into the poaching liquid. Bring to a boil, reduce the heat to very low, cover, and simmer for 5 to 6 minutes, or until the fish has turned white. Remove the pan from the heat.

Remove ½ cup poaching liquid from the pan and reserve for the sauce. Let the fish sit, still on the rack and covered, for 10 minutes. *Leftover poaching liquid can be frozen for up to 3 months, if desired.*

MEANWHILE, MAKE THE SAUCE: Add the vinegar, soy sauce, tomato, ginger, and reserved poaching liquid to a small saucepan. Bring just to a simmer over low heat and cook for 1 minute. Season to taste with pepper, add the butter, and swirl the pan until it has melted. Remove from the heat.

TO SERVE: Carefully remove the rack from the fish poacher or pan and place on a large platter or tray. Lift off the fish fillets and set them aside. Using tongs or a slotted spoon, remove the cooked vegetables and arrange them in the center of four dinner plates, dividing them evenly. Remove any vegetables that may have fallen into the poaching liquid with a slotted spoon. Place the fish fillets on top of the vegetables. Spoon the sauce over the fish, sprinkle with the basil, and serve.

How to Roast
and Peel Peppers

Preheat the broiler. Wash and dry the peppers. Cut off the stem and bottom ends

and slice each pepper into quarters. Remove the seeds and ribs. Place skin side up

on a broiling pan. Broil just until the skins are charred, about 10 minutes. Remove,

cover the pan with a sheet of aluminum foil, and let sit for 20 to 30 minutes so the

peppers steam and the skins loosen. Peel, using a small paring knife to aid in

scraping off the skin. Do not rinse; you will lose too much of the flavor.

Pan-Seared Black Sea Bass with Caramelized Red Pepper Sauce

Black sea bass, which is native to the East Coast, has firm, succulent flesh with a delicate flavor. Lightly coated with cornstarch, its thin skin is panfried to crispness and enhanced by a sweet, smoky roasted red pepper sauce. Serve with sautéed Yukon Gold potatoes and Sichuan Pickled Brussels Sprouts (page 91).

Red snapper, trout, or striped bass can be substituted for the sea bass.

Serves 4

4	7-ounce black sea bass fillets, skin on
4	tablespoons plus 1 teaspoon olive oil
¼	cup vodka
3	tablespoons soy sauce
2	tablespoons grated peeled fresh ginger
2	garlic cloves, sliced
1	small red bell pepper, roasted, peeled, and cut into large dice
2	tablespoons balsamic vinegar
1	cup fish stock or chicken stock
¼	cup cornstarch
1	tablespoon butter, melted
¾	cup julienned peeled daikon, soaked in ice water to crisp
¼	cup sliced (2-inch lengths) fresh chives or chopped fresh flat-leaf parsley

Rinse the sea bass fillets under cold running water and dry well with paper towels. Place the fillets in a shallow dish large enough to hold them in a single layer. Mix 2 tablespoons of the oil, the vodka, soy sauce, and ginger in a small bowl. Pour over the sea bass and turn to coat. Cover and refrigerate for 1 hour, turning once or twice.

Preheat the oven to 450 degrees. Remove the fish from the marinade and place on a plate. Reserve the marinade.

Heat the 1 teaspoon oil in a small saucepan over medium heat. Add the garlic and cook, stirring, until lightly golden, about 30 seconds. Add the red pepper, balsamic vinegar, the reserved marinade, and the stock. Bring to a boil, turn the heat to low, and simmer for about 15 minutes, until the vegetables are very soft.

Remove from the heat and puree in a food processor or blender until smooth. Spoon the sauce into a small saucepan and keep warm.

Sprinkle the cornstarch over the skin side of the fish and pat lightly so it adheres. Heat a large nonstick skillet over high heat. Add the remaining 2 tablespoons oil. When it is hot, add 2 fillets skin side down and cook until the skin is browned and crisp, 2 to 3 minutes. Spoon half the melted butter over the flesh side and transfer the fish, skin side up, to a baking pan large enough to hold all the fillets in a single layer. Repeat with the remaining fillets.

Bake the sea bass for 5 to 7 minutes, depending on the thickness of the fish; the flesh should be white throughout when you test it with a knife.

Place the fillets skin side up on serving plates. Spoon the sauce around the fish, garnish with the daikon and chives or parsley, and serve.

Braised Red Snapper with Thai Curry Sauce

Fresh tomatoes, mushrooms, and basil bring to mind the flavors of Italy. But rather than combining them with a standard tomato sauce, I pair them with a Thai curry sauce, a striking counterpoint to the mild fish.

American red snapper, with its pinkish red skin, delicate, creamy flavor, and firm, meaty texture is preferable for this dish. Native to the southeastern coast, it is fresher and firmer than other kinds of red snapper.

You can substitute wild striped bass, sea trout, black sea bass, sole, flounder, or any mild fresh fish fillets for the snapper. The cooking time will depend on the thickness of the fillets.

Serve with white rice to soak up the curry sauce.

[Serves 4]

4	6-ounce red snapper fillets, skin on
2	tablespoons vodka
1	tablespoon soy sauce
3	tablespoons olive oil
4	ounces white button mushrooms, stemmed and thinly sliced

4	plum tomatoes, peeled (see page 123), seeded, and quartered
	Thai Curry Sauce (recipe follows)
1	cup fresh basil leaves, julienned, or 2 fresh kaffir lime leaves (see page 45), thinly sliced

Rinse the fillets under cold running water and pat dry with paper towels. Spoon the vodka, soy sauce, and 1 tablespoon of the oil into a large zipper-lock bag. Place the fillets in the bag and seal, pressing out the excess air. Turn and gently squeeze to coat the fillets evenly with the marinade. Refrigerate for 1 to 2 hours, turning occasionally.

Drain the fillets well, pat dry, and place on a platter. Heat the remaining 2 tablespoons oil in a large nonstick skillet or flat-bottomed wok over high heat. When it is hot, add 2 of the fillets skin side down and sear for 2 minutes, or until the skin is golden. Remove and place on a plate, then repeat with the other 2 fillets.

Add the mushrooms to the skillet, turn the heat to low, and cook until they are soft, 2 to 3 minutes. Return the fillets to the skillet, skin side up. Place the tomatoes around the fillets and pour the curry sauce over the fish. Cover and simmer for 5 to 10 minutes, or until the fish is just cooked through. Using a spatula, carefully place 1 fillet on each of four dinner plates.

Bring the sauce to a boil and add the basil or lime leaves. Spoon the sauce and vegetables over and around the fish and serve.

Thai Curry Sauce

[*Makes a generous ½ cup*]

The inspiration for this complex sauce was a curry dish I tasted in Bangkok many years ago. It's spicy from hot peppers, tart from lemongrass and lime, pungent from fish sauce, and mellowed by coconut cream — a perfect blend. It's great with chicken as well as fish.

2	garlic cloves, sliced
2	shallots, sliced
2	red serrano peppers, stemmed and thinly sliced
1	stalk fresh lemongrass (see page 150), tender inner part only, thinly sliced
1	tablespoon soybean oil or corn oil
½	cup unsweetened coconut cream (see page 77)
	Grated zest of 1 lime
2	tablespoons fresh lime juice
2	tablespoons fish sauce (see page 43)
½	cup chicken stock or Vegetable Stock (page 56)
	Kosher salt and freshly ground pepper

Put the garlic, shallots, peppers, and lemongrass in a food processor or blender and process until finely minced.

Heat the oil in a small saucepan over medium heat. Add the garlic mixture and cook, stirring, until soft, about 2 minutes. Add the coconut cream and cook, stirring frequently, over medium-low heat until the coconut oil separates from the cream, 3 to 5 minutes.

Add the lime zest, lime juice, fish sauce, and stock to the pan. Turn the heat down to low and cook, stirring occasionally, for 10 minutes. Remove from the heat and cool.

Strain the sauce through a fine sieve, pressing hard on the solids. Discard the solids. Season with salt and pepper to taste.

The sauce can be refrigerated, covered, for 1 day or frozen for up to 2 months. Thaw and reheat for a few minutes before serving.

Baked Pompano with Slow-Roasted Tomatoes

Pompano is a small flatfish with buttery, smooth, succulent flesh. During my college years, when my husband, E-Hsin, and I were first dating, my future mother-in-law often cooked pompano when she invited me for dinner. She pan-seared the fish, then added a Western touch by covering it with a cheesy béchamel sauce.

Other than replacing the condensed milk she used with real milk, I've stayed close to her original recipe, searing the fish, putting it on sliced potatoes, and covering it with fresh tomatoes. This multilayered gratin is an all-in-one meal.

Serves 4

4	5- to 6-ounce pompano fillets, skin on
1	teaspoon kosher salt, plus more to taste
	Freshly ground pepper
1	pound fingerling potatoes or small new potatoes, peeled and cut into ½-inch-thick slices
2	tablespoons butter
1	small onion, thinly sliced

½	cup plus 1 tablespoon all-purpose flour
1½	cups milk
1	teaspoon crushed red pepper flakes
¾	cup freshly grated Parmesan cheese
2	tablespoons olive oil or soybean oil
8	slow-roasted plum tomatoes
½	cup chopped fresh herbs, such as chives or basil

Rinse the pompano fillets under cold running water and dry well with paper towels. Sprinkle with the 1 teaspoon salt and pepper to taste. Let stand at room temperature for about 30 minutes while you prepare the remaining ingredients.

Preheat the oven to 425 degrees. Cook the potatoes in a medium pot of boiling salted water for about 5 minutes, or until barely tender but not mushy. Drain well and set aside.

Melt the butter in a medium skillet over high heat. Add the onion and cook until soft, about 2 minutes. Add the 1 tablespoon flour, stirring it in with a whisk, and cook for about 20 seconds. Whisk in the milk and hot pepper flakes and bring to a boil, then turn the heat to low and simmer for about 5 minutes, or until the sauce is thickened, stirring occasionally. Season with salt and pepper, remove from the heat, and stir in half of the cheese.

Lightly coat the fish fillets on both sides with the ½ cup flour. Heat the oil in a large nonstick skillet over high heat. Add the fillets skin side up (in batches if necessary) and sear for about 2 minutes, until lightly golden on the first side. Turn and sear on the other side, about 2 more minutes. Remove from the pan and drain on paper towels.

Place the potatoes in an even layer in a nonstick baking dish large enough to hold the fillets in a single layer. Place the fish skin side up on the potatoes and pour the sauce over the fish. Cover with the tomatoes, then sprinkle with the rest of the Parmesan cheese. *The fish can be prepared up to this point 1 day ahead, covered, and refrigerated.*

Bake for 10 to 15 minutes, or until the cheese is melted and the fish is cooked through and very hot. Sprinkle with the herbs and serve from the baking dish.

Slow-Roasted
Plum Tomatoes

Plum tomatoes are available all year round, and roasting is the perfect way to accentuate their rich flavor. ✿ TO PEEL AND ROAST PLUM TOMA- TOES: Remove the core and cut a small X in the bottom of each tomato. Blanch in a pot of boiling water for 20 seconds. Plunge into a bowl of ice water to cool. Drain, peel, and halve lengthwise. Using a small teaspoon, remove the seeds. ✿ Sprinkle the cut sides of the tomatoes with salt, pepper, a pinch of fresh or dried thyme, and sugar (about ¼ teaspoon per tomato half). Drizzle with olive oil. Place cut side down in a single layer on a nonstick baking sheet (or one lined with parchment paper) and bake in a preheated 200-degree oven for 1½ to 2 hours, or until the tomatoes have lost most of their moisture but are not dried out. Cool in the baking pan. The tomatoes will keep well for a week or more, tightly covered and refrigerated.

Panfried Skate with Orange Pernod Sauce

The thin wing of the skate, a type of ray, is silky in texture, a sublime contrast to the crisp coating. An anise-flavor orange sauce provides the right touch of sweetness.

Skate wing should be shiny, firm, and almost odorless. It is very perishable, and if you notice a slight smell of ammonia, the fish is no longer fresh. You can substitute black sea bass, lemon or Dover sole, butterfish, or any tender white fish fillets.

[Serves 4]

2	tablespoons vodka		2	tablespoons Pernod
1	tablespoon soy sauce		2	tablespoons butter
1	tablespoon olive oil			Kosher salt
1½	pounds skinless, boneless skate, cut into 4 equal pieces		2	large eggs
1	cup orange juice		½	cup cornstarch
2	tablespoons fresh lime juice		½	cup soybean oil, corn oil, or olive oil
2	shallots, thinly sliced		1	pound pea shoots (see page 52) or baby spinach, washed and drained
	Grated zest of 1 orange			
¼	cup dry white wine		1	navel orange, segments removed (see page 69)
½	cup heavy cream			

Mix the vodka, soy sauce, and olive oil in a large zipper-lock bag. Add the skate, turning to coat with the marinade, and seal the bag, pressing out the excess air. Marinate for 1 to 2 hours in the refrigerator.

Combine the orange juice and lime juice in a medium saucepan, bring to a boil over high heat, and cook until the juice is reduced to about ¼ cup, 5 to 7 minutes. Remove from the heat.

Combine the shallots, orange zest, and white wine in a small saucepan, bring to a boil over high heat, and cook until the shallots are soft and the wine is almost completely evaporated, about 2 minutes. Add the heavy cream and cook, stirring, until reduced by half, 2 to 3 minutes. Add the reduced orange juice mixture, the Pernod, and butter. Stir to melt butter and remove from the heat. Strain the sauce through a fine sieve and season to taste with salt. *The sauce can be made up to 2 days ahead and refrigerated, covered. When ready to use, reheat in a microwave oven or a small saucepan over low heat for a few minutes; do not boil.*

Lightly beat the eggs in a large shallow bowl. Remove the skate from the marinade, draining well. Add the skate to the eggs, turning to coat well. Place the skate in a single layer on one side of a baking sheet. Place the cornstarch in a fine sieve and sprinkle half the cornstarch evenly over the skate. Turn the skate and place on a clean portion of the baking sheet. Cover the second side with the remaining cornstarch.

Fill the bottom of a steamer with water and bring to a boil.

Meanwhile, heat the oil in a large heavy skillet over medium heat until it barely begins to smoke. Carefully add 2

pieces of skate to the pan, in a single layer, and cook for 3 minutes, or until the crust is lightly golden. Turn and cook for 2 to 3 minutes on the second side. Remove the skate from the skillet, drain on paper towels, and keep warm. Cook the other 2 pieces of skate in the same way.

While cooking the second batch of fish, add the pea shoots or spinach to the steamer pot and steam for 1 minute.

Place 1 piece of skate on each of four dinner plates. Arrange the greens on top of the skate. Spoon the sauce around the fish and decorate with the orange sections. Serve immediately.

Soybean Oil

Soybean oil is almost completely odorless and flavorless. It's good for fried dishes when you want crispness without a taste of oil, and it can be heated to high temperatures without smoking and breaking down. It's also high in healthier unsaturated fats. ✿ Soybean oil is readily found in grocery stores and supermarkets. It is often labeled vegetable oil, but check the ingredients list carefully, since not all vegetable oils are pure soybean oil.

Crispy Jumbo Shrimp with Caramelized Orange Sauce

Crispy tempura-battered shrimp and hot caramelized orange sauce: it's no wonder this is the hands-down favorite at my restaurant. Customers complain if I take it off the menu for even a single night.

[Serves 4]

16   jumbo shrimp (11–15 count), peeled and deveined

1   teaspoon kosher salt

1   large navel orange

¼   cup julienned red bell pepper

½   pound baby bok choy, washed

    Soybean oil or corn oil for deep-frying

    Caramelized Orange Sauce (recipe follows)

    Tempura Batter (recipe follows)

Rub the shrimp well with the salt, then rinse thoroughly under cold running water. Dry well with paper towels.

Remove the zest of the orange with a small knife or vegetable peeler. Cut away and discard any white pith still attached to the zest, then slice the zest lengthwise into julienne strips. Remove the orange segments from their membranes according to the directions on page 69. Set the segments aside in a bowl.

Cook the orange zest for 2 minutes in a small saucepan of boiling water. Remove with a slotted spoon, drain well, and place in a small bowl. Cook the red pepper and bok choy separately in the boiling water for about 1 minute each, remove with the slotted spoon, and plunge into a bowl of ice water to stop the cooking. Drain again, place on separate microwaveable dishes or (separately) on a plate.

Heat about 3 inches of oil in a deep fryer or deep skillet to 350 to 375 degrees. Meanwhile, heat the orange sauce in a small saucepan and keep warm.

Dip each shrimp into the batter to coat lightly, making sure it is completely covered, then drain off any excess batter, drop into the hot oil and deep-fry until golden brown, turn-ing once. Do not crowd the pan: cook in 2 batches if necessary. Place on a plate lined with a thick layer of paper towels to drain well.

Warm the bok choy and red peppers in a microwave oven just until hot, about 30 seconds. Or sauté them separately in a small skillet, adding 1 teaspoon soybean or corn oil to keep them from sticking, for 1 to 2 minutes, or just until hot.

To serve, place 4 shrimp in the center of each of four plates. Top with the red pepper and orange zest. Spoon the sauce over all and garnish with the orange segments and baby bok choy.

SIMPLE VARIATION

You can skip the red bell pepper and the bok choy garnish if you like, or substitute spinach or broccoli for the bok choy.

Caramelized Orange Sauce

Makes about ¾ cup

This light golden sauce is also great on fried chicken tenders.

- ½ cup sugar
- 1 garlic clove, minced
- 1 tablespoon grated peeled fresh ginger
- 2 star anise
- 1 tablespoon grated orange zest
- 1 cup orange juice
- 2 tablespoons fresh lemon juice
- 1 tablespoon fish sauce (preferably Three Crabs brand)
- ½ teaspoon cornstarch, mixed with 1 teaspoon cold water

Place the sugar and 2 tablespoons water in a small saucepan. Stir and heat over medium heat until the sugar begins to melt. Shake the pan, wait 1 minute, then stir and cook until it caramelizes and turns a very light golden color, about 5 minutes.

Add the garlic, ginger, and star anise and cook for another 20 seconds. Stir in the orange zest and juice, lemon juice, fish sauce, and cornstarch mixture. Turn the heat to low and stir until any lumps of caramel dissolve. Simmer for 15 to 20 minutes, until the sauce is slightly thickened. Strain through a fine sieve. *The sauce can be made up to 2 days in advance and refrigerated, covered.*

Tempura Batter

Makes about 2 cups

Club soda makes the batter fluffy. Quick and easy, this is good for many things; use it as a coating for a variety of vegetables, such as onion rings, sliced zucchini, bell pepper slices, blanched sliced carrots, and blanched broccoli and cauliflower florets.

- 1 cup all-purpose flour
- ½ cup cornstarch
- ½ teaspoon baking powder
- 1 large egg yolk
- 1 cup club soda, chilled

Sift the flour, cornstarch, and baking powder together into a large bowl. Slowly stir in the egg yolk and club soda. Mix until thoroughly blended. The batter will be thick. *The batter can be prepared up to 2 hours ahead and refrigerated, covered.*

Shrimp with Lobster Sauce

Imagine my surprise when I learned that the traditional recipe for shrimp with lobster sauce contained no lobster at all! The dish was created in this country by Cantonese chefs using the same sauce they made for lobster but substituting shrimp to keep the price down and give it an appealing name. Made with real lobster as well as shrimp, it is sensational. Spoon over plain white rice and serve on a large platter, family-style, with a simple sautéed green vegetable, such as broccoli rabe or spinach.

If you don't want to cook a whole lobster, buy freshly cooked lobster meat at a good fish store. You will need approximately ½ pound for this recipe.

--------[*Serves 4*]--------

1	pound jumbo shrimp (11–15 count)
1	large egg white
1	tablespoon vodka, dry vermouth, or gin
1	teaspoon cornstarch
1	1½-pound lobster
1½	cups chicken stock or Lobster Stock (page 57)
1	teaspoon cornstarch, mixed with 1 tablespoon water
3	tablespoons soybean oil or corn oil
1	tablespoon chopped garlic

1	tablespoon grated peeled fresh ginger
½	cup fresh or frozen peas or peeled fava beans (see page 105)
½	cup grape tomatoes, peeled (see page 123)
2	tablespoons butter
1	teaspoon kosher salt
½	teaspoon freshly ground white pepper
2	scallions, white part only, chopped

Peel the shrimp and remove the veins. Rinse the shrimp under cold running water and pat dry. Lightly beat the egg white in a large bowl and mix in the liquor. Add the shrimp and mix well. Sprinkle with the 1 teaspoon cornstarch and mix well. Cover and refrigerate.

Bring a large deep pot of water to a boil over high heat and plunge the lobster into the pot. Cover and cook for 4 minutes. Remove the lobster and plunge into a large bowl of ice water to stop the cooking; drain.

When the lobster is cool, twist off the claws and tail (save the body for making lobster stock). Using heavy kitchen shears, cut through the shell down the length of the tail and remove the meat. Remove the vein on top of the tail and discard; cut the meat into 1-inch slices. Crack the claws and knuckles and remove the meat. Cut into 1-inch slices.

Heat the stock in a small saucepan, whisk in the cornstarch mixture, and bring to a boil. Reduce the heat and simmer for 15 minutes, or until reduced to about 1 cup. Keep warm.

Heat the oil in a large nonstick skillet over high heat. Add the garlic and ginger and cook, stirring, until soft, about 30 seconds. Add the shrimp and cook until barely firm, 1 to 2 minutes. Add the peas or beans, lobster, tomatoes, and hot stock. Bring to a boil and cook for about 1 minute, or until the lobster is just cooked through but still very tender. Add the butter, salt, and white pepper. Turn off the heat and mix in the scallions, then taste and correct the seasonings and serve.

To Peel Tomatoes

Remove the tomato cores with a sharp paring knife and make a small cross-shaped slit in the bottom of each. Cook in a medium saucepan filled with boiling water for 30 seconds to 1 minute, or just until the skins begin to loosen; plum tomatoes will take about 20 seconds, grape or cherry tomatoes 10 seconds. Plunge into a bowl of ice water to stop the cooking. Drain again, then peel with your fingers or a sharp paring knife; the skins should slip off.

Sichuan Shrimp

Leaving the shells on during cooking keeps the shrimp tender. The sauce, made from oven-dried plum tomatoes, is spicy, sweet, and gingery. Oven-roasting is the perfect way to remove some of the tomatoes' watery acidity; they develop a rich, concentrated flavor.

Serve with Belgian Endive and Orange Salad (page 69) or a simple green vegetable such as Sautéed Baby Bok Choy (page 245) and white rice.

———{ *Serves 4 as a main course or 6 as a first course* }———

2   plum tomatoes, peeled (see page 123), halved lengthwise, and seeded

12 jumbo shrimp (11–15 count), preferably with heads (about 1½ pounds)

¼   cup vodka, gin, or dry vermouth

2   tablespoons soy sauce

1   tablespoon ketchup

1   teaspoon rice wine vinegar or sherry wine vinegar

¼   cup extra-virgin olive oil

3   garlic cloves, thinly sliced

2   jalapeño peppers, stemmed, seeded, and diced

1   tablespoon grated peeled fresh ginger

½   cup diced scallions, white parts only

    Lemon wedges for garnish

Preheat the oven to 250 degrees. Place the tomatoes cut side down in a small nonstick baking pan or a pan lined with parchment and bake for 30 to 40 minutes, turning once, until they have lost some of their moisture. Remove from the oven.

Meanwhile, if the shrimp have heads, cut off the eyestalks with kitchen shears; cut off the legs. Split the shells down the back and remove the black veins. Rinse the shrimp under cold water and dry with paper towels.

Puree the tomatoes with the liquor in a food processor or blender. Add the soy sauce, ketchup, and vinegar and process until blended.

Add 2 tablespoons of the oil to a large nonstick skillet or flat-bottomed wok and heat over medium-high heat. Add half the shrimp with the slit side up, standing them in the skillet,

and cook for 30 seconds, just until the shells turn pink. Turn them on one side and cook for another 30 seconds, then turn on the other side and cook for 30 seconds. The shells should be completely pink, but the shrimp will be undercooked. Remove with tongs and place on a large plate. Add the remaining 2 tablespoons oil to the pan and cook the remaining shrimp.

Add the garlic, jalapeños, and ginger to the skillet and cook, stirring, for 1 minute. Stir in the tomato mixture and return the shrimp to the pan. Turn the heat to high and cook, stirring, until the shrimp are cooked through and completely coated with the sauce (there should be no liquid left), about 3 minutes. Mix in the scallions.

Spoon the shrimp onto individual serving plates, garnish with lemon wedges, and serve.

SEARED SCALLOPS
WITH MUSHROOMS AND CREAMY MUSHROOM SAUCE
PAGE 126

Seared Scallops with Mushrooms and Creamy Mushroom Sauce

This creamy mushroom sauce can make anything taste good. Try it over sautéed chicken breasts or veal tenders. When combined with scallops, wild mushrooms, and Parmesan cheese, it is a rich and extraordinary flavor combination. Serve with steamed baby bok choy.

Serves 2 as a main course or 4 as a first course

1½ cups chicken stock or Mushroom Stock (page 58), mixed with ½ teaspoon cornstarch

1 pound dry-packed scallops (see page 128)

7 ounces maitake, oyster, chanterelle, or morel mushrooms

2 scallions

5 tablespoons extra-virgin olive oil

2 shallots, thinly sliced

5 medium white button mushrooms, coarsely chopped

¼ cup dry vermouth

2 tablespoons sherry wine vinegar

2 tablespoons butter

Kosher salt and freshly ground pepper

2 tablespoons freshly grated Parmesan cheese

Boil the stock mixture in a small saucepan until reduced to ½ cup to concentrate the flavor.

Remove the small muscle flap from the side of each scallop, place in a small bowl, and reserve for making the sauce. Place the scallops on a plate.

Trim off and discard any brown parts from the bottoms of the wild mushrooms. Slice the maitakes into about 3-inch-long florets, break the oyster mushrooms into manageable segments, halve the chanterelles, or leave the morels whole if small, halve if large.

Trim the scallions and dice them, keeping the white and green parts separate.

Heat 2 tablespoons of the oil in a small saucepan over medium heat. Add the shallots and reserved scallop muscle flaps and cook until the shallots are soft, about 30 seconds. Add the button mushrooms and cook, stirring, for 5 minutes, or until they have released their liquid. Add the vermouth and

vinegar and cook until the liquid is almost evaporated, 2 to 3 minutes.

Stir in the stock and bring to a boil. Turn the heat to medium-low and cook until reduced by two thirds, about 20 minutes.

Add the butter and stir until melted, then strain the sauce through a fine sieve, pressing on the solids with the back of a spoon to extract all of the liquid; discard the solids. Cover the sauce to keep warm.

Heat 1 tablespoon of the oil in a large nonstick skillet over high heat. Sear the scallops on both sides until golden, about 2 minutes per side. The centers should still be slightly undercooked; do not overcook, or the scallops will lose their juices and become tough and chewy. Transfer to a plate and keep warm.

Heat the remaining 2 tablespoons oil in the same skillet over high heat. Add the scallion whites and stir-fry for 30 seconds. Add the wild mushrooms and cook for 1 minute, turning to coat well with the oil. Spoon 2 tablespoons of the mushroom sauce over the mushrooms and heat just until hot. Season to taste with salt and pepper.

Mix the Parmesan cheese into the remaining sauce.

Place 4 or 5 scallops on each serving plate and top with the mushrooms. Spoon the sauce over all, sprinkle with the scallion greens, and serve.

Japanese Maitake Mushrooms

The maitake, commonly called hen of the woods, is a large, beautiful, and very unusual mushroom. Weighing about a pound, it resembles a small grayish brown cauliflower. The body consists of a central section holding many branched stems that end in multiple caps. These caps have wrinkled edges and are joined together in clusters, almost like a large gray flower. Maitake mushrooms are usually available year-round, but the best season is from autumn to early spring. With a unique, delicate aroma and a meaty yet firm texture, they are good in soup and excellent either steamed or sautéed. When sautéing, I use a good olive oil and cook them for just a few minutes so they remain firm. 🌀 In ancient Japan, maitake mushrooms were rare and considered valuable — shoguns once traded them pound for pound for silver. Until less than twenty years ago, maitakes grew only in the wild. Today they are cultivated in the mountains of northeastern Japan as well as in North America and Europe. 🌀 Most maitake mushrooms are very clean. To prepare them, cut off the bottom stem or body (which is 4 to 6 inches wide) and save for making sauce or mushroom stock. With a small knife, very carefully cut the mushroom tops into single flowery pieces, or florets. To store maitakes, place a paper towel in the bottom of a large container, add a single layer of florets, and cover with another paper towel. Continue layering the mushrooms with paper towels, top with paper towels, and cover tightly. The paper towels will absorb moisture from the mushrooms, and they will keep in the refrigerator for up to a week.

How to Buy Scallops

There are three common varieties of scallops: bay scallops, calico scallops, and sea scallops. Bay scallops are very small; there can be as many as 80 to 100 per pound. Their meat is delicate and succulent. Nantucket bay scallops are the sweetest and best I have ever tasted. Their season runs from October to March. 🌀 On the West Coast, calico scallops from the Gulf of Mexico are often sold as bay scallops. These processed baby scallops are much smaller and more reasonably priced, but they do not have as much flavor as true bay scallops. 🌀 Sea scallops are much larger, from 6 to 30 per pound; the larger ones are more expensive. Though they are slightly firmer than bay scallops, their meat is sweet and moist. Peak season is mid-fall to mid-spring. 🌀 Once out of the water, scallops perish quickly, so make certain they are really fresh and cook them the day you buy them. If a scallop looks very white, it has probably been processed. Processed scallops, also called wet scallops, are soaked in water with preservatives after they are shucked to increase their weight (and price) and prolong their shelf life. They look shiny, but when you cook them, they release a lot of liquid and shrink. 🌀 The best scallops are dry-packed scallops, with no water or preservatives added. Dry scallops should have no smell at all and should look moist, not wet. Varying from pale beige to a creamy pinkish orange tint, with an appealing sheen, dry scallops do not have as uniform a color as wet scallops, but they are sweet, with no off or bitter flavor. 🌀 Diver scallops are of even higher quality. They are individually hand-picked from the ocean floor by deep-sea divers. Once shucked, they are packed dry. Peak season runs from November to April. 🌀 If you cannot find dry-packed scal-lops, rinse the processed scallops, then place on several layers of paper towels to dry. Change the towels until all the scallops feel dry and the paper towels do not absorb any more moisture.

Shaking Filet Mignon with Sea Scallops

───────── (✺) ─────────

"Shaking beef" is a famous Vietnamese dish. The beef is cut into cubes, stirred and shaken in a wok to coat it with a mixture of fish sauce, ginger, and sugar, and finished with butter. My variation on surf and turf uses cubes of filet mignon and substitutes scallops for the lobster tail. My version is spicy with fresh hot peppers, and I add basil for an herbal flavor.

──────[*Serves 2*]──────

2	tablespoons soy sauce
1	tablespoon whiskey or brandy
1	tablespoon extra-virgin olive oil
6	ounces filet mignon, trimmed well and cut into 1-inch cubes
3	tablespoons chicken stock or beef stock
1	tablespoon sherry wine vinegar
½	teaspoon sugar
8	ounces Brussels sprouts or baby spinach leaves
2	tablespoons butter

3	tablespoons soybean oil or corn oil
8	ounces medium sea scallops (8–12), preferably dry-packed, small muscle flaps removed
¼	cup diced red bell pepper
2	scallions, white part only, diced
2	garlic cloves, chopped
1	jalapeño pepper, stemmed and chopped
¼	cup fresh or frozen white corn
5–6	fresh basil leaves, julienned

In a medium bowl, mix together 1 tablespoon of the soy sauce, the whiskey or brandy, and olive oil. Add the meat and turn until each cube is well coated. Cover and marinate in the refrigerator.

Mix the remaining 1 tablespoon soy sauce, the stock, vinegar, and sugar in a small bowl. Set aside.

Discard the tough outer leaves of the Brussels sprouts, if using. Trim off the bottoms, then separate into individual leaves. Bring a medium pot of water to a boil over high heat. Blanch the Brussels sprout leaves or the spinach for about 1 minute, then drain well. Place in a bowl or saucepan and mix in 1 tablespoon of the butter. Cover to keep warm (if you use a glass bowl, you can reheat the sprouts or spinach in a microwave oven).

Heat 2 tablespoons of the soybean or corn oil in a large nonstick skillet over high heat until very hot. Add the beef and cook, stirring, until seared on all sides, about 2 minutes. Remove with a slotted spoon and place in a bowl. Wipe the skillet clean with paper towels.

Heat the remaining 1 tablespoon oil in the same skillet. Add the scallops and cook for 1 minute, turning once, just until they are lightly seared. Add the red pepper, scallions, garlic, and jalapeño pepper and cook, stirring, for about 30 seconds. Return the beef to the skillet and add the corn and reserved soy sauce mixture. Shake the pan and stir until the scallops and beef are well coated with sauce, about 2 minutes. Stir in the basil and finish with the remaining tablespoon of butter. Turn off the heat.

Meanwhile, reheat the sprouts or spinach.

Arrange the sprouts or spinach in a ring around a serving platter, spoon the filet and scallop mixture in the center, and serve.

Poultry

Oven-Roasted Shantung Chicken

When we were young, my father often reminisced about Shantung chicken, which he had whenever he passed through the small town of Dao Chu, in Shantung Province, where this legendary recipe originated. The chicken was usually sold at train stations, and passengers often bought it to eat for lunch or dinner while on the train.

Whole free-range chickens were deep-fried, marinated with spices, smoked with Chinese medicinal herbs, and then steamed until tender. The chicken had a deep brown color and a lusty, rich flavor. It was so unusual and delicious that anyone who tried it couldn't forget it.

My version calls for searing the chicken before marinating it with the spices so it turns a deep brown, then oven-roasting it. I like to serve it with white rice, a green vegetable, and two or three relishes, such as Pickled Rhubarb with Ginger (page 288), Cucumber Mint Relish (page 288), and Pan-Roasted Poblano Peppers (page 281).

[Serves 4]

2	tablespoons toasted sesame oil
¼	cup soy sauce
1	tablespoon maltose (malt sugar) or 2 tablespoons honey
¼	cup brandy, whiskey, or dry sherry
½	cup soybean oil or corn oil
1	4-pound free-range chicken, rinsed, dried, and cut into 8 pieces (see page 134)

5	garlic cloves, crushed
1	onion, thinly sliced
1	2-inch piece fresh ginger, thinly sliced (do not peel)
3	star anise
3	cardamom pods, crushed
1	3-inch piece cinnamon stick
1	tablespoon butter, melted

Maltose

Produced in China since the second century, maltose is the Chinese equivalent of corn syrup. Less sweet than other sugars, it is used mainly in preparing roasted meats; it gives Peking duck its lacquered look. The thick amber liquid is made by fermenting germinated grain, such as wheat, barley, millet, or rice. The process converts the grain's natural starch into maltose and dextrose. Sold in glass jars or plastic containers, maltose can be found in Asian markets and some health food stores.

Mix the sesame oil, soy sauce, maltose or honey, and liquor in a small bowl, stirring until the sugar is dissolved.

Heat the soybean or corn oil in a large skillet or flat-bottomed wok over high heat until hot. Fry the chicken in batches, skin side down, until golden brown, 6 to 8 minutes. Turn and brown the flesh side, about 3 minutes. Place the browned chicken in a single layer in a large roasting pan.

Drain the extra oil from the skillet, leaving just a scant tablespoon. Turn the heat to medium-low and add the garlic, onion, ginger, star anise, cardamom, and cinnamon. Cook, stirring, for about 3 minutes, until the onion and garlic are soft and the spices have released their aroma. Pour in the soy sauce mixture and cook for 3 to 4 minutes, until the sauce thickens. Pour in ¼ cup water, scrape the bottom of the pan well to deglaze, and cook for 1 minute.

Pour the mixture over the chicken and turn until evenly coated. Cool a little, then cover and refrigerate for 4 to 8 hours or overnight, turning the chicken occasionally in the marinade. Remove from the refrigerator about 30 minutes before cooking.

Preheat the oven to 375 degrees. Turn all the chicken pieces skin side down and cover the pan with a double sheet of aluminum foil. Bake for 30 minutes.

Turn the oven up to 400 degrees. Take out the pan, carefully remove the aluminum foil, and turn all the pieces skin side up. Brush with the melted butter. Return the pan to the oven and roast for 5 to 8 minutes, until the skin is well browned. Remove the chicken and place on a serving platter.

Pour the pan juices through a fine strainer into a small bowl. Spoon over the chicken and serve hot.

Cutting Up a Chicken

Place the chicken breast side down on a cutting board and, using a sharp boning knife, cleaver, or poultry shears, cut down along one side of the backbone from neck to tail. Remove the backbone by cutting down the other side of the bone from neck to tail. Reserve the backbone for making stock, if desired. ✦ With the chicken still breast side down, push down on the breastbone with your hand to loosen it. Then crack the breastbone and remove it with your fingers, loosening any attached cartilage. ✦ Cut down the center of the breast with your knife, separating the chicken into 2 halves. Turn skin side up and cut apart the breast and leg sections on each half of the chicken; you will have 4 pieces. ✦ Remove the wings from the breast sections by cutting around the ball and socket of the first joint to separate them. Cut off the wing tips (reserve for making stock). Remove the drumsticks from the thigh sections by cutting though the joint connecting them. ✦ If the breasts are very large, you can cut each in half crosswise, for 10 pieces.

Roast Chicken with Peppercorn Rub

Brining a chicken before roasting it ensures a beautifully moist bird. I add flavor to the skin by rubbing it with an aromatic Sichuan peppercorn–coriander blend. Placing it on a rack and roasting it over stock also keeps the meat juicy, while the skin gets crisp and brown. Root vegetables are roasted in the stock at the same time. The result is an easy one-pot meal. If you don't have the time for brining, you can use a kosher chicken, which is already soaked and salted and will remain moist when roasted.

Serve with steamed white rice or crusty French bread.

[Serves 4]

1	3½- to 4-pound free-range chicken, brined (see page 137)
4	tablespoons (½ stick) butter, softened
1	tablespoon Sichuan peppercorns (see page 93) or black peppercorns
1	tablespoon coriander seeds
2	cups chicken stock
8	ounces celery root, peeled and cut into 1-inch cubes
2	sweet potatoes (about 8 ounces), peeled and cut into 1-inch cubes
1	pound potatoes, preferably Yukon Gold, peeled and cut into 1-inch cubes
4	ounces small white button mushrooms
3	sprigs fresh thyme
	Kosher salt and freshly ground pepper
¼	cup chopped fresh cilantro

Preheat the oven to 400 degrees. Rinse the chicken and pat dry. Rub the skin with 2 tablespoons of the butter.

Heat a small dry skillet over medium-low heat. Add the peppercorns, swirl, and toast for about 2 minutes, or until fragrant. Add the coriander seeds and toast for another minute. Remove from the heat and cool.

Grind the spices almost to a powder in a spice grinder or coffee mill. Rub the mixture all over the bird.

Pour the stock into the bottom of a roasting pan and place the chicken breast side up on a rack over the liquid. Roast for 30 minutes, or until the skin begins to brown. Remove the chicken from the roasting pan and place on a plate. Remove the rack and spread the celery root, sweet potatoes, potatoes, mushrooms, and thyme in the roasting pan. Spoon a little stock over the vegetables to moisten them, then dot with the remaining 2 tablespoons butter. Return the rack to the roasting pan and place the chicken on it breast side down.

Roast for another 45 minutes, or until the skin is nicely browned and an instant-read meat thermometer inserted into the thigh reaches 170 degrees. Place the chicken on a large plate or platter, cover loosely with foil, and let sit for 15 minutes. Remove the rack and discard the thyme. Spoon the vegetables into a serving bowl and cover with foil to keep warm. Or keep them warm in a 325-degree oven.

Carefully pour the broth into a bowl and skim off and discard any fat floating on the surface.

If the vegetables or broth have become too cool, warm them in a microwave oven until hot. Reheat the broth in a small saucepan over medium heat for 1 to 2 minutes, until hot. Season the vegetables to taste with salt and pepper.

Carve the chicken and divide among four dinner plates or shallow bowls. Spoon the vegetables and broth around the chicken, sprinkle with the cilantro, and serve.

Cantonese Salt-Water Chicken with Soy Ginger Vinaigrette

One of the most famous Cantonese dishes, salt-water chicken is first soaked, then cooked in a brine made with salt, ginger, Shaoxing wine, and spices. The timing of this dish is very precise, resulting in meat that is velvety, silky, juicy, and very tender. The skin is pale, almost colorless. The chicken is always served cold or at room temperature.

If the chicken is brined a day ahead, the flavors of the brine will penetrate the meat better. The chicken can be boiled or steamed: I prefer to boil it in the brining liquid. I adapted this recipe from one by Mr. Lee, a Cantonese chef in my restaurant.

The cooked chicken is great to have around for sandwiches or salads. It can also be warmed in a microwave oven (or a preheated 325-degree oven) and served as a main course. Serve with Sautéed Baby Bok Choy (page 245), Artichoke Pasta with Broccoli Rabe, Tomatoes, and Artichokes (page 200), or Herbed Israeli Couscous (page 199).

Serves 4

BRINE

2/3	cup kosher salt
1	tablespoon sugar
1	2- to 3-inch piece fresh ginger, crushed
5	star anise
2–3	sprigs fresh thyme
2	scallions, crushed and cut into 2-inch lengths
	Fennel fronds (optional)
1/2	cup sake, dry sherry, or Madeira

1	2½- to 3-pound free-range chicken, washed well
	Soy Ginger Vinaigrette (recipe follows)

TO BRINE THE CHICKEN: Add 3 quarts water, the salt, sugar, crushed ginger, and star anise to a tall, narrow 6-quart or larger pot with a cover. Bring to a boil and let boil for 5 minutes. Cool.

Add the thyme, scallions, fennel (if using), and liquor. Add the chicken, submerging it in the brine; the liquid should cover it completely. Refrigerate, covered, for 12 hours.

TO COOK THE CHICKEN: Set the pot containing the brine and chicken over high heat and bring to a boil, skimming off any scum that forms. Boil the chicken for 30 to 35 minutes, or until an instant-read thermometer inserted into the thigh reaches 170 degrees.

Fill a bowl large enough to hold the chicken with ice water. Carefully remove the chicken from the hot brine and plunge it into the ice water to stop the cooking. When the chicken is cool, drain well, and dry. Wrap well and refrigerate. *The cooked chicken will keep in the refrigerator for 3 days.*

Meanwhile, strain the brine through a fine sieve into a bowl. Cool, then discard the layer of fat on top. Reserve 3 tablespoons of the brine for the vinaigrette. *Freeze the rest in a plastic container, if desired. It can be used again to make this recipe. Add enough water to make 3 quarts of liquid and an additional tablespoon or more of salt. The flavor of the brine gets better each time it is used.*

TO SERVE: Cut the chicken into serving-sized pieces and cut the breast meat into slices. Arrange the chicken on four plates, spoon the vinaigrette over the meat, and serve.

The Chinese Way
of Brining

Brining has only recently become popular in America, but it's been practiced in China for thousands of years. Whereas in the West its main purpose is to make pork or poultry juicier and tenderer, in China brining is done not only for this reason but to infuse flavor. Consequently, Chinese brines are generally very highly seasoned. ✦ The brine is typically prepared by seasoning a large pot of water with a combination of salt, Shaoxing wine, ginger, scallions, fresh herbs, and such spices as star anise, Sichuan peppercorns, cinnamon bark, fennel seeds, and cloves, and slowly simmering it until flavorful. (This kind of brine is called a white brine; the addition of soy sauce turns it into a dark brine, which imparts a deeper color to the meat.) After the brine is cooled, the ingredient to be brined — chicken, duck, squab, pork, or even beef — is added and marinated for several hours before being steamed or slowly poached in the same liquid.

Soy Sauce

Soy sauce is an important ingredient in Chinese cooking, replacing salt and adding depth of flavor to a dish. It also acts as a tenderizer and moistens meat. There are several different types of soy sauce, with varying degrees of saltiness, color, and flavor. My mother and grandmother used only regular soy sauce, and this is what I prefer. I use Kikkoman soy sauce, which is widely available and has just the right amount of saltiness and body. The darker varieties of soy sauce and tamari (a Japanese dark soy sauce) are too heavy for my taste, obscuring the flavors of other ingredients and darkening the color too much. Be sure that the soy sauce you buy is naturally fermented and that the label lists only soybeans, wheat, water, and salt with just a small amount of preservative. Avoid soy sauces with ingredients such as hydrolyzed soy protein and caramel — tip-offs that they have been processed from chemicals rather than naturally aged. Store soy sauce in a cool place once opened.

Soy Ginger Vinaigrette

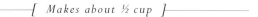

[Makes about ½ cup]

This traditional vinaigrette is also good over a salad of baby greens, a fresh tomato salad, plain steamed fennel, or grilled tuna.

2	garlic cloves, minced
1	tablespoon olive oil
1	teaspoon toasted sesame oil
1	tablespoon soy sauce
2	teaspoons rice wine vinegar
1	teaspoon sugar
2	tablespoons julienned peeled fresh ginger (preferably young ginger)
2	scallions, white part only, thinly sliced
3	tablespoons reserved brine (from page 136) or chicken stock
10	fresh cilantro leaves, cut into julienne

Mix the garlic, olive oil, and sesame oil in a small glass bowl and microwave on high power for 1 minute. Or place in a small saucepan and cook over medium heat for 1 to 2 minutes, or until the garlic is soft. Add the soy sauce, vinegar, sugar, ginger, scallions, and brine. *The vinaigrette can be made 1 to 2 days ahead, covered, and refrigerated.* Just before serving, mix in the cilantro.

PAN-SEARED CHICKEN BREASTS
WITH MOREL SAUCE
PAGE 140

Pan-Seared Chicken Breasts with Morel Sauce

In the spring, from early March until early June, fresh cultivated morels are available in many specialty markets. They have spongy, cone-shaped caps, 1 to 4 inches in length, and range in color from light tan to dark brown. I love their smoky, earthy, nutty flavor and springy texture.

I prefer small morels, since they are more flavorful and have a firmer texture than the larger ones. (They also tend to be lighter in color.) If you can't get fresh morels, dried are an excellent alternative. They have a more intense flavor but not the texture of fresh ones.

Since most boned chicken breasts have been skinned, buy breasts with the skin and bones and ask your butcher to remove the bones for you, or bone them yourself and save the bones for making stock.

Serve the chicken with sautéed broccoli rabe or baby bok choy and rice.

[Serves 4]

CHICKEN AND MARINADE

4	boneless chicken breast halves, with skin (about 6 ounces each)
3	tablespoons soy sauce
2	tablespoons olive oil
2	tablespoons vodka, sake, or vermouth
2	garlic cloves, minced

MOREL SAUCE

8	ounces fresh morels or 1 ounce dried morels
2	shallots, finely diced
2	tablespoons unsalted butter
½	cup chicken stock
½	cup whisked unsweetened coconut milk (heavy cream can be substituted)
	Kosher salt and freshly ground pepper
½	cup cornstarch
3	tablespoons soybean oil or corn oil, or more if needed
2	teaspoons truffle oil (optional)
	Fresh cilantro sprigs for garnish

TO MARINATE THE CHICKEN: Place each chicken breast between two sheets of plastic wrap and pound lightly with a flat mallet or the back of a cleaver until it is about ¼ inch thick. Place the breasts in a shallow pan or bowl. Add the soy sauce, olive oil, liquor, and garlic and turn to coat well. Marinate, covered and refrigerated, for 2 to 4 hours.

MEANWHILE, FOR THE SAUCE: If using fresh morels, brush them lightly to remove any sand and dirt. Cut lengthwise in half if they are very large. Set aside. If using dried morels, place them in a small bowl and pour boiling water over them to cover. Soak for 15 to 20 minutes, then lift out of the liquid and set aside.

Drain the chicken, reserving the marinade. Lightly dust with the cornstarch on the skin side only.

TO COOK THE CHICKEN: Preheat the oven to 250 degrees. Heat 2 tablespoons of the soybean or corn oil in a large nonstick skillet over high heat. Add 2 chicken breasts skin side down and sear until the skin is golden and crisp, 2 to 3 minutes. Turn and cook for 2 minutes, or until cooked through. Remove and place skin side up on a baking sheet. Add the remaining tablespoon of oil to the skillet and repeat with the other 2 chicken breasts. Keep warm in the oven until ready to serve.

TO FINISH THE SAUCE: Add the shallots to the skillet

in which you cooked the chicken and sauté over high heat for
1 minute, or until translucent. Add the morels and butter and
sauté for another minute.

If using fresh morels, remove with a slotted spoon and
place in a bowl. If using dried, leave them in the skillet. Pour
the chicken stock, reserved marinade, and coconut milk into
the skillet and bring to a boil. Turn the heat to low and cook
for 3 to 5 minutes, until the liquid is slightly reduced. Add the
fresh morels, if using, and cook for 1 minute. Season to taste
with salt and pepper.

TO SERVE: Place 1 piece of chicken on each of four dinner plates and spoon the sauce and mushrooms on top. Drizzle ½ teaspoon truffle oil over each portion, if desired. Garnish with the cilantro and serve.

Tung An Chicken

———————(☼)———————

Tung An chicken is a classic spicy stir-fry created in 1800 by a famous general in the revolutionary army who was born in the county of Tung An, in Hunan Province. My mother-in-law often cooked this dish. She loved to tell us about how she collected wild mushrooms for it from the local forests near where she lived when growing up.

In the traditional version, a young free-range mountain chicken (similar to a pheasant) is blanched, skinned, and cut into bite-sized pieces with the bones intact. The chicken is then sautéed with fresh hot peppers, wild mushrooms, young spring ginger, spring bamboo shoots, and Chinese black vinegar. I use a free-range poussin (a tender baby chicken) or a Cornish hen, and I substitute tangy fresh rhubarb for the black vinegar. Crunchy, nutty-tasting fresh artichoke hearts take the place of the bamboo shoots (fresh bamboo shoots are difficult to get in this country). And I remove most of the bones from the chicken to make it easier to eat.

—————[*Serves 2 as a main course*]—————

1	1- to 1¼-pound poussin or a 1- to 2-pound Cornish hen (buy the smallest available)
1	large egg white
1	tablespoon cornstarch
¼	cup extra-virgin olive oil
½	cup thinly sliced (¼-inch-thick) rhubarb (about 1 stalk)
1	teaspoon sugar
4	ounces wild mushrooms, such as morels or small shiitakes, stemmed
¼	cup chicken stock
1	tablespoon soy sauce
1	tablespoon vodka
1	1-inch piece fresh ginger, peeled and thinly sliced
4	small fresh hot red peppers, such as serrano or bird's-eye chiles, stemmed and halved
1	large artichoke, prepared as described on page 239

Bring a medium pot of water to a boil over high heat. Add the poussin or Cornish hen and cook for 5 minutes. Drain and cool.

Using a sharp knife, cut along one side of the backbone, then cut along the other side and remove the backbone. Cut off the wing tips. (Reserve the backbone and wing tips for stock, if desired.) Cut each wing into 2 pieces and remove the skin. Slice off each breast, including the rib cage. Remove the skin and cut each breast in half crosswise through the bone. Cut off the legs and thighs, cut the legs and thighs apart, and peel the skin from the meat. You will have 12 small pieces: 4 sections of breast meat, 2 legs, 2 thighs, and 4 wing sections.

Mix the egg white, cornstarch, and 1 tablespoon of the olive oil in a medium bowl. Add the chicken pieces, using your hands to coat them well with the mixture. Refrigerate, covered, if not immediately proceeding with the recipe.

Mix the rhubarb with the sugar in a small bowl and let sit at room temperature. If using shiitakes, cut into quarters. Leave small morels whole.

Mix the chicken stock, soy sauce, and vodka in a small bowl.

Heat the remaining 3 tablespoons oil in a large skillet or flat-bottomed wok over high heat. Add the ginger and hot peppers and cook, stirring, for 30 seconds. Add the chicken legs, thighs, and wings, turn the heat to medium, and cook for about 4 to 5 minutes, turning often, until the pieces are well browned and almost cooked through. Add the breasts and cook until browned and cooked through, 2 to 3 minutes.

Drain the artichoke and add to the pan along with the mushrooms. Stir-fry for about 2 minutes, or until the artichoke is just cooked through. Pour in the soy sauce mixture and the rhubarb and cook, stirring, for 1 to 2 minutes, or until hot. Serve.

Rhubarb

It's a shame to limit versatile rhubarb to desserts. I use it in salads, make it into relish, serve it as a vegetable, sauté it in a wok along with chicken and duck, and add it to braised meat dishes. There are several varieties; I prefer the kind called strawberry rhubarb, which has cherry red stalks, because it is less fibrous than the others. Choose crisp stalks that are brightly colored. If possible, buy rhubarb with the leaves still on the stalks, so you can judge its freshness; the leaves should be fresh-looking and blemish-free. But be sure to remove the leaves, since they are poisonous. Before cooking, peel a thin layer from the tough outside of the stalks.

Braised Chicken with Thai Curry Sauce

This delightfully fragrant curry combines lemongrass, ginger, coriander seeds, turmeric, garlic, and shallots, ground into a wet paste, then cooked with coconut milk. Unlike chicken breasts, which are leaner and dry out with long, slow simmering, boneless chicken thighs stay succulent. Serve with white rice.

[Serves 4 to 6]

- 2 tablespoons soy sauce
- 2 tablespoons vodka
- 1 large egg yolk
- 2 pounds skinless, boneless chicken thighs, cut into 1-inch cubes
- 2 large Yukon Gold or Red Bliss potatoes (about 6 ounces each)
- 1 stalk fresh lemongrass (see page 150), tender inner parts only, thinly sliced
- 2 garlic cloves, sliced
- 1 tablespoon fresh coriander seeds or chopped cilantro roots or 1 teaspoon dried coriander

- 3 shallots, sliced
- 1 tablespoon minced peeled fresh ginger
- 3 fresh or dried hot red peppers
- 3 tablespoons fish sauce (preferably Three Crabs brand)
- ¼ cup whisked unsweetened coconut milk
- ¼ cup soybean oil or corn oil
- ½ teaspoon ground turmeric
- 1 tablespoon Thai red curry paste (see page 107)
- 1 cup chicken stock

Add the soy sauce, vodka, and egg yolk to a large bowl and mix well. Add the chicken and stir to coat. Cover and refrigerate.

Peel the potatoes and cut into 1-inch cubes. Submerge in a bowl of cold water to keep them from discoloring.

Put the lemongrass, garlic, coriander or cilantro, shallots, ginger, and red peppers in a spice grinder or coffee mill and coarsely chop. Or chop by hand. Place in a small bowl.

Mix the fish sauce and coconut milk in another bowl.

Heat the oil in a large nonstick skillet or flat-bottomed wok over high heat. Add the chicken and stir-fry for about 2 minutes, until the cubes are lightly seared. Add the lemongrass mixture and cook, stirring, until slightly fragrant, about 2 minutes. Add the turmeric and curry paste and cook, stirring, until the chicken pieces are well coated, about 1 minute.

Drain the potato cubes well and add them, along with the fish sauce mixture, to the pan and cook for about 2 minutes. Add the chicken stock, cover, turn the heat to low, and simmer for 15 minutes, or until the potatoes are soft and the chicken is tender, stirring occasionally to keep from sticking.

Serve hot.

Cilantro

In mid- to late July, the tops of my cilantro plants
are heavy with green coriander seeds, which I collect
and grind in my spice grinder. They have a mild, pleasant
citrus flavor, quite different from the dried seeds. They're
perfect for Braised Chicken with Thai Curry Sauce or for
marinades or grilled meats. I always freeze a package of
whole seeds so I can enjoy them in the winter; they keep
for at least 3 months. ✿ If you don't have fresh coriander seeds, you can use fresh coriander (cilantro) roots,
which Asians consider to be the best part of the plant.
Many markets and supermarkets sell cilantro with the
roots attached. They have a much stronger flavor than the
leaves and are great for grinding into sauces, curries, and
pastes. To store, place the plant in a container of water,
cover the greens with a loosely fitting plastic bag, and
refrigerate for up to 1 week. Or, to store cilantro that
has no roots, wrap in a damp paper towel and
refrigerate it in a perforated plastic
bag for up to 5 days.

Chicken Soong

—— (✻) ——

For this pretty dish, which I often serve as an appetizer or for lunch, the chicken is diced, marinated, and sautéed with aromatic vegetables, such as celery, carrots, and crunchy water chestnuts, and buttery pine nuts, then nestled in lettuce cups. You can substitute or add your own vegetable combinations, using, for example, diced asparagus, snow peas, red bell peppers, or beets.

—— [*Serves 4*] ——

8	ounces skinless, boneless chicken breast		1/2	cup diced (1/4-inch) carrots
3	tablespoons soy sauce		1/2	cup diced (1/4-inch) fresh water chestnuts or jicama
1	teaspoon cornstarch		1/2	cup diced (1/4-inch) celery
1	tablespoon white vinegar		1/4	cup pine nuts
1/4	teaspoon sugar			Lettuce leaves (preferably iceberg), trimmed into cups
2	tablespoons soybean oil or corn oil			Brandy-Infused Hoisin Sauce (page 169) or hot pepper sauce
1	garlic clove, minced			
1	teaspoon minced peeled fresh ginger			

Place the chicken breast in the freezer for about 1 hour to make slicing easier.

Using a Japanese Benriner, mandoline, or sharp knife, cut the chicken into very thin slices, then cut the slices into 1/4-inch-thick julienne. The chicken will look almost shredded. Place in a large bowl. Mix in 1 tablespoon of the soy sauce and the cornstarch and marinate while you prepare the other ingredients.

Mix the remaining 2 tablespoons soy sauce, the vinegar, and sugar in a small bowl.

Heat the oil in a large skillet or flat-bottomed wok over high heat. Add the garlic and ginger and stir-fry for 30 seconds. Add the chicken and stir-fry just until it changes color, about 2 minutes. Remove with a slotted spoon.

Add all of the vegetables and the pine nuts to the pan. Cook, stirring, for about 2 minutes. Return the chicken to the pan, add the soy sauce mixture, and stir-fry until hot.

Spoon into the lettuce leaves and serve with small bowls of the hoisin sauce or hot pepper sauce on the side.

Fresh Water Chestnuts

Once found only in cans in this country, water chestnuts can now be bought fresh. These dark brown-skinned, walnut-sized corms (underwater bulbs) are cultivated throughout China, grown in muddy ponds or around the edges of rice paddies. They must be rinsed well and peeled before using. They have a mild, slightly sweet taste and crunchy texture. Choose rock-hard water chestnuts with tight unwrinkled skins — if they are soft, they are usually old or rotten. Don't use any that have discolored flesh. Fresh water chestnuts will keep, unpeeled, in a paper bag stored in the refrigerator for up to 2 weeks. ✿ If you can't find fresh water chestnuts, canned can be substituted, but only in a cooked dish where they will play a minor part. A better substitute is crunchy fresh jicama, which is readily available in Hispanic markets and most supermarkets.

Crisp Roasted Poussin with Leeks and Potatoes

Here, I have adapted some of the basic techniques of a Cantonese dish, briefly simmering the poussins in a flavorful liquid, painting the skin with a syrup glaze, air-drying them, and roasting the birds to a crisp dark mahogany sheen. I also stuff a flavorful mixture under the skin.

The birds are roasted on a rack placed over the vegetables and stock, and the vegetables absorb the juices that drip from the birds, enriching their flavors. Serve with Cranberry-Ginger Relish (page 282), Mango-Kumquat Relish (page 283), or Pickled Rhubarb with Ginger (page 288).

[Serves 4]

4	poussins (about 1 pound each)
2	tablespoons honey
3	tablespoons soy sauce
1	tablespoon grated peeled fresh ginger
1	stalk fresh lemongrass (see page 150), tender inner part only, thinly sliced
2	shallots, thinly sliced
6	sprigs fresh lemon thyme or regular thyme, finely chopped
½	teaspoon Tabasco sauce

¼	teaspoon five-spice powder
1	tablespoon kosher salt, plus more to taste
1	tablespoon olive oil
2	tablespoons butter, softened
3	medium leeks
12	small new potatoes, peeled
2	carrots, peeled and cut into 1-inch lengths
2	cups chicken stock
	Freshly ground pepper

Wash the birds well under cold running water and dry with paper towels.

Combine 4 cups water, the honey, and soy sauce in a large skillet or flat-bottomed wok, bring to a boil, stirring, and simmer for 5 minutes to blend the flavors.

Place 1 bird in the pan and ladle the liquid over it until well coated, about 2 minutes; the skin will turn pale yellow. Place the poussin breast side up on a rack over a baking sheet, and repeat with the other birds.

Bring the liquid back to a boil, then reduce the heat and simmer until thickened and reduced to about 1 cup, about 20 minutes. Pour the syrup into a bowl and cool.

Meanwhile, mince the ginger, lemongrass, shallots, and thyme in a food processor or spice grinder. Spoon into a small bowl and mix in the Tabasco, five-spice powder, salt, and olive oil.

Loosen the skin from the breast and thighs of the birds by carefully running your fingers between the meat and the skin, and spread the herb mixture evenly over the flesh. Brush the cooled syrup over the outside of the poussins.

Place the birds, uncovered, on a rack set on a baking sheet in the refrigerator for at least 4 hours, or until the skin is very dry.

Preheat the oven to 375 degrees. Massage the butter into the skin of the poussins. Trim off the green tops of the leeks to within 1 inch of the whites; trim off the roots.

Cut the leeks into 1-inch pieces. Wash well to make sure there is no dirt between the layers.

Put the leeks, potatoes, and carrots in a roasting pan with a rack. Pour the stock over the vegetables and place the rack on top. Set the birds breast side up on the rack and roast for 30 minutes.

Turn the birds over and roast for another 30 minutes, or until the skin is golden and crisp and an instant-read thermometer inserted into the thigh reaches 170 degrees.

Place each bird on a large dinner plate. Season the roasted vegetables with salt and pepper to taste, spoon them around the birds, and serve.

SIMPLE VARIATION

Omit the vegetables and serve the birds with Vegetable Rice with Shiitakes and Broccoli Rabe (page 209).

Lemongrass

Lemongrass has a light, refreshing lemon flavor and an intriguing lemony perfume without the bite of lemon. These qualities make it a good partner with garlic, chiles, and cilantro. ✿ Fresh lemongrass stalks can be found in Asian markets and large supermarkets. They have plump bases and long, bladelike gray-green leaves. Strip off the tough outer leaves and cut off the bottom root portion. Use only the relatively tender inner white base up to where the leaves begin to branch. ✿ Wrap fresh lemongrass in plastic wrap and store in the refrigerator for several weeks. If you can't get fresh lemongrass, frozen (available in Asian markets) is better than dried.

Roasted Squab with Port Wine Sauce

Coriander and fennel seeds combine in this aromatic spice rub. The port wine–honey-vinegar glaze gives the roasted squab a beautiful caramel-like coating. Refrigerating the seasoned birds allows time for the flavors to penetrate the meat; Cornish hens or poussins can be substituted for the squab.

[Serves 4]

4	squab (about 1 pound each; or see above)		3	shallots, minced
1	tablespoon kosher salt		1½	cups tawny port
1	tablespoon coriander seeds		¼	cup honey
1	tablespoon fennel seeds		3	tablespoons white vinegar
1	tablespoon soybean oil or corn oil			Fresh rosemary sprigs for garnish (optional)

Rinse the squab and pat dry. Use shears or a sharp knife to remove the neck and any fat from the back.

Heat a small heavy skillet over medium-low heat and add the salt and coriander and fennel seeds. Toast the mixture, shaking the pan, until the spices darken and smell pungent, about 3 minutes. Transfer to a bowl and cool, then grind to a powder using a spice grinder or coffee mill.

Rub each squab inside and out with the spice powder. Place the birds on a platter, cover with plastic wrap, and refrigerate for at least 4 to 6 hours, or overnight.

Heat the oil in a medium saucepan over medium heat. Add the shallots and cook, stirring, until they are soft, about 3 minutes. Pour in the port and cook until the sauce thickens and reduces by two-thirds, about 20 minutes. Strain through a fine sieve into a small saucepan.

Preheat the oven to 450 degrees. In a small bowl, whisk together the honey and vinegar. Place the squab breast side down on a rack in a roasting pan. Brush generously with the honey-vinegar mixture and roast for 15 minutes.

Turn the birds over, brush again, and roast for another 10 minutes, or until they are nicely browned. The meat will be rare at this stage; if you prefer it more well done, continue to roast for another 5 minutes.

Reheat the port sauce.

Meanwhile, using poultry shears or a cleaver, cut along both sides of each squab backbone and remove. Cut the squab in half, cutting through the breastbone. Place the squab halves on a platter.

Spoon the port sauce around the birds. Garnish with rosemary sprigs, if desired, and serve.

SIMPLE VARIATION

You can substitute 2 tablespoons Sichuan peppercorns (see page 93) for the coriander and fennel seeds. Toast them with the salt in a small dry skillet over medium heat until they are almost black, about 5 minutes, then cool and grind.

Stuffed Quail with Cabbage, Cured Ham, and Roasted Fuyu Persimmons

Quail are sold whole or partially boned, with just the drumsticks and wing bones intact. The meat is very lean, with a light gamy flavor. These extremely tasty and tender little birds are perfect for stuffing.

Cured ham or prosciutto and wild mushrooms add body and flavor to the cabbage stuffing. It absorbs the flavor of the meat and releases some liquid, so the quail taste especially succulent. I make this in the fall after the first frost, when cabbage becomes sweet. The Fuyu persimmons brighten the dish with their beautiful orange color.

[Serves 4]

8	semi-boneless quail (see above)
3	tablespoons olive oil
3	tablespoons soy sauce
2	tablespoons brandy
2	large Fuyu persimmons (see page 155)
2	tablespoons butter
1	teaspoon sugar

½	pound shiitake, morel, or chanterelle mushrooms
½	small tender green cabbage
3	shallots, thinly sliced
2	ounces cured ham or prosciutto, cut into ¼-inch dice
	Kosher salt and freshly ground pepper
2	tablespoons truffle oil (optional)
2	tablespoons chopped fresh thyme

Wash the quail under cold running water. Dry well with paper towels.

Pour 2 tablespoons of the olive oil, the soy sauce, and brandy into a large bowl and mix well. Turn the quail inside out, so that the flesh will better absorb the marinade. Add the quail to the marinade and turn until they are well coated. Cover and refrigerate for at least 20 minutes and up to 1 hour.

Trim the stems from the persimmons. Peel off the skin with a vegetable peeler. Cut the persimmons into quarters and remove the cores. Slice each quarter into 3 sections. Wash in cold water, drain, and dry well with paper towels to prevent them from turning brown.

Heat a large skillet over high heat. Add the butter and, once it melts, add the persimmons and cook, turning once, until lightly golden, about 2 minutes. Remove from the heat and sprinkle with the sugar. *The persimmons can be prepared up to 4 hours ahead of time. Place in a glass bowl and warm in a microwave oven before serving; or reheat in a 325-degree oven for about 5 minutes.*

Remove the stems from the shiitake or morel mushrooms (save them for mushroom stock, if desired), or trim the chanterelles. Cut each mushroom into quarters.

Remove any tough outer leaves from the cabbage. Cut out and discard the core. With a Japanese Benriner, mandoline, or sharp knife, slice the cabbage into julienne; you should have 4 packed cups. Bring a large pot of water to a boil. Add the cabbage and cook for 20 seconds. Drain and plunge into a bowl of ice water to stop the cooking, then pour into a colander and drain well; squeeze out the excess water with your hands.

Heat the remaining 1 tablespoon olive oil in a medium skillet over high heat until hot but not smoking. Add the shallots and sauté for about 1 minute, just until soft, then mix in

the ham or prosciutto. Add the cabbage and mix well. Season to taste with salt and pepper. Remove from the heat, divide the stuffing into 8 portions, and cool.

Preheat the oven to 425 degrees. Remove the quail from the marinade and turn them so that the skins are now facing out. Reserve the marinade.

Stuff each quail with a portion of the stuffing. Then, using the tip of a knife, make small incisions about ¼ inch from the left and right of the bottom cavity, near the legs. Cross the quail legs and tuck the tips inside the holes. *The recipe can be made to this point up to 1 day in advance. Refrigerate the quail, the marinade, the mushrooms, and the persimmons separately, covered.*

Place the quail in a roasting pan, preferably nonstick or lined with foil. Roast in the lower third of the oven for about 6 minutes, or until the quail turn golden brown. Turn and continue to roast for another 4 minutes, or until the quail are cooked through. (Check, using the tip of a knife to see if the thigh juices run clear; an instant-read thermometer inserted in the thigh should reach 170 degrees.)

Meanwhile, heat the reserved marinade in a medium skillet over high heat. Add the mushrooms and cook for 2 minutes, or until just barely soft. Remove from the heat and season to taste with salt and pepper. Add the truffle oil, if desired.

Arrange 2 quail on each plate, along with 6 slices of persimmon. Spoon the mushrooms over the quail, then sprinkle with the thyme and serve.

Fuyu Persimmons

Persimmons rank high among the favorite fruits in China, and they are now common in American supermarkets. Fuyu and Hachiya are the two main varieties, though they have completely different characteristics.  Fuyu persimmons are bright orange, with a round tomato shape. They are sweet, with none of the harsh tannins that are present in Hachiyas. The fruit is crisp even when fully ripe and has a refreshing, mild flavor; no other fruit is quite like it. Fuyus can be peeled and eaten out of hand like apples, and they are excellent in chutney or pickles. They can even be roasted to use as a side dish. Choose Fuyu persimmons that are deep orange, with shiny skin free of black spots or bruises, and that are firm to the touch. Those that are pale orange have probably been picked too soon and will not be sweet. If you have a choice, buy bigger ones, as they are usually sweeter. Store them in the refrigerator for up to 1 week. Hachiya persimmons have a domed shape and a pointed end and are bright red-orange. Impossibly astringent when unripe, they can be soft and sweet when fully ripened. But even then, they often taste bitter, so I avoid them.

Nanking Salt-Brined Duck

—— (✿) ——

Raising and cooking ducks have always held a special and important place in Chinese cuisine. Most Westerners are familiar with Beijing's Peking duck, but other regions of China have their own equally famous duck recipes. Nanking is known for salt-brined duck, which is marinated with aromatic spices and then steamed. Because the brining process acts like a cure, the meat stays beautifully pink and moist.

Salt-brined duck is usually thinly sliced and served cold at the beginning of the meal, as an appetizer, accompanied by other cold foods such as salad, seafood, and nuts. Or it can be served family-style as part of a meal.

—— [*Serves 4 as a main course or 8 to 10 as part of an appetizer plate*] ——

1	4½- to 5-pound duck (preferably a Pekin/Long Island duck)
½	cup plus 2 teaspoons kosher salt
1	tablespoon plus 1 teaspoon Sichuan peppercorns (see page 93)
2	cinnamon sticks

2	tablespoons anise seeds
5	star anise
5	cloves
1	3-inch piece fresh ginger, thinly sliced
1	bunch scallions, trimmed

Remove any pinfeathers from the duck. Wash and dry well.

Heat a small heavy skillet over medium-low heat and add 2 teaspoons of the kosher salt and 1 teaspoon of the Sichuan peppercorns. Toast, shaking the pan, until the peppercorns turn very dark brown, almost black, and smell pungent. Transfer to a bowl and cool, then grind to a powder using a spice grinder or coffee mill.

Rub the duck with the peppercorn-salt mixture. Cover and refrigerate for at least 4 hours, or overnight.

Tie the remaining 1 tablespoon Sichuan peppercorns, the cinnamon sticks, anise seeds, star anise, and cloves tightly in cheesecloth. Bring 1 gallon water to a boil in a large pot over high heat, add the spice package, turn the heat to medium, and simmer for about 20 minutes. Mix in the remaining ½ cup salt, remove from the heat, and cool.

Add the duck to the brine, cover, and refrigerate for 12 hours.

Drain the duck and dry well. *If you like, you can save the brine and use it again. Bring the liquid to a boil and cook for 5 minutes, then cool. The brine can be frozen for up to 3 months.*

Bring a large pot of water to a boil over high heat and add the ginger and scallions. Add the duck and bring to a boil, then turn the heat to medium and simmer for about 45 minutes, or until the meat is tender and an instant-read thermometer registers 170 degrees when inserted into the thigh. Remove from the heat and cool the duck in the liquid.

When the duck is cool, remove from the liquid and dry well. Cut the duck breasts from the carcass and remove the legs and place on a serving platter. Cut the breast meat into thin slices, place next to the legs, and serve.

Using the Whole Duck

Every part of the duck is precious. After rinsing and drying the duck, remove any excess fat and save for rendering. Duck fat has a lot of flavor and is wonderful for sautéing meats, potatoes, and vegetables. 🌀 To cut up a duck, place it breast side up on a cutting board. Using a sharp boning knife or cleaver, remove each leg in one piece by cutting through the skin and then the joint connecting it to the carcass. Use the thigh and drumstick portions for braised dishes. 🌀 Detach the wings by cutting around the ball and socket of the first joint to separate them from the breasts. Save the wings for stock. 🌀 Remove the breasts one at a time by cutting along the front of the breastbone to free the meat. With your fingers, separate the meat from the carcass and remove each breast section. The boneless breast meat is good in sautéed dishes; see the recipes on pages 159 and 160. 🌀 Chop the carcass with a cleaver or large chef's knife into 2- to 3-inch pieces and save it, along with the wings and giblets (except the liver), for stock. Save the liver for sautéing or a quick pâté. Chop any pieces of skin into 1-inch squares and save for cracklings (see page 53).

SIMPLE VARIATION

You can also roast the duck instead of poaching it. Preheat the oven to 350 degrees. Cut the scallions into 1-inch pieces. Stuff them, along with the ginger, into the cavity of the duck. Truss with butcher's twine to help keep the stuffing inside the bird.

Place a rack over a large shallow pan (a broiling pan with a rack works well) filled halfway with water. (The water will prevent the grease from the duck from making a mess in your oven and keep the smoke in your kitchen to a minimum.) Set the duck breast side down on the rack and roast for 45 minutes. Turn the duck and roast breast side up for another 45 minutes, or until it is lightly golden and the meat is tender and an instant-read thermometer inserted into the thigh reaches 170 degrees. Add more water to the pan if needed.

Simple Grilled Duck Breasts

Several different kinds of duck are available in the market: Long Island, mallard, Muscovy, and Moulard. Long Island ducks, which I like best, are actually descendants of the Pekin duck, a breed with pure white feathers. The whole breasts weigh about ¾ to 1 pound, and their meat is much tenderer than that of other breeds, with fewer tendons. Mallard, Muscovy, and Moulard ducks have much larger breasts, but the meat is tougher.

Here the duck breasts are marinated, pan-seared to remove some of the fat and crisp the skin, and finished on a grill. If you don't have a grill, a large heavy skillet will also work. I like duck breast cooked to medium-rare, so it remains tender and juicy. The skin becomes deliciously dark and crisp as the honey caramelizes under the high heat.

[Serves 4]

- 4 single duck breasts (preferably from Pekin/Long Island duck; 7–8 ounces each)
- 2 tablespoons soy sauce
- 2 tablespoons brandy
- 1 teaspoon honey

- 3 tablespoons olive oil or soybean oil, plus more for the grill
- 3 garlic cloves, finely chopped
- 1 scallion, green part only, cut into 1-inch pieces
- 1 small bunch fresh thyme

Remove the excess fat along the edges of the duck skin and discard. Rinse the breasts well, then dry with paper towels. With a sharp knife, score the skin in a crisscross pattern about ⅛ inch deep at 1-inch intervals.

In a small bowl, mix the soy sauce, brandy, honey, 1 tablespoon of the oil, the garlic, scallion, and thyme. Pour into a large zipper-lock bag, add the duck breasts, and seal, squeezing out the excess air, then turn to coat all sides. Refrigerate for 2 to 4 hours, turning the bag over a few times to redistribute the marinade.

When you are ready to cook, remove the duck from the marinade and scrape off the garlic and thyme.

Preheat a grill or griddle until hot and brush with a thin coating of oil. Heat the remaining 2 tablespoons oil in a large heavy skillet over high heat until hot. Add the duck breasts skin side down and sear for about 2 minutes, or until the skin is lightly browned. Turn and sear the flesh side for about 1 minute. Transfer to a large plate.

Grill the duck breasts flesh side down for about 4 minutes. Turn skin side down and grill for another 4 minutes; the duck breasts will be medium-rare. If you like your meat more well done, increase the cooking time by a minute or so.

Slice and serve hot or at room temperature.

Smoked Duck Breasts

(☼)

Smoking duck breasts indoors is simple, and the results are superb. Unlike the Western technique of cold-smoking, Chinese hot-smoking is fast, usually a matter of minutes. Rice, flour, and sugar are the basic smoking ingredients, but a great variety of aromatics can be added, such as tea leaves, orange peel, dried herbs and spices, or flavorful wood chips.

Generally the smoking mixture is placed directly in the bottom of a wok. I like to use a large heavy cast-iron pot (lined with aluminum foil) with a tight-fitting lid, which produces superior results. A rack is inserted, the duck breasts are placed on top, and the pot is tightly covered. The sugar and flour produce a good amount of smoke, while the rice aerates the mixture, causing it to burn more evenly. Several cooking methods happen at the same time — smoking, baking, and dry-steaming — producing a subtle aroma and moist, tender meat. During this process, the duck gives off a lot of smoke — make sure your kitchen is well ventilated.

Served medium-rare, the breasts are much tenderer and juicier than if well done.

{ Serves 4 as a main course or 8 as a first course }

DUCK

4   teaspoons coarse sea salt or kosher salt

2   teaspoons Sichuan peppercorns (see page 93) or black peppercorns

2   12-ounce whole duck breasts (preferably Pekin/Long Island)

SMOKING MIXTURE

¼   cup all-purpose flour

¼   cup sugar

¼   cup long-grain white rice

¼   cup tea leaves, preferably jasmine

TO PREPARE THE DUCK: Heat a small heavy skillet over medium-low heat and add the salt and peppercorns. Toast the mixture, shaking the pan, until the peppercorns turn very dark brown and smell pungent. Transfer to a bowl and cool, then grind to a powder using a spice grinder or coffee mill.

Wash the duck breasts and pat dry. Rub the breasts all over with the salt-peppercorn mixture. Refrigerate, well covered, overnight (or up to 12 hours) so that the flavor of the rub penetrates the flesh.

TO SMOKE THE DUCK: Line a cast-iron or other heavy Dutch oven with heavy-duty aluminum foil. Mix all the ingredients for the smoking mixture together and spread on the foil. Have ready a rack that will fit into the pot, about 2 inches above the smoking mixture. Support the rack on crumpled aluminum foil, if necessary.

Heat the smoking mixture over high heat until wisps of smoke begin to appear, about 5 minutes. Place the rack in the pot and set the duck breasts on it skin side up. Cover the pot with another piece of heavy-duty aluminum foil, then with a heavy lid to prevent any smoke from escaping. Turn the heat down to medium and smoke for 7 minutes. Remove from the heat and let sit for 5 minutes before removing the lid.

TO SERVE: Remove the duck breasts and, using a paper towel, wipe off any remaining peppercorn mixture. Slice and serve warm or cold as an appetizer or as part of a cold plate; the duck will be very rare. *The duck can be refrigerated, well wrapped, for 3 to 4 days. If desired, reheat by placing the breasts skin side up under a hot broiler for 5 minutes, or until the skin is well browned and the meat is medium-rare. Or reheat them in a dry skillet: cut 3 lengthwise slits into the skin of each breast and cook skin side down for about 5 minutes per side over medium-high heat.*

Star Anise Duck and Soybean Stew

The aromatic cooking liquid, redolent of star anise, along with the flavorful juices from the duck penetrate the beans during the slow braising process. Dried soybeans are essential for this recipe. Unlike other beans, which become mushy and starchy and disintegrate when cooked too long, soybeans retain their shape no matter how long you simmer them.

For this dish, you can buy packaged duck legs, but I prefer to start with whole ducks and save the breasts for smoking (see page 160) or grilling (see page 159) and the bones for making stock. Serve with white rice.

[Serves 4]

1½	cups dried yellow soybeans (see page 232)
4	whole duck legs (thighs and drumsticks)
3	tablespoons corn oil or light olive oil
1	small onion, diced (1 cup)
3	garlic cloves, sliced
¼	cup soy sauce
¼	cup brandy
2	tablespoons balsamic vinegar
5	star anise

2	bay leaves, crushed
1	sprig fresh rosemary, leaves only, chopped, or ½ teaspoon dried rosemary
2	carrots, peeled and diced
2–3	cups Duck Stock (page 58) or chicken stock
2	medium tomatoes, peeled (see page 123), seeded, and diced
5	fresh basil leaves, julienned

Soak the soybeans for at least 8 hours, or overnight, in a large bowl of cold water to cover by at least 6 inches. Add more water if needed to keep the beans well covered. Drain well.

Bring a large pot of water to a boil over high heat. Add the soybeans, turn the heat to medium-low, and cook, uncovered, for 2 hours. Drain well. Rinse well under cold running water to remove any scum that might have formed during cooking, then drain again.

Cut each duck leg into 2 pieces, separating the thighs from the drumsticks.

Heat the oil in a large casserole or braising pan over high heat. Add the duck pieces, skin side down, and brown well. Turn and continue to cook until the second side is browned, about 5 minutes total. Pour off all but 2 tablespoons of the duck fat.

Add the onion and garlic to the pot and cook until soft, about 2 minutes. Add the soy sauce, brandy, vinegar, star anise, bay leaves, and rosemary, turn the heat to very low, and cook for about 20 minutes, skimming off any fat or foam.

Add the soybeans, carrots, and 2 cups of the stock. Bring to a boil, then lower the heat and simmer, covered, for 45 minutes to 1 hour, or until the duck is tender. Stir occasionally and turn the duck over halfway through the cooking time; add more stock if needed.

Remove and discard the star anise. Mix in the tomatoes and bring to a boil. Remove from the heat, add the basil, and serve.

Meats

Braised Lion's Head Meatballs

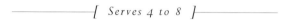

These classic Chinese meatballs are big, about the size of a fist, and unevenly shaped. Some say they resemble a lion's head, which is how they got their name. Juicy, bursting with flavor, and very soft (almost to the point of melting in your mouth), they are made with ground pork and silken tofu, along with shiitake mushrooms and fresh water chestnuts. Layered with napa cabbage, they are slowly braised.

When I make this dish, I coarsely grind the meat myself. The ground meat in most markets is too fine and does not retain much liquid, making the meatballs dry. If you don't have a meat grinder, ask your butcher to grind the pork for you using a coarse setting. A food processor does not chop the meat properly.

{ Serves 4 to 8 }

1	large head napa cabbage (about 2 pounds)
1	tablespoon kosher salt
4	ounces silken tofu
1	3-inch piece fresh ginger
1½	pounds boneless pork butt, with some fat
3	tablespoons soy sauce
3	tablespoons whiskey or brandy
1	tablespoon toasted sesame oil

4	ounces shiitake mushrooms, stemmed and finely chopped
2	ounces peeled fresh or canned water chestnuts, patted dry and finely chopped
½	cup cornstarch or all-purpose flour
½	cup soybean oil or corn oil
1	bunch scallions, trimmed and cut into 2-inch lengths
½	cup chicken stock or beef stock, or more if needed

Preheat the oven to 375 degrees. Cut off the base of the cabbage so that the leaves come loose. Cut big leaves lengthwise in half, then cut all the leaves crosswise into 1-inch strips. Place the cabbage in a large strainer, sprinkle with the salt, and set over a bowl. Let stand for 1 hour, or until the cabbage is softened slightly.

Meanwhile, place several layers of paper towels on a large plate. Place the tofu on top, cover with another layer of paper towels, and let sit for 30 minutes. Replace the paper towels as necessary when they become wet.

Peel and grate the ginger. Wrap it in a piece of cheesecloth and squeeze out the juice; you need 2 tablespoons. Discard the solids and set the juice aside.

Wash the pork butt and dry with paper towels. Cut it

into 2-inch pieces. Grind through a meat grinder with a coarse blade.

Combine the ground pork, soy sauce, whiskey or brandy, ginger juice, and sesame oil in a large bowl and mix well, then slowly add 3 tablespoons cold water. Keep stirring in one direction, to loosen the mixture, until the liquid has been totally absorbed by the meat. Mix in the shiitake mushrooms and water chestnuts. Add the drained tofu and mix until combined.

Divide the mixture into 8 portions. Shape into 8 large meatballs and lightly roll in the cornstarch or flour.

Rinse the cabbage under cold running water and squeeze to remove excess water.

Heat the oil in a nonstick heavy Dutch oven or casserole

Pork Butt

Even though it's called butt, this cut of meat comes from the upper part of the front leg of a hog. Depending on the region of the country you're in, it can be called Boston butt, shoulder picnic, or shoulder butt. Weighing 6 pounds (boneless) to 8 pounds (bone in), this economical, rectangular cut is marbled with enough fat to keep it moist during slow cooking, so it is perfect for braising or roasting. ✧ Most Americans are more familiar with pork loin or tenderloin. Don't make the mistake of substituting these cuts (or chops) for butt; they do not have enough fat for slow cooking and will become dry and tough. Pork butt is available in Asian markets and other ethnic grocery stores and in many butcher shops and supermarkets, or your market can probably special-order it.

over high heat. When it is hot, add half the meatballs and cook, turning, until golden on all sides, about 8 minutes. Lift out onto a large plate and repeat with the remaining meatballs.

Drain all the oil from the casserole. Add the cabbage, top with the meatballs, then the scallions, and pour the stock over all.

Cover the pot and bake for 40 to 45 minutes, checking halfway and adding more stock if needed to keep the meatballs moist. Serve hot.

Pork Chops with Spicy Tomato Sauce

This recipe combines two techniques, one Chinese, one French. Following the Chinese tradition, I marinate the pork chops in an egg–soy sauce mixture before braising them with vegetables (in this case, tomatoes and roasted red bell pepper). Then I borrow from the French, browning the chops to produce caramelized, meaty flavors. The liquid and vegetables are pureed to make a sauce, and the chops are simmered in the liquid for a short time. Serve with Mashed Taro Root (page 266) and sautéed broccoli rabe.

Serves 4

¼	cup soy sauce
1	large egg yolk
3	tablespoons olive oil
4	12- to 14-ounce bone-in loin pork chops, each ¾ inch thick
1	large onion, chopped (about 1½ cups)
3	garlic cloves, peeled and crushed
1	pound tomatoes, peeled (see page 123) and quartered

1	large red bell pepper, roasted and peeled (see page 110)
2	jalapeño peppers, diced, or 1 teaspoon crushed red pepper flakes
½	cup dry sherry
½	cup chicken stock
	Fresh oregano sprigs
	Kosher salt and freshly ground pepper

Mix the soy sauce, egg yolk, and 1 tablespoon of the olive oil in a small bowl.

Cover each pork chop loosely with a piece of plastic wrap and pound the meat with a mallet to flatten it to ½ inch thick. Peel off the plastic wrap and place the pork chops in a zipper-lock bag. Pour the soy sauce mixture into the bag, seal well, squeezing out the excess air, and rub with your hands to distribute the marinade. Refrigerate for 2 to 4 hours.

Remove the pork chops from the marinade, saving the liquid.

Heat 1 tablespoon of the oil in a large nonstick skillet or flat-bottomed wok over moderately high heat. When it is hot, add 2 of the chops and brown for about 1½ minutes on each side. Transfer to a platter or baking sheet. Repeat with the remaining 2 chops.

Add the remaining 1 tablespoon oil to the same pan. Add the onion and garlic and cook, stirring, until softened, about 3 minutes. Add the tomatoes, roasted red pepper, jalapeños or crushed pepper flakes, sherry, and the reserved marinade and stir to mix. Reduce the heat to low, cover tightly, and simmer for 10 minutes.

Add the stock and oregano to the pan, scrape up the brown bits from the bottom and sides, and cook for 2 minutes. Transfer the cooking liquid and vegetables to a blender or food processor and puree. *You can make the recipe to this point up to 1 day ahead. Wrap the pork chops well and refrigerate. Put the puree in a covered container and refrigerate.*

Return the sauce to the pan, add the pork chops, cover, and simmer for 10 minutes, or until they are tender, turning once. Season to taste with salt and pepper.

Arrange a pork chop on each of four plates, spoon the sauce over them, and serve.

Moo-Shu Pork with Fresh Mushrooms

My grandmother often talked about raising her family in Ping Yao, in Shanxi Province. The family was very large, and because meat was expensive, moo-shu pork was one of the dishes she could serve, since it was made with very little pork and lots of other flavorful ingredients. I substitute brandy for the more traditional Shaoxing wine and balsamic vinegar for black vinegar. My grandmother used lots of napa cabbage for bulk; I prefer smoked pressed tofu for its smoky flavor. If you can't get dried lily buds, just leave them out, since there is no good substitute.

[Serves 4]

8	ounces boneless pork loin, fat and silverskin removed
3	tablespoons soy sauce
3	tablespoons soybean oil, corn oil, or olive oil
2	tablespoons brandy
1	teaspoon cornstarch
2	large eggs, lightly beaten
1/2	cup dried lily buds, soaked in warm water for 30 minutes
2	teaspoons balsamic vinegar
1/4	cup chicken stock

2	large or 4 small shiitake mushrooms, stemmed and julienned (about 1/2 cup)
1/2	cup julienned red bell pepper
2	scallions, trimmed and cut into julienne
2	ounces smoked pressed tofu (see page 229), cut into 1/8-inch-thick julienne
1/2	cup loosely packed fresh cilantro leaves
12	10-inch flour tortillas warmed for serving
	Brandy-Infused Hoisin Sauce (recipe follows)

Place the pork loin in the freezer for about 1 hour, until half-frozen, to facilitate slicing.

With a sharp knife, slice the pork loin into 1/8-inch-thick slices, then julienne the slices. In a medium bowl, mix together 1 tablespoon of the soy sauce, 1 tablespoon of the oil, and the brandy. Add the pork and mix well. Mix in the cornstarch. Cover and refrigerate.

Heat 1 tablespoon of the oil in a large skillet or flat-bottomed wok over medium heat. Make a thin egg crepe by pouring in the beaten eggs and swirling them around until the eggs have set. Flip the crepe onto a cutting board and cut into 3 strips. Thinly slice each one into pieces about 1/8 inch wide. *The crepe can be made up to 1 day ahead, tightly wrapped, and refrigerated.*

Drain the soaked lily buds and cut off and discard the hard tips of the stems with scissors. Dry well and set aside.

Mix the remaining 2 tablespoons soy sauce, the balsamic vinegar, and the stock in a small bowl.

Heat the remaining 1 tablespoon oil in the skillet or wok over high heat. When the oil is very hot, add the marinated pork. Cook, stirring to separate the pieces of meat, just until the pork turns white, 1 to 2 minutes. Add egg crepe, lily buds, mushrooms, red pepper, scallions, and tofu and stir-fry for 1 minute. Pour in the soy sauce mixture and stir-fry until the vegetables are very hot, 2 to 3 minutes.

Spoon the moo-shu pork onto a large platter and sprinkle with the cilantro. Serve with the tortillas along with the hoisin sauce. Let each person spoon some of the filling into the wrappers, top with hoisin sauce, and roll up.

Brandy-Infused Hoisin Sauce

I don't care for the flavor of hoisin sauces straight from the jar — they are too sugary, pasty, and floury for my taste. I learned to doctor them from a Shanghai cooking teacher when I was in college. I add garlic, brandy, vinegar, and stock and simmer the mixture slowly; the sauce becomes much lighter and tastier. You can use this improved version in any recipe that calls for hoisin sauce.

2 tablespoons corn oil

5 garlic cloves, minced

1 16-ounce jar (2 cups) hoisin sauce

2 tablespoons toasted sesame oil

1/2 cup brandy

2 tablespoons balsamic vinegar or dry red wine

1 cup chicken stock or beef stock

Heat the corn oil in a medium saucepan over high heat. Add the garlic and cook, stirring, until golden, about 30 seconds; be careful not to let it brown. Add the hoisin sauce and sesame oil and bring to a boil, stirring constantly. Reduce the heat to medium, add the brandy and vinegar or red wine, and cook for 5 minutes, stirring constantly to keep the sauce from sticking to the pan.

Add the stock and reduce the heat to low. Cook, stirring occasionally, for 15 minutes, until the sauce is well blended and thickened.

Cool and pour into a jar with a tight-fitting lid. The sauce will keep well, refrigerated, for up to 1 month.

Dried Lily Buds

In China, the slim buds of lilies are picked just before they open into flowers and are then sun-dried. (They are a different variety from the tiger lilies in this country.) Two to three inches long and a lightly burnished gold, they have a delicate, earthy flavor. Also known as golden needles, the dried buds are great in stir-fries, soups, and braised meat dishes. (When slow-braising them along with meat, tie the individual buds together to prevent them from falling apart.)

Dried lily buds are sold in most Asian food markets, packed in 4- to 8-ounce plastic bags. Buy only those with a bright whitish yellow color. If they have turned brown or black, they are too old to use — and they will taste musty and ruin the flavor of the dish.

The dried buds keep for up to 6 months refrigerated in a sealed container, or they can be frozen for up to 1 year. To use, soak in warm water until soft, about 30 minutes. With small scissors, trim off and discard the hard tips of the stems.

Braising

This is a method of slow moist cooking that develops flavors and tenderizes foods by breaking down their fibers. Long popular with Chinese home cooks, braising is one of my favorite ways to cook meat and poultry. Braising works best for inexpensive cuts of meat, such as shoulder, ribs, and pork belly, as well as poultry and some leg cuts of beef, pork, veal, and lamb.

In the classic Chinese method of braising, the meat is first blanched to rid it of any impurities. It is then slowly simmered for hours with soy sauce, black vinegar, ginger, rock sugar, Shaoxing wine, and spices. Sometimes the meat is further cooked by steaming for another hour or two, so that more fat is rendered out. I follow this traditional technique but have also adopted the common European method of searing the meat to give it deeper flavor before I add aromatic vegetables, soy sauce, and liquid.

The charm of braising is its utter simplicity. For best results, keep the following pointers in mind.

1. You will need a good heavy-duty braising pot, Dutch oven, or casserole; it can be made of cast iron, enameled cast iron, stainless steel with an extra-thick aluminum base, or even copper. It should have a heavy tight-fitting lid that forms a good seal. My own favorite is an 8-quart heavy-duty cast-iron pot that I have had for over fifteen years. These pots can last forever, so it's worthwhile to invest in a good one.

2. Cuts of meat such as shanks, chuck, rib roast (bone in), short ribs, leg rump roast, shoulder blade steaks, and round tip roasts are preferable for braising because they are well marbled with collagen and fat, which dissolves during the long cooking, making the meat superbly tender. Buy well-marbled meat with some fat or connective tissue. The flesh should be pink and the fat white. Bones, such as shinbones and oxtails, will add even more body and flavor. When braising a whole leg of lamb, choose a small leg weighing no more than 5 pounds. If braising poultry, keep the skin on, since it protects the meat from drying out.

3. Other additions to the pot include flavoring agents such as aromatic vegetables (onions, scallions, leeks, celery, shallots, lemongrass, and garlic), herbs and other aromatics (rosemary, cilantro, thyme, and even orange zest), and spices (star anise, cloves, and cinnamon). Flavorful vegetables include tomatoes, mushrooms, parsnips, daikon, and celery root. Fruits such as apples, oranges and lemons, lime juice and zest, or even tamarind lend a wonderfully fresh note to the braising liquid. (Some fruit-and-meat combinations, such as apples and pork, are meant for each other.)

4. No water or stock should be added; the braising liquid comes directly from the natural meat and vegetable juices as well as the soy sauce, vinegar, and liquors, such as brandy, whiskey, dry sherry (not cooking sherry, which is too harsh), port, or Madeira. Inferior red wine will change the flavor of the meat, and if I'm spending the money for a good bottle of red wine, I'd much rather drink it with my dinner than cook with it. When I want sweetness, I add port, parsnips, sweet potatoes, or fruits, not sugar.

5. For a clearer sauce, blanch large cuts of meat, such as lamb or pork shanks, shoulder, beef short ribs, and pork belly, briefly in boiling water before braising to remove fatty impurities that would cloud the sauce. Rinse well, then add the braising liquid.

6. Brown smaller or cut-up pieces of meat over high heat to caramelize the surface and heighten the flavor. Once the meat is seared, though, the braising liquid must simmer only, not boil, because boiling would toughen the meat, make it dry, and cause it to lose the good juices present. Braising should not be hurried.

Braised Pork Belly

— (✿) —

When we were young and living in Taiwan, my father often took us to a Shanghai restaurant because he loved this effusively flavored dish — and he would sigh, shout, and groan with pleasure whenever he ate it. The pork belly is cut into squares and slowly braised with sherry, soy sauce, and rock sugar, a technique known as "red cooking." Steamed for hours, the fat slowly melts, making the pork sweet and mellow. Before serving, the fat is skimmed off, leaving a clear, extraordinarily rich sauce.

I prefer to leave the skin on the pork belly. If you like, you can remove the bottom layer of fat and skin.

[*Serves 4 to 6*]

4	pounds pork belly
2	tablespoons kosher salt
1	cup soy sauce
2	cinnamon sticks
5	star anise
1/4	cup rock sugar (see page 99) or honey

2	cups dry sherry
1	bunch scallions, trimmed and cut into 2-inch lengths
1	2- to 3-inch piece fresh ginger
3	tablespoons Chinese black vinegar (see page 183) or balsamic vinegar

Cut the pork belly into 2-inch squares. Rub the meat with the salt and then rinse under cold running water to remove any bloody juices. Tie each piece with butcher's twine to help it retain its shape.

Cook the pork belly in a large pot of boiling water for about 3 minutes, until the pork turns white. Drain, rinse the pork belly under cold running water to remove the scum, and then drain well again.

Combine the pork belly, soy sauce, cinnamon, star anise, sugar or honey, sherry, scallions, ginger, and vinegar in a medium Dutch oven or other heavy pot and bring to a boil over high heat. Turn the heat to very low, cover tightly, and simmer for 3 hours, turning the pork from time to time.

Using a slotted spoon or tongs, transfer the meat to a large plate. Remove the twine and cover to keep warm.

With a spoon, skim off all the fat and oil on the surface of the cooking liquid. Strain, discarding the solids.

This dish can be made 2 days in advance; it will be easier to remove the fat from the braising liquid when it is cooled. Refrigerate the meat and broth together, so the meat will remain moist. Reheat in a microwave or regular oven.

Serve the meat on individual plates or a serving platter. Spoon some of the braising liquid over the meat and serve the rest in a sauceboat.

Pork
Belly

The belly comes from the section of the pig below the loin.
(When salted and smoked, this cut of meat becomes bacon.)
A boneless slab of meat, the belly features alternating layers of
fat and lean meat, and when it is slowly braised, the fat melts
into the meat, making it exquisitely tender. Its Chinese name
translates poetically as five-flower pork, and while the reason
is elusive, it sums up the meat's special character far better
than the English words. Whatever you call it, this is a
superb cut. Look for it in Asian markets or
order it from your butcher.

Roasted Five-Spice Pork Tenderloin

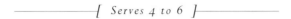

Jalapeño peppers, coriander seeds, and five-spice powder give this marinade a lively fragrant note. It penetrates the meat, contributing character and a bold, sweet-tangy flavor. If I have fresh coriander seeds on hand, I use them in place of dried. Serve with Pickled Napa Cabbage (page 276) or Cranberry-Ginger Relish (page 282).

[Serves 4 to 6]

1 teaspoon coriander seeds	2 tablespoons brandy or whiskey
¼ cup soybean oil or corn oil	1 tablespoon honey
2 garlic cloves, thinly sliced	1 teaspoon five-spice powder
2 jalapeño peppers, stemmed and thinly sliced	2 1-pound pork tenderloins, fat and silverskin removed, rinsed and dried
1 tablespoon kosher salt	

Place the coriander seeds in a small dry skillet and toast over medium heat, tossing and stirring constantly, until they darken slightly and become fragrant. Transfer to a small bowl to cool.

Heat 2 tablespoons of the oil in a small skillet over high heat. Add the garlic and jalapeño peppers and cook, stirring often, until soft, about 1 minute. Add the salt, liquor, honey, and toasted coriander seeds and mix well. Remove from the heat and puree in a mini processor or blender. Transfer to a small bowl and mix in the five-spice powder.

Rub the spice mixture all over the tenderloins. Marinate, covered, in the refrigerator for at least 4 hours, or overnight.

Preheat the oven to 425 degrees. Heat the remaining 2 tablespoons oil in a large ovenproof skillet over high heat. When it is hot, sear the tenderloins until well browned on all sides, 3 to 5 minutes.

Transfer the pan to the oven and roast for 10 minutes, or until an instant-read thermometer inserted into the center of a tenderloin reaches 155 degrees; the meat should still be pink inside. Remove from the oven, cover with aluminum foil, and let stand for a few minutes to allow the meat to absorb the juices, then slice and serve.

Spicy Pork Tenderloin with Poblanos and Plums

The combination of succulent pork tenderloin and the fresh sweet-sour taste of plums is heavenly. You can substitute Fuyu persimmons or nectarines. Serve over white rice or Homemade Buckwheat Noodles (page 201).

[Serves 4]

- 2 tablespoons olive oil
- 3 tablespoons soy sauce
- 1 tablespoon brandy or whiskey
- 1 pound pork tenderloin, fat and silverskin removed, rinsed and dried and cut into ½-inch-thick rounds
- 1 tablespoon plus 1 teaspoon cornstarch
- 1 tablespoon Chinese oyster sauce
- ¼ cup chicken stock
- ¼ cup soybean oil or corn oil

- 1 teaspoon Chinese fermented black beans, rinsed, drained, and squeezed dry
- 2 garlic cloves, minced
- 1 large poblano pepper, stemmed, seeded, and julienned
- 1 jalapeño pepper, stemmed and cut into ⅛-inch slices
- ½ red bell pepper, julienned
- 2 scallions, white part only, cut into 1-inch pieces
- 2 small firm red plums, pitted and cut into ¼-inch-thick slices

Mix the olive oil, 2 tablespoons of the soy sauce, and the liquor in a large bowl. Add the pork tenderloin and turn until all the meat is well coated with the marinade. Sprinkle with 1 tablespoon of the cornstarch and mix well. Cover and refrigerate for 1 hour or up to 4 hours.

Mix the oyster sauce, the remaining 1 tablespoon soy sauce, the stock, and the remaining 1 teaspoon cornstarch in a small bowl. Set aside.

Heat the oil in a large skillet or flat-bottomed wok over high heat until very hot. Add half the marinated pork and sear on all sides until light brown, about 2 minutes. Remove with a slotted spoon and place on a plate. Cook the remaining pork and add to the plate. Pour off all but 1 tablespoon of the oil.

Add the black beans, garlic, peppers, and scallions to the pan and cook over high heat, stirring constantly, for about 1 minute, or until the peppers are heated through.

Add the plums, pork, and oyster sauce mixture to the pan. Cook, stirring, for 2 to 3 minutes, until the pork is well coated with the sauce. Serve.

Wuxi-Style Braised Beef Short Ribs

Shanghai is famous for its braising techniques, and one of the most famous of its classic braised dishes is Wuxi-style spareribs. Wuxi is a suburb of Shanghai, and every family takes pride in its own version of this dish. The ribs are first blanched, then slowly simmered for hours with dark soy sauce, spices, rock sugar, and Shaoxing wine until the meat is tender and all the fat melts away.

I cook beef short ribs in much the same way. But since I don't like the sweetness rock sugar imparts to this dish, I use port instead of sugar. The leftover sauce is good for braising tofu, potatoes, daikon, or any root vegetable.

[Serves 4 to 6]

4	pounds beef short ribs
4	garlic cloves
1	2-inch piece fresh ginger, peeled and thinly sliced
1	cup sake, gin, or brandy
½	cup tawny port

½	cup soy sauce
¼	cup sherry wine vinegar
5	star anise
1	2- to 3-inch cinnamon stick

Fill an 8-quart heavy pot with a heavy lid with water and bring to a boil over high heat. Add the short ribs and cook for 2 minutes. Transfer the ribs to a colander to drain. Discard the water and rinse out the pot.

Add the garlic, ginger, liquor, soy sauce, vinegar, star anise, cinnamon, and short ribs to the pot. Bring to a boil. Turn the heat to the lowest possible setting and cover tightly with the lid (if the lid does not fit tightly, cover the pot first with a piece of aluminum foil, then put on the lid). Slowly simmer for 2 hours, turning the ribs from time to time so all sides of the meat are covered with the sauce.

Using a slotted spoon or tongs, remove the ribs to a large plate and cover to keep warm. With a spoon, skim off all the fat and oil from the surface of the liquid and discard. Strain the sauce, discarding the solids, and pour into a sauceboat. (Or, if you have a fat separator, remove the garlic, gin-ger, star anise, and cinnamon, then pour the sauce into the separator. Allow to settle for a few minutes, then pour the clear sauce into a sauceboat.) *This dish can be made up to 2 days in advance. Reheat the ribs in the sauce in a microwave oven or a pre-heated 375-degree oven. Any leftover sauce can be frozen for 1 month.*

Serve the ribs on individual plates or a serving platter. Pour some of the sauce over the ribs and serve the rest on the side.

SIMPLE VARIATIONS

Substitute pork spareribs for the beef short ribs, and reduce the cooking time to 1 hour and 20 minutes.

You can add 8 ounces of diced silken tofu to the braising liquid during the last 15 minutes, if desired.

Quick-Seared Sichuan Beef Tenderloin Stew

Small tenderloin tips are preferable to filet mignon here, because they have some marbling, and the fat adds flavor when they are braised. Unlike most long-simmered beef stews, this dish cooks quickly. Searing the meat, then simmering it with aromatics and spices produces a flavorful, spicy stew, with a hint of orange in the sauce. Cutting the dried peppers into halves will make the stew spicier, but you can leave them whole if you prefer. Serve over Homemade Buckwheat Noodles (page 201) or any broad noodle.

Serves 8

3	pounds beef tenderloin tips
2	tablespoons soybean oil or corn oil, or more if needed
4–6	star anise
3	dried hot red peppers, halved
3	garlic cloves, sliced
4	shallots, halved
2	tablespoons julienned peeled fresh ginger

2	tablespoons grated orange zest
¼	cup soy sauce
2	tablespoons balsamic vinegar
2	tablespoons brandy
1	tablespoon sugar
3	scallions, trimmed and cut into 1-inch lengths

Trim the fat and sinews from the beef (once trimmed, the meat should weigh about 2½ pounds). Cut the meat into 1-inch pieces.

Heat 1 tablespoon of the oil in a large heavy pot over high heat until hot. Add half the beef (do not crowd the pan) and quickly sear on all sides until lightly browned, 3 to 4 minutes. Remove and set aside. Add the remaining 1 tablespoon oil and sear the rest of the meat.

Return all the beef to the pan. Add the star anise, red peppers, garlic, shallots, ginger, and zest and cook until lightly browned, 2 to 3 minutes. Add the soy sauce, vinegar, brandy, and sugar, turn the heat to low, and cook for 5 minutes. Add 1 cup water, cover, and simmer until the beef is tender, checking for doneness after 20 minutes.

Stir in the scallions and remove from the heat. Discard the star anise and hot peppers, skim off the fat, and serve.

Korean-Style Grilled Sirloin in Pear Jalapeño Marinade

My daughter-in-law, Nancy, makes an unusual Korean marinade for grilled steak using hot peppers, a pureed pear, and toasted sesame seeds. The heat of the jalapeños and cayenne is balanced by the sweetness of the pear and the mellow nuttiness of the sesame seeds. Serve with French-Fried Parsnips (page 259) or Cold Chinese Eggplant Salad with Sesame Soy Vinaigrette (page 85).

[Serves 4]

POACHED PEAR

1/3	cup sugar
1	tablespoon fresh lemon juice
1	1/2-inch slice fresh ginger, crushed
1	1-inch piece cinnamon stick
1	medium firm Anjou or Bartlett pear, peeled and cored

STEAKS

1/4	cup sesame seeds
1	teaspoon kosher salt
3	tablespoons vegetable oil
2	jalapeño peppers, stemmed
1	large garlic clove, peeled
2	medium scallions, trimmed and cut into 1-inch pieces
1/4	cup soy sauce
1	tablespoon toasted sesame oil
1	teaspoon sugar
1/2	teaspoon cayenne pepper
4	8- to 10-ounce sirloin steaks, about 1 inch thick

TO POACH THE PEAR: Place 1 cup water, the sugar, lemon juice, ginger, and cinnamon stick in a small saucepan. Bring to a boil over high heat, then reduce the heat and simmer for 5 minutes. Place the pear in the hot liquid, cover, and simmer until tender, about 10 minutes. Drain well and cool.

TO PREPARE THE STEAKS: Toast the sesame seeds in a small dry skillet over medium-low heat until golden, about 3 minutes. Remove from the pan, sprinkle with the salt, and cool, then crush in a mortar or spice grinder or coffee mill; do not process for too long, or you will end up with sesame paste. Transfer to a small bowl.

Add 1 tablespoon of the vegetable oil and the whole jalapeño peppers to the same skillet and cook over medium heat, turning the peppers often, until soft, about 3 minutes. Remove from the pan and cool.

Place the poached pear in a food processor or blender, add the jalapeño peppers, garlic, and scallions, and process until pureed. Transfer to a small bowl.

Combine 2 tablespoons of the crushed sesame seeds (save the rest for later), the pear puree, soy sauce, the remaining 2 tablespoons vegetable oil, the sesame oil, sugar, and cayenne in a large heavy zipper-lock bag and add the steaks. Seal the bag, squeezing out the excess air, and turn to coat the meat. Refrigerate for 4 to 8 hours, turning occasionally to keep the steaks covered with the marinade.

Set the rack of a grill 4 to 6 inches from the heat source,

lightly oil it, and preheat the grill until very hot. Remove the steaks from the marinade and grill for about 4 minutes on each side for rare meat, 5 to 6 minutes if you like your meat more well done.

TO SERVE: Sprinkle the steaks with the remaining sesame seeds and serve.

SIMPLE VARIATION

Instead of poaching a fresh pear, you can use a canned pear in light syrup, drained well.

Grilled Beef Tenderloin with Rosemary Soy Marinade

(✿)

Beef tenderloin is tender but not especially flavorful. Marinating the meat in a mixture of cooked garlic and jalapeños pureed with soy sauce, brandy, and fresh rosemary, and then grilling it over high heat gives the meat a robust fla- vor. The scallion-tomato sauce, which is made from the marinade, is very quick and fresh-tasting.

[Serves 4]

¼ cup olive oil	2 tablespoons brandy
2 jalapeño peppers, stemmed	1 tablespoon balsamic vinegar
3 garlic cloves	2 tablespoons coarsely chopped fresh rosemary
2 pounds center-cut beef tenderloin, trimmed and silverskin removed	1 cup grape tomatoes, preferably peeled (see page 123) and halved
3 tablespoons soy sauce	2 scallions, white parts only, diced

Heat 2 tablespoons of the oil in a small saucepan over high heat. Add the whole jalapeños and garlic, turn the heat to medium-low, and cook slowly, stirring often, until soft, about 5 minutes. Transfer to a small bowl and cool.

With a sharp knife, cut the tenderloin crosswise into 8 slices.

Transfer the jalapeños and garlic, with the cooking oil, to a blender or food processor, add the soy sauce, brandy, vinegar, rosemary, and the remaining 2 tablespoons olive oil, and puree.

Place the meat in a single layer in a shallow baking pan and pour the rosemary soy marinade over the meat. Turn so that each piece is coated with marinade. Refrigerate for 30 minutes to 1 hour.

Lightly oil a charcoal or gas grill and heat until very hot. Remove the beef from the marinade, draining it well, and transfer to a plate. Pour the marinade into a small saucepan.

Grill the beef about 4 inches from the coals, 2 minutes on each side for rare meat, 3 minutes per side for medium.

Meanwhile, bring the marinade to a boil and cook for about 1 minute. Add the tomatoes and scallions and cook for 2 minutes.

Transfer the beef to four large plates, top with the scallion-tomato sauce, and serve.

SIMPLE VARIATION

You can also broil the steaks. Preheat the broiler. Heat a large skillet until very hot, add 2 tablespoons butter, then add half the meat and sear quickly on both sides. Remove and place on a broiler pan. Repeat with the remaining meat, using an additional 2 tablespoons butter. Broil for 3 minutes per side for rare meat or up to 5 minutes for medium, turning once.

Braised Lamb Blade Chops with Tomatoes and Parsnips

This recipe is based on a Mongolian lamb stew made with black vinegar and daikon. I prefer parsnips to daikon because of their sweetness. Lamb blade chops have an internal layer of fat and bones, making them perfect for braising. The tightly sealed pot captures all of the juices from the meat and vegetables, forming a natural, flavorful sauce.

Unlike many braised dishes, this one is most aromatic when served the day it's made.

[Serves 4]

2	tablespoons olive oil or corn oil
4	10- to 12-ounce lamb shoulder blade chops
3	garlic cloves, sliced
3	1/8-inch-thick slices peeled fresh ginger
4	star anise
1/4	cup soy sauce
1/2	cup cream sherry or dry sherry
2	tablespoons balsamic vinegar or black vinegar
1	teaspoon sugar
1	pound parsnips, peeled and cut into 1-inch pieces
1	bunch scallions, white part only, cut into 2-inch pieces
3	large vine-ripened tomatoes, peeled (see page 123) and quartered

Heat the oil in a 6-quart Dutch oven or other heavy pot over high heat. Add the lamb and sear until well browned, for about 5 minutes, turning once.

Add the garlic, ginger, and star anise, then mix in the soy sauce, sherry, balsamic vinegar, and sugar. Cover, turn the heat to very low, and simmer for about 25 minutes.

Turn the lamb over, cover, and cook for 25 minutes longer.

Add the parsnips, cover, and continue to cook, stirring occasionally, for 20 minutes. Add the scallions and tomatoes, cover, and cook for 5 to 10 minutes, until the parsnips are tender and the flavors are well blended. Spoon onto a large platter and serve.

Chinese Black Vinegar

Chinese black vinegar is somewhat similar to balsamic vinegar, for it has a complex, almost sweet flavor and a distinctive aroma. It is made from fermented grains, such as sorghum, millet, or wheat, and sometimes fermented jujube dates and is aged for years. Shanxi Province, where my father comes from, is famous for its black vinegar. Cooks there add it to almost every dish, and drinking this aged vinegar is considered good for health and digestion. The locals claim the people who work in and live around the vinegar factories never get sick or catch cold. Today many different brands of very reasonably priced black vinegar can be found in most Asian markets. I usually buy Gold Plum's Chinkian or Shanxi vinegar.

Grilled Lamb Chops with Roasted Sesame Marinade

Lamb shish kebab is quite popular in Inner Mongolia, where my mother's family originated. Large chunks of lamb tenderloin, marinated in a combination of roasted sesame paste, fermented bean curd, soy sauce, and wine, are threaded onto long skewers and grilled over an open pine or fruitwood fire. I use tender rib chops, marinating them with toasted sesame seeds, honey, and fresh rosemary, and grill them over charcoal. The lamb is juicy, with a pronounced herbal flavor.

Serve with Broccoli Rabe with Sun-Dried Tomatoes (page 246), Beet, Rhubarb, and Grapefruit Salad (page 78), or Frisée and Peach Salad with Honey Mustard Vinaigrette (page 70), and with Saffron Basmati Fried Rice (page 210).

[Serves 4]

¼ cup sesame seeds

1 small piece fresh ginger (about 1 inch)

8 rib lamb chops, trimmed (2 pounds total)

¼ cup olive oil, plus additional for grilling

¼ cup soy sauce

1 tablespoon honey

1 tablespoon toasted sesame oil

1 tablespoon chopped fresh rosemary

Toast the sesame seeds in a small dry skillet over low heat, stirring often, until light brown, about 5 minutes. Pour into a bowl and cool, then grind to a paste in a spice grinder or coffee mill.

Peel and grate the ginger. Wrap it in a piece of cheesecloth and squeeze out the juice; you need 2 tablespoons. Discard the solids and set the juice aside.

Place the chops on a rimmed platter or baking dish large enough to hold them in a single layer.

Combine the oil, sesame paste, and all the remaining ingredients in a medium bowl and mix thoroughly. Pour over the lamb chops and marinate at room temperature for 30 minutes, turning once.

Put the rack of a charcoal or gas grill 4 to 6 inches from the heat source, brush generously with oil and heat the grill until hot. Remove the chops from the marinade and grill for 3 to 4 minutes. Turn the chops and cook for 3 to 4 minutes on the second side for meat that is medium-rare. Serve hot.

Mongolian Lamb with Leeks, Chinese Eggplant, and Fennel

Lamb has always been a favorite meat in Inner Mongolia. In the fifteenth century, the Mongols invented a round iron grill with grates made of welded iron rods, on which they grilled thinly sliced lamb that had been marinated in soy sauce, garlic, scallions, leeks, and sesame paste.

In the early 1960s, Mongolian barbecue restaurants became popular in Taiwan. In the modern version, a sumptuous spread, consisting of a variety of raw vegetables and aromatics, different kinds of thinly sliced meats, and a huge selection of oils and flavorful sauces, is set up around a gigantic hot grill. Customers choose whatever ingredients they want, place them in a big bowl, and take it to the waiting chefs, who, armed with large Chinese spatulas, grill them.

I have adapted the procedure to home cooking by stir-frying the meat in a large skillet or flat-bottomed wok. Serve with white rice or flatbread.

{ Serves 2 }

LAMB AND MARINADE

- 1 pound lamb tenderloin or boneless leg of lamb
- 1 tablespoon soy sauce
- 2 tablespoons olive oil or corn oil
- 1 tablespoon brandy
- 1 tablespoon cornstarch

VEGETABLES

- 1 Chinese eggplant (see page 84), stemmed (Sicilian eggplant or white eggplant can be substituted)
- 2 jalapeño peppers, stemmed and thinly sliced
- 2 garlic cloves, minced
- 1 tablespoon fermented black beans, soaked in warm water and drained
- 1 small leek, white part only
- 1 fennel bulb
- 1 small red bell pepper, cored, seeded, and julienned
- 2 tablespoons balsamic vinegar
- 1 tablespoon soy sauce
- 1 tablespoon brandy
- 3 tablespoons soybean oil or corn oil

TO MARINATE THE LAMB: Place the lamb in the freezer for about 30 minutes, or until it is almost half-frozen, to facilitate slicing.

Slice the lamb about ⅛ inch thick. Mix the soy sauce, oil, and brandy in a large bowl, add the lamb, and mix until well coated. Sprinkle the cornstarch over the meat and mix well. Cover and refrigerate.

TO PREPARE THE VEGETABLES: Cut the eggplant lengthwise in half, then slice on the diagonal into ½-inch-thick slices and place in a bowl.

Mix the jalapeños and garlic together in a small bowl. Place the black beans in a small bowl.

Slice the leek lengthwise in half, then cut on the diagonal into slices about 2½ inches long and about ⅛ inch thick. Soak the leek in a bowl of cold water for a few minutes, then lift out and drain well in a colander.

Discard the tough outer parts of the fennel and cut in half lengthwise. Reserve one half for another purpose. Using a Japanese Benriner, mandoline, or sharp knife, thinly slice the fennel.

Place the leek, fennel, and red pepper in a medium bowl and toss to mix.

Mix together the balsamic vinegar, soy sauce, and brandy in a small bowl.

Heat 2 tablespoons of the oil in a large skillet or flat-bottomed wok over high heat until very hot. Add the lamb and cook, stirring, until lightly browned, about 2 minutes. With a slotted spoon, transfer to a plate.

Turn the heat to medium-low, add the remaining 1 tablespoon oil, the jalapeño-garlic mixture, and the eggplant and cook, stirring until the eggplant is soft, about 3 minutes. Add the black beans and the vegetables, turn the heat to very high, and cook, stirring and turning the ingredients, for about 30 seconds; the vegetables should be barely cooked.

TO SERVE: Add the lamb and the balsamic vinegar mixture and cook, stirring, for about 2 minutes, until very hot. Spoon out onto a large platter and serve.

How to Julienne a Bell Pepper

Cut the top off the pepper. Cut the pepper lengthwise in half and remove the seeds and ribs. Slice each half lengthwise in half again. Turn the pepper so the skin side faces down, then thinly slice crosswise into strips that are about ⅛ inch wide.

Noodles, Rice, and Other Side Dishes

Cold Soba Noodles with Lime Coriander Vinaigrette

— (✿) —

Dried soba noodles stand up nicely to cold preparations, absorbing the vinaigrette but remaining agreeably firm. Here they get a Chinese twist with cucumber, bean sprouts, and toasted sesame seeds.

—[*Serves 4 to 6*]—

6	ounces soba noodles
1	tablespoon soybean oil or corn oil
	Lime Coriander Vinaigrette (recipe follows)
8	Belgian endive leaves
4	radicchio leaves (optional)

½	cup julienned cucumber
½	cup bean sprouts, root ends pinched off
2	tablespoons chopped fresh cilantro
¼	cup sesame seeds, toasted (see page 64)

Soba Noodles

The soba noodles we are familiar with today, made from a mixture of buckwheat and wheat flours, first appeared in Japan in the mid-1500s, but actually they originally came from northern China. Now the finest soba comes from Shinshu, the mountainous area of central Japan. ✿ Dried soba noodles are widely available and cost anywhere from $1.50 to $5.00 a pound. The color of the noodles can sometimes explain the difference in price: the darker ones are usually better. The cheaper ones become very soft after cooking and do not have as much flavor. I try to buy soba noodles from a Japanese store rather than from a Chinese or Asian market, because they are generally of better quality. I prefer the brand Shinshu Hachiwari, imported by the Hudson (Toko) Trading Company. The dried noodles can be kept for many months.

Cook the noodles in a large pot of boiling salted water just until tender, about 3 minutes. Drain, rinse the noodles under cold running water, and drain again. Toss the noodles with the oil. *The noodles can be cooked 1 day in advance and refrigerated, covered.*

Mix the noodles with the lime vinaigrette in a large bowl.

Place 2 Belgian endive leaves and 1 radicchio leaf, if using, on each of four plates. Top with the noodles. Decorate with the cucumber, bean sprouts, cilantro, and sesame seeds and serve.

Lime Coriander Vinaigrette

—————————[*Makes about ¾ cup*]—————————

This piquant dressing stands up to and complements the earthy flavor of the soba noodles. The spicy ingredients in the recipe are Thai, but the method of cooking the dressing with a little cornstarch to keep it from separating is Chinese.

2	tablespoons extra-virgin olive oil
2	garlic cloves, thinly sliced
1	jalapeño pepper, stemmed and coarsely chopped
2	shallots, chopped
¼	cup chicken stock
½	teaspoon cornstarch, mixed with 1 teaspoon cold water
3	tablespoons fresh lime juice
2	tablespoons fish sauce (preferably Three Crabs brand)
¼	cup fresh cilantro leaves, blanched in boiling water for 30 seconds, rinsed under cold running water, drained, and squeezed dry
1	teaspoon honey

Heat the oil in a small skillet over high heat. Add the garlic, jalapeño, and shallots and cook, stirring, until soft and lightly golden, about 1 minute. Add the stock and cornstarch mixture, stir well, turn the heat to low, and continue to cook for 5 minutes, stirring frequently. Remove from the heat and cool.

Transfer to a food processor or blender. Add the lime juice, fish sauce, cilantro, and honey and process until finely pureed. Cover and refrigerate if not using immediately; stir vigorously before serving. *The vinaigrette will keep, refrigerated, for up to a week.*

Soba Noodles with Ginger, Scallions, and Shrimp

This simple stir-fry is based on a traditional lo mein dish: shrimp and vegetables are cooked in a flavorful sauce and blended with noodles. I substitute soba for the fresh Chinese noodles typically used — they give more body and texture (you can use either dried soba or fresh buckwheat noodles, page 201). The diced tomatoes are also my own touch.

[Serves 4]

6	ounces soba noodles
2	tablespoons soybean oil or corn oil
2	tablespoons soy sauce
1	tablespoon oyster sauce
1	teaspoon toasted sesame oil
1	tablespoon vodka
1/2	cup chicken stock or Vegetable Stock (page 56)
1	garlic clove, minced
1	teaspoon minced peeled fresh ginger

2	scallions, finely chopped
1/2	pound medium shrimp (31–35 count), peeled and deveined
1	cup baby spinach leaves or 1/2 cup julienned snow peas
2	medium tomatoes, peeled (see page 123), seeded, and diced
	Kosher salt and freshly ground white pepper
2	tablespoons finely chopped fresh cilantro

Cook the noodles in a large pot of boiling water until just tender, about 3 minutes. Drain well, place in a bowl, and add 1 tablespoon of the soybean or corn oil, tossing to separate and coat the noodles; cool.

Mix together the soy sauce, oyster sauce, sesame oil, vodka, and stock in a small bowl.

Heat the remaining 1 tablespoon soybean or corn oil in a large skillet or flat-bottomed wok over high heat. Add the garlic, ginger, and scallions and cook, stirring, for about 1 minute, until soft. Add the shrimp and cook, stirring, until they turn white, about 1 minute. Mix in the noodles, soy sauce mixture, spinach or snow peas, and tomatoes and stir and toss until just heated through, 1 to 2 minutes. Season with salt and white pepper, mix in the cilantro, and serve.

Pasta with Cilantro Pesto, Zucchini, and Tomatoes

Choose any small firm pasta that is about the same size as the cut vegetables. Have all the ingredients ready before you begin, as the recipe takes very little time from start to finish. And if you use fresh or frozen pasta rather than dried, start the vegetables cooking first. You can also add 1 cup blanched broccoli florets along with the zucchini.

{ Serves 4 }

8   ounces cavatelli, gemelli, or gnocchetti sardi

2   tablespoons olive oil

2   shallots, minced, or ½ cup diced onion

1   garlic clove, minced

3   small zucchini, quartered lengthwise, then cut into ¼-inch slices

Kosher salt and freshly ground pepper

½   cup grape tomatoes, peeled (see page 123) and halved

¼   cup pine nuts, toasted (see page 64)

¼   cup Cilantro Pesto (recipe follows), or more to taste

½   cup freshly grated Parmesan cheese, or more to taste

Cook the pasta in a large pot of boiling salted water according to the package directions until al dente.

Meanwhile, heat the oil in a large skillet or flat-bottomed wok over medium heat. Add the shallots or onion and garlic and cook, stirring, for about 1 minute, until soft. Mix in the zucchini, season with salt and pepper, and cook, stirring, for about 2 minutes, until crisp-tender.

Drain the pasta, reserving 1 cup of the cooking water. Stir the pasta into the zucchini, adding some of the pasta water as necessary to thin the mixture. Mix in the tomatoes and pine nuts and turn off the heat.

Stir in the pesto (do not cook it, or it will lose its fresh taste). Mix in the cheese, taste to correct the seasonings, and serve. Pass a bowl of grated Parmesan on the side.

Cilantro Pesto

This pesto keeps well and can be used to perk up many dishes. Try it on grilled or poached salmon or grilled pork. It is also good with jasmine rice or soba noodles. Never heat it; it will lose its freshness.

———————[*Makes about 1 ¾ cups*]———————

½   cup raw peanuts, skins removed

1   cup soybean oil or corn oil

4   garlic cloves, thinly sliced

1   1-inch piece fresh ginger, peeled and thinly sliced

3   shallots, thinly sliced

1   packed cup fresh Thai basil or regular basil leaves

1   packed cup fresh cilantro leaves

2   small fresh hot red peppers, stemmed and thinly sliced

3   stalks fresh lemongrass (see page 150), tender inner parts only, thinly sliced

Grated zest of 2 limes

1   teaspoon sugar

Kosher salt and freshly ground pepper

Preheat the oven to 325 degrees. Spread the peanuts on a small baking sheet and toast in the oven, stirring occasionally, until lightly golden, about 10 minutes. Remove.

Heat the oil in a small heavy skillet over high heat until it is nearly smoking. Remove from the heat, add the garlic, ginger, and shallots to the hot oil, and allow them to sit for 30 seconds; they should be very lightly cooked. Remove with a slotted spoon and place in a small bowl. Pour the flavored oil into another small bowl.

Blanch the basil and cilantro in a medium pot of boiling water over high heat for 30 seconds. Pour into a colander and rinse under very cold water. Drain and squeeze out the excess water.

Add the peanuts to a food processor or blender and process until a coarse paste forms. Pour in half of the flavored oil, add the garlic mixture, hot peppers, and lemongrass, and puree for 1 minute. Add the blanched herbs, lime zest, sugar, and the remaining flavored oil and blend until a coarse paste forms, about 2 minutes.

Transfer to a bowl and season to taste with salt and pepper. *The pesto will keep in a sealed jar, covered with a little oil, in the refrigerator for 1 to 2 weeks, or it can be frozen for up to 3 months.*

Braised Orzo with Diced Vegetables and Toasted Pine Nuts

——————————————(✿)——————————————

Leeks, celery root, carrots, fresh water chestnuts, and toasted pine nuts add color and crunch to this risotto-like dish, and the fish sauce, lime, and coconut cream–butter mixture unite in a tangy, lemony, Thai-influenced sauce to dress up the orzo. Serve with grilled fish or braised lamb or as a light lunch.

——————————[*Serves 4*]——————————

½	cup pine nuts
1	cup orzo
1	tablespoon plus 1 teaspoon extra-virgin olive oil
¼	cup diced (¼-inch) well-washed leek greens
¼	cup diced (¼-inch) peeled celery root (regular celery can be substituted)
¼	cup diced (¼-inch) carrots
3	tablespoons fish sauce (preferably Three Crabs brand)

2	tablespoons fresh lime juice
¼	cup chicken stock or Vegetable Stock (page 56)
2	tablespoons unsweetened coconut cream (see page 77) or heavy cream
2	tablespoons butter, melted and cooled
2	shallots, minced
¼	cup fresh peeled water chestnuts or jicama, julienned
2	tablespoons chopped fresh chives or cilantro

Preheat the oven to 300 degrees. Spread the pine nuts on a baking sheet and toast in the oven, stirring occasionally, for about 10 minutes, until lightly golden. Transfer to a plate and cool.

Cook the orzo in a medium pot of lightly salted boiling water until just barely al dente, about 7 minutes. Drain, then transfer to a bowl and toss with 1 teaspoon of the olive oil to keep the grains separate.

Blanch the leek greens, celery root, and carrots in a medium pot of lightly salted boiling water for about 1 minute. Drain and plunge into a bowl of ice water to stop the cooking and set the color. Drain again and place in a bowl.

Mix together the fish sauce, lime juice, and stock in a small bowl. Mix together the coconut cream or heavy cream and butter in another small bowl.

Heat the remaining 1 tablespoon oil in a large skillet or flat-bottomed wok over high heat. When it is hot, add the shallots and cook for about 30 seconds, just until fragrant. Add the orzo, fish sauce mixture, blanched vegetables, and water chestnuts or jicama. Lower the heat to medium and cook until the orzo absorbs all the liquid, about 3 minutes. Add the cream-butter mixture and continue to cook for 1 to 2 minutes, just until hot.

Remove from the heat, mix in the toasted pine nuts and the chives or cilantro, and serve.

Orzo with Cilantro Pesto and Peanuts

This recipe incorporates all the fresh flavors of springtime, is easy to assemble, and is good with almost anything.

[*Serves 4*]

¼   cup unsalted roasted peanuts

1   cup orzo

1   tablespoon extra-virgin olive oil

¼   cup Cilantro Pesto (page 195)

Kosher salt and freshly ground pepper

Preheat the oven to 325 degrees. Spread the peanuts on a small baking sheet and toast in the oven, stirring occasionally, until lightly golden, about 10 minutes. Cool, then coarsely chop.

Cook the orzo in a medium pot of lightly salted boiling water for about 8 minutes, until just al dente. Drain.

Place the pot in which you cooked the orzo back on high heat and add the olive oil. Add the orzo and mix well to coat. Turn off the heat and mix in the pesto and chopped peanuts. Taste and add salt and pepper if needed. Spoon into a bowl and serve hot.

Herbed Israeli Couscous

(✿)

The first step in this recipe, soaking and draining the couscous, is important — it not only softens the couscous but washes away some of its starchy coating, making for a cleaner-tasting result.

[*Serves 4 to 6*]

1 cup Israeli couscous

1 tablespoon soybean oil or corn oil

1 large shallot, finely diced

2 garlic cloves, finely diced

2 tablespoons butter

1 cup chicken stock or Vegetable Stock (page 56)

1/2 cup chopped fresh flat-leaf parsley or cilantro

1/2 cup chopped fresh basil

1 teaspoon kosher salt

Freshly ground pepper

Soak the couscous in 4 cups cold water for about 10 minutes. Drain and rinse under cold running water.

Heat the oil in a large nonstick skillet over high heat. Add the shallot and garlic and cook until soft, about 1 minute. Stir in the couscous, then the butter, and cook, stirring, for about 1 minute, until all the couscous grains are well coated with butter. Add the stock, stirring constantly so that the couscous does not stick to the bottom of the skillet, and bring to a boil. Turn the heat to medium-low and cook, uncovered, until the couscous completely absorbs all the liquid; this should take about 5 minutes.

Turn off the heat and add the parsley or cilantro and basil. Sprinkle with the salt and pepper to taste, mixing it in well. Spoon into a bowl and serve.

Israeli Couscous

We tend to think of couscous as a grain, but it is not. It is made from durum wheat semolina (the same kind of hard-wheat flour used to make pasta) processed into very fine granules. Israeli couscous is much larger than the more commonly known type; it is about the size of barley. (Osem, an Israeli firm in Tel Aviv, created this product in the 1950s; hence its name.) The round pieces of pasta are extruded, then toasted until dry. When cooked, Israeli couscous has a firm, chewy texture and absorbs flavors easily.

Artichoke Pasta with Broccoli Rabe, Tomatoes, and Artichokes

Whenever I visited my son Jimmy at college, I would cook a whole week's worth of dinners for him. Once I found a type of pasta made with artichokes at a local Whole Foods market and made it for him, with fresh artichoke hearts and broccoli rabe. It was supposed to last for two nights, but he ate it all in one meal. Since it was such a hit, I decided to try it out on my restaurant menu.

If you can't find artichoke pasta, substitute any pasta made with semolina flour that has a firm texture. The one I use, Foglie di Carciofo (artichoke leaf pasta), is shaped somewhat like orecchiette. It is a product of Castellana Rustic Italian Pasta, made in Agulia, Italy (see sources, page 320).

{ *Serves 4* }

¼	cup olive oil
2	shallots, thinly sliced
2	garlic cloves, minced
¼	cup dry white wine
2	large artichokes, cleaned according to the directions on page 239
	Kosher salt and freshly ground pepper

8	ounces dried artichoke pasta (see above)
1	small red onion, diced
½	bunch broccoli rabe, trimmed and cut into 2-inch pieces
¼	cup Vegetable Stock (page 56) or chicken stock
1	cup grape tomatoes or cherry tomatoes, halved
1	tablespoon butter
1	cup shaved Parmesan cheese

Heat the oil in a medium skillet over medium-high heat and sauté the shallots and garlic for 1 minute, just until soft. Add the white wine and increase the heat to high.

Drain the artichokes, add to the pan, and cook for about 2 minutes, just until the artichokes are slightly tender.

Add salt and pepper to taste, transfer to a bowl, and cool. *The artichokes can be prepared up to 3 days ahead of time, covered, and refrigerated.*

Cook the pasta in a large pot of boiling salted water according to the package directions until just al dente. Drain well.

Spoon 2 tablespoons of the artichoke cooking liquid into a large skillet. Heat over medium heat until warm, then add the red onion and cook until soft, 2 to 3 minutes. Add the broccoli rabe, stock, pasta, and artichokes, along with any remaining artichoke liquid, and cook, stirring, until the broccoli rabe is tender, 2 to 3 minutes. Turn the heat to high, add the tomatoes and butter, and cook until the liquid is absorbed, 2 to 3 minutes. Season to taste with salt and pepper.

Divide among four plates, top the pasta with shaved Parmesan cheese, and serve.

Homemade Buckwheat Noodles

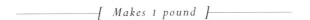

Buckwheat noodles are eaten only in the northern region of the country, where my family comes from. Buckwheat has been cultivated in China for more than a thousand years. The triangular seeds of the grain are ground into a dark, gritty flour, which my family calls *chao mei*.

When my cousin and mother visited me here, we bought a bag of buckwheat flour from a specialty store, and they showed me how to make these noodles. They mixed the buckwheat flour with a small amount of wheat flour and water, kneaded it, rolled it out thin, and cut it into narrow strips about the thickness of linguine. The light brown noodles have a nutty, earthy flavor and an addictively chewy, somewhat slippery texture. I always toss them with a bit of good olive oil, even if I am going to serve them right away, to prevent them from sticking together.

Serve with almost any saucy meat dish, such as Spicy Pork Tenderloin with Poblanos and Plums (page 176), Braised Lamb Blade Chops with Tomatoes and Parsnips (page 183), or Quick-Seared Sichuan Beef Tenderloin Stew (page 178).

[*Makes 1 pound*]

1 cup semolina flour

1 cup buckwheat flour

1 large egg

About ½ cup all-purpose flour

1 tablespoon olive oil

Place the semolina and buckwheat flours in a food processor and pulse just to mix.

Mix the egg with ½ cup cold water in a small bowl. With the motor on, slowly pour the mixture into the processor; continue to process until the mixture forms a ball. Transfer to a lightly floured surface. Knead the dough for a few minutes, sprinkling with the all-purpose flour until the dough is no longer sticky.

Cut the dough into 4 equal pieces, seal in plastic wrap, and refrigerate for about 2 hours.

Set the rollers of a pasta machine to the widest setting and roll 1 piece of dough through it. Adjust the machine to the next setting and pass the dough through it. Continue to roll the dough, reducing the setting each time you pass the dough through the machine, until the dough is about ⅛ inch thick. Place the strip on a lightly floured surface and repeat with the remaining dough.

Using the linguine cutter, cut the strips into noodles. Place the noodles on a large baking sheet sprinkled with all-purpose flour and toss lightly to prevent them from sticking together. Set aside at room temperature until ready to cook. *The noodles can be frozen at this point. Place in zipper-lock bags and freeze for up to 3 months. Do not defrost before cooking.*

Cook the noodles in a large pot of boiling salted water, stirring to be sure they are well separated, for about 1 minute, just until al dente. Drain well. Sprinkle with the oil, tossing to coat, and serve.

SIMPLE VARIATION

If you don't own a pasta machine, roll the dough by hand into 4 large rectangles. Dust with flour and roll up into long sausages, then cut into thin strips with a knife. Place on a well-floured baking sheet and toss well to unravel the strips.

Rice Noodle Flan

We tend to think of flan as a dessert, but it can also be a soft, creamy savory dish. The custard that forms the base of this one is typically French, seasoned with leeks and garlic; here Chinese rice noodles give the flan body and texture. It's the ultimate party dish, since it can be prepared well ahead of time, goes with almost any main course, and reheats beautifully (it can even be frozen for up to 1 month). Serving is a breeze, as the individual portions are easy to unmold. Deliciously rich and sumptuous, the flan is a welcome change from the usual potato, rice, or noodle side dish.

Serve with Korean-Style Grilled Sirloin in Pear Jalapeño Marinade (page 180), Roasted Five-Spice Pork Tenderloin (page 175), Smoked Duck Breasts (page 160), or plain roast chicken.

{ Serves 6 }

4	ounces thin dried rice noodles
1½	teaspoons soybean oil or corn oil
1	tablespoon finely chopped onion
1	shallot, finely chopped
1	cup chicken stock or Vegetable Stock (page 56)
	Kosher salt and freshly ground pepper
1	tablespoon butter

1	very small leek, white part only, cut into 2-inch sections, washed, and cut into fine julienne
½	teaspoon minced garlic
1	large egg
¾	cup heavy cream
4	ounces Swiss or Parmesan cheese (or a mixture), grated

Preheat the oven to 325 degrees. Grease six 4-ounce 3-inch-diameter soufflé cups or molds. Soak the rice noodles in warm water for about 10 minutes, then drain well.

Heat the oil in a medium saucepan over high heat. Add the onion and shallot and sauté until soft, 1 to 2 minutes. Add the stock and drained noodles and bring to a boil. Turn the heat to low and cook for about 5 minutes, stirring often so that the noodles don't stick to the bottom of the pan, until they absorb all of the liquid. Season to taste with salt and pepper. Spread the hot noodle mixture out onto a large platter or flat pan and cool.

Melt the butter in a small skillet over medium heat. Add the leek and garlic and cook, stirring, just until soft, 2 to 3 minutes. Cool.

Beat the egg and cream together in a large bowl. Add the noodle mixture, the leek and garlic mixture, and the grated cheese and mix well. Pack evenly into the prepared molds, smoothing the tops.

Place the molds in a baking pan and add enough hot water to come halfway up the sides. Bake for 30 to 35 minutes, or until firm. Remove from the oven and cool for a minute or so.

Run a small knife around the edge of each mold and turn out onto a serving plate. Serve hot.

The flans can be unmolded, cooled, wrapped in plastic wrap, and refrigerated for a few days. Defrost and reheat just until hot in a microwave oven, or place on a buttered baking sheet and bake in a preheated 325-degree oven for about 10 minutes, or until hot. If frozen, defrost before heating.

Pork Lo Mein with Tomatoes and Fresh Herbs

This is Chinese home cooking at its best. In a well-prepared lo mein dish, there is no extra gravy or liquid: the noodles are cooked until they are al dente, then stir-fried with the vegetables and meat so they absorb all the juices and seasonings and become smooth, chewy, and very tasty.

Since the noodles are long, I julienne the other ingredients to match their shape. You can also make a vegetarian lo mein with all kinds of herbs and garden vegetables or use chicken or cured ham in place of the pork. Heat leftovers in a microwave oven or serve at room temperature.

For this dish, you need fresh pasta or noodles instead of dried ones, because fresh noodles have a natural sweetness and more easily absorb the seasonings of the other ingredients in the stir-fry. The best kinds are long, thin, round strands made from durum wheat semolina with no eggs; their texture is firm and chewy. Do not use fresh egg noodles; they are too soft and become mushy during the cooking. I like the fresh long Chinese noodles sold in Chinatown or Asian markets. Sometimes called Shanghai noodles or lo mein noodles, they come in 1-pound packages. They can be found refrigerated or frozen.

[Serves 4]

8	ounces pork loin, trimmed of all fat
8	ounces fresh long noodles (lo mein), cut in half
3	tablespoons soy sauce
1/4	cup soybean oil, corn oil, or olive oil
1	teaspoon cornstarch
2	tablespoons oyster sauce
2	tablespoons vodka, gin, or vermouth

1	small onion, cut in half and thinly sliced
1	cup julienned green cabbage (about 1/4 small head)
2	scallions, trimmed and cut into 1/2-inch lengths
1/2	cup chicken stock
1	large tomato, cut into 1/4-inch cubes
1/2	cup chopped fresh cilantro, basil, or other herb

Wrap the pork loin in plastic wrap and place in the freezer for 2 hours to facilitate slicing.

Cook the noodles in a large pot of boiling water until just al dente; check for doneness after 4 minutes. Drain and rinse under cold running water to separate the strands.

Place the pork tenderloin on a cutting board. Using a sharp knife, slice it crosswise into 1/8-inch-thick slices, then cut into julienne. Put the pork in a medium bowl, add 2 tablespoons of the soy sauce, 1 tablespoon of the oil, and the cornstarch, and mix well.

In a small bowl, mix the remaining 1 tablespoon soy sauce with the oyster sauce and liquor.

Heat the remaining 3 tablespoons oil in a large skillet or flat-bottomed wok over high heat. Add the pork and cook, stirring, until the meat loses its pink color, about 2 minutes. With a slotted spoon, transfer to a small bowl.

Add the onion to the pan and cook, stirring, until soft, about 2 minutes. Add the green cabbage, noodles, scallions, pork, and oyster sauce mixture and cook, stirring, for 2 minutes. Add the stock and tomato and stir-fry for 3 to 5 minutes, until the noodles are hot and all the liquid has been absorbed. Sprinkle with the cilantro or basil and serve.

Pad Thai

This is the most famous of all Thai noodle dishes. The flat rice noodles, sautéed with fish sauce, tamarind, fried tofu, Chinese preserved vegetables, and shrimp, are sensationally flavored but light. I tasted the best version I've ever had in a famous noodle shop in Bangkok that had been in business for over fifty years. It sold only one dish: pad thai. This is as close as you can come to what that vendor made.

I prefer to use raw peanuts and roast them myself in a 325-degree oven for about 10 minutes, or until they are golden and cooked through. Commercially roasted or salted peanuts are often kept too long in stores and lose their fresh, sweet taste. They have a very short shelf life, no matter what the sell-by date on the package says.

[Serves 4]

8	ounces dried flat rice noodles (1/8 to 1/4 inch wide)
8	ounces large shrimp (21–25 count), shelled and deveined
1	teaspoon kosher salt, plus more to taste
1/4	cup soybean oil or corn oil
2	large eggs, lightly beaten
1	tablespoon tamarind puree or paste (see page 208)
3	tablespoons fish sauce (preferably Three Crabs brand)
2	tablespoons fresh lime juice
1	tablespoon sugar
4	ounces firm tofu, rinsed, pressed and weighted between paper towels to drain, and cut into 1/4-inch dice
2	shallots, thinly sliced
1	garlic clove, thinly sliced

1	tablespoon finely chopped soaked dried shrimp (see page 75)
1	serrano pepper or fresh hot red pepper, stemmed and thinly sliced
1/4	cup Chinese preserved vegetables, prepared as described on opposite page (optional)
1	cup chicken stock, Vegetable Stock (page 56), or water
2	cups (about 4 ounces) fresh bean sprouts, root ends pinched off
	Freshly ground pepper
1/4	cup fresh cilantro leaves
1/4	cup chopped unsalted roasted peanuts (see above)

Soak the noodles in cold water to cover in a medium bowl for 15 minutes, or until softened. Drain in a colander.

Rub the fresh shrimp with the teaspoon of salt and immediately rinse under cold running water until the liquid runs clear. Pat the shrimp dry and cut lengthwise in half.

Heat 1 tablespoon of the oil in a large nonstick skillet or flat-bottomed wok over medium heat. When it is hot, pour in the beaten eggs and slowly swirl to cover the bottom of the skillet, forming a thin crepe. Cook for 2 to 3 minutes, or until set. Transfer the crepe to a cutting board and cool, then

cut into 3 pieces. Slice the pieces crosswise into strips about 1/8 inch wide. Place in a bowl.

Mix the tamarind, fish sauce, lime juice, and sugar in a small bowl.

Heat 1 tablespoon of the oil in the same skillet over high heat. Add the tofu and cook, shaking the pan, until it is light golden, about 2 minutes. Place in a bowl.

Heat the remaining 2 tablespoons oil in the skillet or wok over high heat. Add the shallots, garlic, dried shrimp, and hot pepper and cook, stirring, until fragrant, about 20 seconds. Add the shrimp and cook, stirring, until they have turned white, about 2 minutes. Add the tamarind–fish sauce mixture, noodles, egg strips, preserved vegetables (if using), and tofu and stir and toss to mix well.

Slowly add the stock or water, then cook until the noodles are al dente and have absorbed all the stock, about 5 minutes. Stir in the bean sprouts and salt and pepper to taste. Sprinkle with the cilantro and peanuts and serve.

Chinese Preserved Vegetables

Preserved vegetables have long been used to add flavor to Chinese dishes. Made with members of the cabbage, mustard, and radish families, they are cured primarily with salt. They come whole, julienned, or diced and are sold in small crocks or cans or packed in 1-pound plastic bags. They may be variously labeled "preserved vegetables" (this usually means mustard greens) or "preserved turnips" (radishes). Tientsin preserved vegetables, which I prefer, are made with cabbage, garlic, and salt and sold in 1-pound, 5-ounce decorative crocks. They will keep for at least 6 months, refrigerated. ✧ Before using, soak the vegetables in cold water for 5 minutes, then drain, rinse two or three times to wash off some of the salt, and squeeze dry.

Tamarind

Because of its natural tartness, tamarind imparts a uniquely sour taste to many dishes. It can be used in sauces, for braises, or in marinades, where it acts as both a tenderizer and a flavoring ingredient. You can buy three different forms of tamarind at Asian markets: fresh pods, dried seedless pulp, and paste. ✿ Fresh tamarind pods are available in the summer. They are shaped like broad beans, but the pods are brittle and dark brown. The flesh within the pods is fibrous and full of hard brown seeds. This is the purest form of tamarind and provides the best quality of pulp, but it requires a lot of effort. First you have to open the pods and remove the seeds and pulp, then soak and cook them. I did this once, and it was so much work I never tried it again. ✿ The dried seedless tamarind pulp that comes packed in 4-by-6-inch 16-ounce blocks wrapped in plastic is preferable. You can keep the blocks in the refrigerator for months. Break off and soak the portion needed to make the desired amount of puree and keep the rest refrigerated. ✿ Tamarind paste, which comes in a glass jar and is imported from Thailand (Suree Pantai is a good brand), is the easiest of all to use, but it lacks the fresh flavor of the puree.

Tamarind Puree

[*Makes about 3¼ cups*]

If you want to make your own tamarind puree, this is the easiest way to do so.

1   cup dried seedless tamarind pulp

Soak the pulp in 6 cups hot water for 30 minutes.

Transfer the soaked tamarind with the liquid to a medium saucepan and bring to a boil over high heat. Turn the heat to low and simmer for 15 minutes. Remove from the heat and cool.

Push the tamarind and liquid through a strainer, pressing to extract as much of the liquid as possible. Discard the solids. *The puree will keep, refrigerated in a covered jar, for 2 weeks.*

Vegetable Rice with Shiitakes and Broccoli Rabe

Jasmine rice is an aromatic variety native to Thailand. In fragrance and flavor, it is similar to basmati rice, but it's usually much cheaper. It's now grown in this country and can be found in many supermarkets.

Make sure the broccoli rabe is very dry before adding it to the rice; otherwise, it will release too much moisture while cooking, and the rice will be overdone and mushy.

[Serves 6 to 8]

4	ounces broccoli rabe
2	tablespoons soybean oil, corn oil, or light olive oil
3	shallots, thinly sliced
4	ounces shiitake mushrooms, stemmed and thinly sliced
1	teaspoon kosher salt
1/4	teaspoon freshly ground pepper

	Pinch of ground cloves
4	tablespoons (1/2 stick) unsalted butter
1 1/2	cups jasmine rice or long-grain white rice, rinsed and drained
1 1/2	cups chicken stock

Trim off the stem ends of the broccoli rabe and remove any tough or yellow outer leaves. If the stems are large and tough, peel them with a paring knife or vegetable peeler. Wash well, drain, and spread out on several layers of paper towels. Let dry for about 15 minutes.

Place 2 stalks of broccoli rabe side by side with the stem ends even on a cutting board and, with a sharp knife, cut the stems and florets into 1/4- to 1/8-inch dice. Repeat with the rest of the rabe.

Heat the oil in a medium saucepan over high heat. Add the shallots, and cook until soft, about 1 to 2 minutes. Add the shiitake mushrooms, salt, pepper, and cloves and cook until the mushrooms are soft, about 1 minute. Add the butter; once it is melted, stir in the rice and mix well to coat all the grains.

Add the stock and 1 cup water, bring to a boil, and stir, then reduce the heat to low. Place the broccoli rabe on top of the rice, cover, and simmer until all the liquid has been absorbed and the rice is just tender, about 15 minutes.

Taste to correct the seasonings, toss gently to mix, and serve.

Saffron Basmati Fried Rice

In this Indian-style pilaf, apricots add sweetness, almonds provide crunch, and saffron brings color and flavor. I also add scrambled egg.

Substituting basmati, an aromatic, slender long-grain rice with a firm texture and nutty flavor, for Chinese short-grain rice gives the dish a firmer texture.

Basmati rice can be found in Indian grocery stores, many Asian markets, and some supermarkets. I prefer to buy it in Indian markets, as it is usually the freshest. You can substitute long-grain jasmine rice.

[Serves 8]

¼	cup half-and-half
	Pinch of saffron threads
3	tablespoons soybean oil or corn oil
2	tablespoons finely chopped shallots
1	tablespoon finely chopped garlic
½	cup diced dried apricots
1½	cups basmati rice, rinsed and drained (see above)

1	teaspoon kosher salt, plus more if needed
2	large eggs, lightly beaten
4	scallions, green parts only, cut into ¼-inch lengths
	Freshly ground pepper
¼	cup sliced almonds, toasted (see page 64)
2	tablespoons chopped fresh chives, flat-leaf parsley, or cilantro

Heat the half-and-half and saffron in a small glass bowl in a microwave oven for 30 seconds. Or warm in a small saucepan over low heat for 1 minute.

Heat 2 tablespoons of the oil in a medium saucepan with a tight-fitting lid over high heat. When it is hot, add the shallots, garlic, and apricots and cook, stirring, for 1 minute, just until the garlic is soft. Add the rice and salt and mix well. Add the saffron mixture and 1½ cups water and bring to a boil. Stir, cover, turn the heat to low, and simmer for 10 to 12 minutes, or until the rice has absorbed all the liquid. Remove from the heat and fluff the rice with a fork.

Heat the remaining 1 tablespoon oil in a large skillet or flat-bottomed wok over medium heat. Pour in the beaten eggs and swirl to cover the bottom of the pan, then stir with a spatula to scramble the eggs until they are set and have formed small, firm lumps, 2 to 3 minutes. Mix in the scallions and cook, stirring, for 1 minute. Stir in the rice mixture and continue to cook, stirring, for 2 minutes, or until the rice is hot.

Remove from the heat and season to taste with salt and pepper. Mix in the toasted almonds and herbs and serve.

Leftover rice can be refrigerated, covered, for 1 to 2 days. Reheat, covered, in a microwave oven.

Cauliflower Risotto with Wild Mushrooms

This is a Chinese version of risotto, without all the stirring. Chinese sweet rice is the only type of rice that is soaked and steamed before cooking. It will remain firm, much as Arborio rice does in a well-made risotto. The coconut cream keeps the grains nicely oiled and separate. This dish is full of the flavors of fall. Serve as a main course or as a side dish with seafood.

[Serves 4]

- 1 cup sweet (glutinous) rice
- 3 tablespoons unsweetened coconut cream (see page 77)
- 4 ounces chanterelle, oyster, or shiitake mushrooms
- 1 cup milk
- 2 cups cut-up cauliflower florets (½-inch pieces)
- 2 tablespoons butter
- 2 tablespoons extra-virgin olive oil
  Kosher salt and freshly ground pepper
- 1 small onion, finely chopped
- ¼ cup freshly grated Parmesan cheese
- 1 cup baby arugula or watercress leaves, washed and dried

Soak the rice in 6 cups of water in a large bowl for 2 to 4 hours. Drain well.

Prepare a steamer by placing a layer of cheesecloth in the bottom of the rack. Spread the rice in an even layer over the cheesecloth. Fill the bottom of the steamer with water and bring to a boil over high heat. Place the rack on top, cover, and steam for 5 minutes; the rice will still be very firm.

Transfer the rice to a bowl and add the coconut cream. Mix well to separate the grains of rice. *The rice can be prepared to this point up to 3 days in advance. Store in a tightly closed container, refrigerated.*

Using a soft brush, clean any dirt from the mushrooms. Cut large mushrooms into halves or quarters. Discard the stems if using shiitakes.

Bring the milk to a boil in a large saucepan over medium heat. Add the cauliflower and 1 tablespoon of the butter, turn the heat down to a simmer, cover, and cook for about 10 minutes, stirring frequently, until the cauliflower is very soft. Remove from the heat.

Heat 1 tablespoon of the oil in a large nonstick saucepan over high heat. Add the mushrooms and cook, stirring, for 1 to 2 minutes to coat them with oil and heat them through; they should be barely cooked. Transfer to a bowl and sprinkle with a little salt and pepper.

Add the remaining tablespoon of oil to the saucepan. When it is hot, add the onion and cook, stirring, until soft, about 2 minutes. Stir in the rice and the cauliflower, along with any remaining milk, and cook until heated through. Stir in the mushrooms and the remaining tablespoon of butter. Mix in the Parmesan cheese. Season to taste with salt and pepper.

Spoon the risotto into four shallow bowls. Garnish with the arugula or watercress and serve.

Braised Chestnuts

———————————(✿)———————————

Braising fresh chestnuts with a little butter, sugar, and stock heightens their flavor and softens their texture. These braised chestnuts make a delicious addition to savory bread pudding (opposite page). On their own, they are a fine accompaniment to roasted meats or poultry.

——————[*Serves 4 as a side dish*]——————

8	ounces whole chestnuts, peeled		1	teaspoon sugar
1	cup chicken stock		2	tablespoons butter

Place the chestnuts, stock, and sugar in a medium saucepan and bring to a boil over high heat. Lower the heat, cover, and simmer for 15 to 20 minutes, or until the chestnuts are tender.

Stir in the butter and continue to cook, uncovered, until most of the liquid is evaporated, about 5 minutes. *The chestnuts can be cooked and refrigerated, covered, for up to 1 day. Reheat before serving.*

Peeling Chestnuts

With a sharp paring knife, make a ⅛-inch-deep cut almost all the way around the circumference of each chestnut. Wrap the chestnuts in aluminum foil and roast in a preheated 400-degree oven for 20 to 25 minutes, or until the shells just open. ✿ Remove the chestnuts a few at a time from the foil. (The nuts should be kept hot so they can be more easily removed from their shells and brown papery inner skins.) Hold each chestnut in a thick towel to protect your hands, and using a small knife, peel off the shell and inner skin.

Chestnut Bread Pudding

———(✿)———

I'm fond of bread pudding in any form — sweet or savory. I usually use plain white bread to make this pudding, but sweet buttery brioche also works well. I cook the pudding in a water bath and cover the pan with a sheet of buttered waxed paper to keep a crust from forming so the pudding stays soft through-out. The chestnuts add richness and mellowness. Serve with Roasted Squab with Port Wine Sauce (page 151), any type of roast bird, or even alongside the Thanksgiving turkey.

———⌐ *Serves 12* ⌐———

1	pound white bread, crusts removed, cut into ¹/₂-inch cubes
2	teaspoons soybean oil or corn oil
1	very small onion, finely chopped
2	tablespoons unsalted butter
4	ounces white button mushrooms, halved and thinly sliced
1	tablespoon brandy
1	tablespoon chopped fresh thyme

¹/₂	cup finely chopped celery
1	large egg, lightly beaten
³/₄	cup chicken stock
¹/₄	cup chopped fresh flat-leaf parsley
	Kosher salt and freshly ground pepper
	Braised Chestnuts (opposite page), halved

Preheat the oven to 300 degrees. Butter twelve 4-ounce ramekins, muffin cups, or soufflé cups or an 8-inch square pan. Cut out twelve circles of waxed or parchment paper to cover the tops of the ramekins. If using the square pan, line it with a sheet of buttered waxed paper large enough to fold over and cover the top of the pudding.

Place the bread cubes in a large bowl.

Heat the oil in a medium skillet over medium heat. Add the onion and cook over medium heat, stirring, until soft, 2 to 3 minutes. Add the butter and mushrooms and cook, stirring, until the mushrooms are soft, 3 to 4 minutes. Add the brandy, thyme, and celery and continue to cook, stirring, for 3 minutes.

Add the onion mixture to the bread cubes. Stir in the egg, stock, and parsley, mixing well. Season to taste with salt and pepper. Let stand, stirring occasionally, for 5 minutes. Mix in the chestnuts.

Divide the bread mixture evenly among the ramekins or place it in the square pan. Top with the paper rounds or fold the waxed paper over, if using the pan. Place the ramekins or pan in a large baking pan filled with 1 inch hot water. Bake for 45 minutes, or up to 50 minutes if using the pan, or until firm. Remove from the water bath.

To unmold the ramekins, remove the paper and run a knife around the sides of each pudding, shake to loosen, and invert the puddings onto individual plates or a serving plat-ter. Cut the square pudding into 12 portions and serve.

The puddings can be made 2 days in advance and refrigerated, covered. Warm the puddings in a microwave oven until hot. Or reheat, covered, in a 325-degree oven for about 10 minutes, until warm. Store any leftover cooked bread pudding, tightly wrapped in several layers of plastic wrap, in the freezer. It will keep for 1 month.

Creamy Coconut Polenta

Most people don't associate corn with Chinese cuisine, but it has been grown in northern China for centuries. It's not the sweet variety that Americans are familiar with but a kind of field corn. In the fall, the kernels are dried and ground into a coarse flour, which is used throughout the long winter in steamed breads.

For this recipe, I use very finely ground instant polenta. Adding coconut milk instead of water gives the dish a creamy soft texture and a slightly sweet, nutty flavor. The polenta can be served immediately, while still soft and creamy, or it can be cooled, cut into pieces, and sautéed in a little corn oil until crisp.

Serve with Pan-Seared Black Sea Bass with Caramelized Red Pepper Sauce (page 111), Salmon Braised with Soy and Ginger (page 98), Roasted Squab with Port Wine Sauce (page 151), or Wuxi-Style Braised Beef Short Ribs (page 177).

Serves 9

4 cups chicken stock or Vegetable Stock (page 56)
1 13.5-ounce can unsweetened coconut milk, whisked
2 teaspoons kosher salt
1/2 teaspoon finely ground white pepper

1 cup instant polenta (preferably Ferrara brand)
2 tablespoons butter
Corn oil (if serving firm polenta)

Bring the stock and coconut milk to a boil in a medium saucepan over high heat. Turn the heat to medium-low and whisk in the salt, white pepper, and polenta. Whisk constantly until the mixture is thick and creamy, about 7 minutes. Whisk in the butter.

Pour the polenta out onto a platter and serve immediately, or spread in a 9-by-13-inch glass or ceramic container. Cool, then cut into 9 pieces. *Store in a sealed container with waxed paper between the layers until ready to heat and serve.*

To serve the firm polenta, heat 1 tablespoon corn oil in a large nonstick skillet over high heat. Add a few pieces of polenta (do not crowd the pan) and pan-sear until lightly browned on the first side, then turn and sear the other side, 2 to 3 minutes per side. Transfer to a plate and keep warm. Repeat until all the pieces are nicely crusted, and serve.

Tofu and Eggs

Firm Tofu

Fresh tofu has a faint soybean aroma and a subtle, almost bland, milky flavor.
Most of the tofu found in supermarkets is vacuum-packed. Check the label to
make sure the sell-by date has not passed. ❧ In Asian markets and health food
stores, firm tofu is sold as loose cakes submerged in a container of water; it is usually
fresher and cheaper than that found in supermarkets. Rinse and store it in clean cold
water in a covered container in the refrigerator, changing the water daily. It will keep
for about 1 week. Before using, rinse tofu under cold running water and dry it on
layers of paper towels or clean kitchen towels. If you need it to be really dry,
drain between layers of paper towels with a weight on top to press
out the excess moisture. To ensure even cooking, cut the
tofu into pieces of the same size.

Wok-Braised Tofu with Tomatoes and Mushrooms

The most important thing about this dish is the technique; the tofu must be first seared in very hot oil before the vegetables and sauce are added. You can easily substitute other vegetables (zucchini, shiitake mushrooms, celery, or briefly cooked broccoli florets or carrots) for those called for in the recipe, but cut each vegetable into similar-sized pieces.

[Serves 4]

- 4 ounces firm tofu
- 1 medium tomato, peeled (see page 123) and cored
- 2 tablespoons soy sauce
- 1 teaspoon balsamic vinegar
- 3 tablespoons mirin (Japanese sweet wine)
- 2 tablespoons sake or vodka
- 3 tablespoons olive oil or soybean oil
- 3 garlic cloves, thinly sliced
- 2 jalapeño peppers, stemmed and thinly sliced
- 1/2 cup small stemmed and halved white button mushrooms
- 1/2 cup sugar snap peas, strings removed
- 1/4 cup julienned red bell pepper
- 1/2 cup fresh basil leaves, julienned

Rinse the tofu under cold running water. Wrap well in several layers of paper towels and place on a plate; place a second plate on top to press out some of the excess water. Let sit for 20 minutes.

Cut the tofu in half, then cut each half crosswise into 4 pieces, each about ½ inch thick.

Cut the tomato crosswise in half, then cut each half into 4 wedges.

Mix the soy sauce, vinegar, mirin, and sake or vodka in a small bowl.

Heat the oil in a large nonstick skillet or flat-bottomed wok over high heat. Carefully lay the tofu in the skillet and sear until lightly golden, about 1 minute. Turn and sear until golden on the second side, about 1 minute. Add the garlic and jalapeño peppers and stir-fry for about 30 seconds, just until the garlic is softened. Add the mushrooms, sugar snap peas, bell pepper, and soy sauce mixture. Cook, stirring gently, until the tofu is well coated with the sauce, about 2 minutes. Add the tomato and cook for 1 minute.

Remove from the heat, mix in the basil, and serve hot.

Warm Crisp-Fried Tofu Salad with Fresh Spinach and Spicy Peanut Sauce

This salad is a mix of spicy and bland, soft and crunchy. Raw carrots, scallions, and spinach are tossed with crisp fried tofu and fresh green soybeans and topped with a spicy peanut sauce and a sprinkling of crunchy peanuts.

[Serves 4]

PEANUT SAUCE

1	tablespoon soybean oil or corn oil
2	garlic cloves, thinly sliced
2	fresh hot red peppers, stemmed and thinly sliced
2	tablespoons soy sauce
¼	cup whisked unsweetened coconut milk (see page 77)
1	tablespoon finely ground unsalted roasted peanuts
1	teaspoon sugar
1	tablespoon rice wine vinegar

TOFU SALAD

½	cup shelled fresh or frozen soybeans (edamame)
1	cup soybean oil or corn oil
8	ounces firm tofu, rinsed, drained, and dried with paper towels
½	cup julienned carrots
1	scallion, cut into small dice
2	cups baby spinach or baby arugula, washed and dried
2	tablespoons coarsely crushed unsalted roasted peanuts
2	tablespoons julienned fresh cilantro leaves

TO MAKE THE SAUCE: Heat the oil in a small saucepan over high heat. Add the garlic and hot peppers and cook until softened, about 1 minute. Add the soy sauce, coconut milk, peanuts, sugar, and rice wine vinegar, mix well, and bring to a boil. Remove from the heat.

TO MAKE THE SALAD: Soak the soybeans in a bowl of cool water for about 10 minutes. Drain, and with your fingers or a sharp paring knife, remove the skins. Cook the soybeans in a small saucepan of boiling water for about 3 minutes, or until tender. Drain.

Heat the oil to 350 degrees in a large skillet or flat-bottomed wok. Pat the tofu dry again if necessary. Add the tofu to the oil and cook until golden on both sides, about 5 minutes. Remove with a slotted spoon and place on paper towels to drain.

Cut the tofu into ½-inch cubes. Place in a large bowl, add the soybeans, carrots, and scallion, and mix well.

TO SERVE: Divide the spinach or arugula among four plates and spoon the tofu mixture over it. Pour the sauce over the top. Sprinkle with the roasted peanuts and cilantro and serve immediately.

Tofu Chili

Forget what you think vegetarian chili tastes like; this version is nothing like any you've ever eaten. It's a startling blend and balance of Eastern and Western spices and ingredients. It's very spicy; if you prefer a milder version, reduce the amount of jalapeño peppers.

About half the size of a kidney bean and dark red in color, adzuki (or azuki) beans have a white ridge along one side. The Chinese call them red beans. You can buy dried adzuki beans in Asian markets and health food stores. Choose beans that have a shine to them. Avoid them if they are a dull red; they have been on the shelf too long. Eden canned adzuki beans have a better texture and flavor than other canned varieties and can be found in many supermarkets, but I prefer to buy dried beans and cook them myself.

[Serves 4]

½	cup dried adzuki beans, soaked overnight in water to cover, or a 15-ounce can adzuki or black beans (preferably Eden brand), drained
2	tablespoons soybean oil or corn oil
1	cup chopped onion
2	garlic cloves, minced
½	cup finely chopped red bell pepper
8	ounces firm tofu, rinsed, excess water pressed out, and cut into ¼-inch dice
4	jalapeño peppers, stemmed, seeded, and finely chopped
1	teaspoon freshly ground white pepper
1	teaspoon ground cumin
2	tablespoons red wine vinegar
2	tablespoons soy sauce
2	large ripe tomatoes, peeled (see page 123) and diced, or a 14½-ounce can diced tomatoes
1	cup chopped scallions
½	cup chopped fresh cilantro

If using dried beans, drain, place in a medium saucepan, and cover with cold water. Bring to a boil over high heat, turn the heat to low, and simmer, uncovered, for 1 hour, or until the beans are tender. Drain. *The beans can be cooked up to 2 days ahead and refrigerated, covered.*

Heat the oil in a large skillet or flat-bottomed wok over medium-low heat. Add the onion, garlic, and bell pepper and cook, stirring, until the onion is softened, about 4 minutes.

Add the tofu, jalapeños, white pepper, cumin, vinegar, and soy sauce and cook, stirring, until the tofu is well coated with the spices, about 3 minutes.

Add the tomatoes and beans and cook for about 10 minutes, stirring occasionally. Add the scallions, and when the chili returns to a boil, turn off the heat. Stir in the chopped cilantro and serve.

Crispy Panfried Silken Tofu with Creamy Sun-Dried Tomato Sauce

Panfrying silken tofu gives it a crisp crust, creating a sensational contrast with the piping hot, soft, silky interior. Because of its custardy texture, silken tofu can't be pan-seared without a coating. Draining off some of the liquid on paper towels before you coat it will make it easier to work with.

This dish should be served very hot. You can panfry the tofu ahead of time, then reheat in a preheated 425-degree oven.

Wait until the last minute to julienne the basil leaves for the garnish, or they will turn brown.

[Serves 4]

1	package (about 16 ounces) silken tofu
1/2	cup all-purpose flour
1/4	cup soybean oil or corn oil
1	large shallot, minced
1	scallion, white part only, minced
2	plum tomatoes, peeled (see page 123) and diced

1	teaspoon soy sauce
1	teaspoon sugar
	Freshly ground pepper
1/2	cup Creamy Sun-Dried Tomato Sauce (recipe follows)
4	fresh basil leaves

Place several layers of paper towels on a large plate. Drain as much liquid as possible from the container, carefully remove the silken tofu, and gently place on top of the paper towels. Cover with another layer of towels and let drain for 30 minutes, replacing the paper towels with dry ones as needed.

Cut the block of tofu into 8 equal pieces.

Place the flour on a plate. One by one, gently roll the tofu pieces in the flour to form a light coating.

Heat 1 tablespoon of the oil in a small skillet over high heat. Add the shallot and scallion and cook until soft, about 1 minute. Turn the heat to low and add the tomatoes, soy sauce, and sugar. Simmer, stirring, for 2 minutes, then add pepper to taste. Remove from the heat.

Heat the remaining 3 tablespoons oil in a large nonstick skillet or flat-bottomed wok over high heat. When the oil is very hot, gently add the tofu and panfry until golden and crisp on the first side, 3 to 4 minutes. Turn the tofu over and panfry until the second side is golden and crisp, 3 to 4 minutes.

Meanwhile, reheat the sun-dried tomato sauce. Cut the basil leaves into julienne.

Spoon the sun-dried tomato sauce onto the center of each of four plates and place 2 pieces of tofu on each one. Spoon the shallot-tomato mixture on top of the tofu, then scatter the julienned basil over all and serve immediately.

Creamy Sun-Dried Tomato Sauce

This sauce will perk up almost anything. Leftovers can be stored in the refrigerator for a day or two, or they can be frozen in a tightly sealed container for a few months.

2	tablespoons olive oil
2	garlic cloves, thinly sliced
2	dried hot red peppers
4	sun-dried tomato halves, chopped
½	cup dry white wine
1	cup chicken stock or Vegetable Stock (page 56)
1	tablespoon tomato paste
¼	cup heavy cream
2	tablespoons butter
	Kosher salt and freshly ground pepper

Heat the oil in a medium saucepan over high heat. Add the garlic, hot peppers, and sun-dried tomatoes and cook until the garlic is soft, 1 to 2 minutes. Add the white wine and cook until it is almost evaporated, 2 to 3 minutes. Add the stock and tomato paste, turn the heat to low, and simmer for about 20 minutes, or until the liquid is reduced by one third.

Stir in the cream and butter. Remove from the heat and cool.

Puree the sauce in a blender or a food processor, then strain through a fine sieve. Season to taste with salt and pepper. Reheat in a small saucepan over low heat or in a microwave oven just until hot.

Silken Tofu

The texture of silken, or soft, tofu is creamier and more like custard than that of regular firm tofu. It is very fragile, so handle with care. Created by the Japanese, silken tofu is prepared with thicker soybean milk and, unlike regular tofu, is made without draining off all the excess liquid. Usually sold in vacuum-packed cartons, it is often ultra-pasteurized and will last in the refrigerator unopened for about 3 months. (Check the sell-by date on the package before purchasing.) Do not substitute regular tofu. ✿ Drain off the excess liquid from the package first, then place the tofu on a layer of paper towels. Cover the top with another layer; let sit for about 30 minutes. Replace with dry towels as needed. This will make the tofu much easier to work with.

Dried Shiitake Mushrooms

Dried shiitake mushrooms have a deeper flavor, a more intense aroma, and a chewier texture than fresh ones. Found in Asian markets, gourmet stores, and many supermarkets at reasonable prices, they are great for soups or braises, since they absorb the flavors of other ingredients when sautéed. Dried shiitakes keep in a sealed container for a long time. ❧ Because they are so hard and chewy, they require soaking and usually need 20 to 30 minutes of cooking to soften them. ❧ TO SOAK DRIED SHIITAKE MUSHROOMS: Rinse the mushrooms under cold running water to remove any dirt. Soak in cold water for about 20 minutes, with a plate on top to weight them down so they are all submerged. ❧ Lift out the mushrooms and gently squeeze out the excess water. Carefully drain off the liquid (leaving any grit in the bottom of the bowl) and save for making sauce or stock. Trim off the mushroom stems and discard, or save them for making sauce or stock.

Braised Pressed Tofu, Shiitake Mushrooms, and Soybeans

If you can't find fresh or frozen soybeans, you can use peas, fava beans, or lima beans.

[*Serves 4*]

6	dried shiitake mushrooms, soaked in water for 20 minutes, drained, and stemmed
1/2	cup fresh or frozen shelled soybeans (edamame)
6	ounces pressed tofu (any kind)
2	tablespoons soy sauce
2	tablespoons sake or dry vermouth

1/2	teaspoon sugar
1/4	cup chicken stock or Vegetable Stock (page 56)
2	tablespoons soybean oil or corn oil
2	garlic cloves, thinly sliced
2	scallions, trimmed and cut into 1/2-inch lengths

Fill the bottom of a steamer with water and bring to a boil. Place the mushrooms in a shallow bowl or plate in the steamer basket, cover, turn the heat to low, and steam for 20 minutes, or until tender. Remove and cool.

Cut the mushrooms into ⅛-inch-thick slices.

Place the soybeans in a bowl of cool water for about 10 minutes. Drain, and with your fingers or a sharp paring knife, remove the thin skins. Rinse under cold running water and drain again.

Cut the pressed tofu in half crosswise and then slice crosswise into ⅛-inch-thick pieces.

Mix the soy sauce, sake or vermouth, sugar, and stock together in a small bowl.

Heat the oil in a large skillet or flat-bottomed wok over high heat. Add the garlic and cook until soft, about 30 seconds. Add the mushrooms, tofu, soybeans, scallions, and soy sauce mixture. Turn the heat down and simmer for about 5 minutes, stirring occasionally, until the soybeans are tender and the tofu is well coated with the sauce.

Spoon onto a serving plate and serve hot.

Pressed Tofu

A specialty of northern China, pressed tofu has been weighted to force out all the excess water and compressed into a very dense, firm cake. It has a chewy texture and is much more flavorful than regular tofu, with a completely different taste. Pressed tofu is usually sold in blocks. It comes in white or brown; whitish yellow is the natural product, while brown is flavored. Many companies flavor it by smoking; others add five-spice powder or hot peppers and spices. Pressed tofu is delicious braised with beef or pork. I also dice it or cut it into julienne strips and stir-fry it along with meat and vegetables for added flavor and texture.

White Corn with Pressed Tofu, Peas, and Tomatoes

The traditional version of this dish is braised and contains yellow field corn, carrots, fermented soybean paste, and cooked dried yellow soybeans, along with diced pork. I give it a fresher flavor by stir-frying it and adding diced fresh tomato, peas, and sweet white corn. I also substitute pressed tofu for the cooked soybeans because I like the smoky taste that it adds.

[Serves 4]

1½	tablespoons soy sauce
1	teaspoon balsamic vinegar
2	tablespoons chicken stock or Vegetable Stock (page 56)
3	tablespoons extra-virgin olive oil
1	small red onion, finely diced
2	garlic cloves, minced
1	12-ounce block smoked pressed tofu, cut into ¼-inch dice

1½	cups fresh white corn
½	cup fresh or frozen peas
1	large tomato, peeled (see page 123), seeded, and diced
2	scallions, trimmed and diced
1	teaspoon crushed red pepper flakes
	Kosher salt and freshly ground pepper

Mix the soy sauce, vinegar, and stock in a small bowl.

Heat the oil in a large skillet or flat-bottomed wok over high heat. Add the onion and garlic and cook, stirring, for about 1 minute, or until soft. Add the tofu and soy sauce mixture and cook for about 2 minutes, until the flavor of the sauce penetrates the tofu. Turn the heat to low and add the corn, peas, tomato, scallions, and red pepper flakes. Cook, stirring, for 4 to 5 minutes, until the peas are tender. Season to taste with salt and pepper.

Spoon out onto a large platter. Serve hot or cold. *The dish can be refrigerated in a tightly covered container for up to 3 days.*

SIMPLE VARIATION

You can include ½ cup diced carrots, zucchini, or celery root in place of or in addition to any of the vegetables — vary the dish according to what is in season and what you have on hand.

Homemade Soybean Milk

You can buy soybean milk in supermarkets, but I don't like the taste of any of the commercially pre-pared products. They lack the sweet milky flavor and fresh soybean aroma of the kind I grew up with, and they're much too thick. This homemade version is just right.

[Makes about 2 quarts]

1   cup dried yellow soybeans
½   cup sugar, or more to taste

Place the soybeans in a large bowl, cover generously with water, and soak overnight. The soybeans will swell to about twice their size. Drain in a colander and rinse well.

Puree the drained beans with 3 cups water in a food processor. The liquid will become milky.

Add the puree and 9 cups water to a 6- to 8-quart pot and bring to a boil over high heat, stirring constantly to prevent the soybean solids from sticking to the bottom and burn-ing. Turn the heat down to a simmer and cook, stirring often, for 30 minutes.

Strain the soy milk through a fine sieve; discard the solids. Add the sugar and mix well. If you prefer, add more sugar to taste.

Cool and store in a plastic container. *The soy milk keeps for about 3 days in the refrigerator.*

Dried Yellow Soybeans

Dried yellow soybeans are the size and shape of small white beans but are a creamy light tan. Soaked for several hours, they absorb a lot of water and double in size. They take a long time to cook — about 3 hours, longer than most other dried beans. But unlike other dried beans, they do not get soft or mushy in long-simmered dishes. Dried soybeans are often sold in 1- to 5-pound bags and are available in Asian markets and health food stores and many supermarkets.

Stir-Fried Eggs and Tomatoes

———(⟳)———

In China and Taiwan, eggs are often served for lunch or dinner. Stir-fried scrambled eggs are cooked over high heat along with a variety of ingredients, depending on what is available. I love the sweetness of the tomatoes mixed with the eggs, and I frequently serve this dish for brunch.

—{ *Serves 3 or 4* }—

¼ cup soybean oil or corn oil

2 shallots, thinly sliced

6 large eggs, lightly beaten

3 vine-ripened tomatoes (about 1 pound), peeled (see page 123), cored, and cut into 8 wedges each

Kosher salt and freshly ground pepper

Heat the oil in a large skillet or flat-bottomed wok over medium heat. Add the shallots and cook until soft, about 1 minute. Add the eggs, swirling to spread them around the bottom of the pan. Continue to swirl and cook until the eggs are set on the bottom, about 3 minutes.

Add the tomatoes, mixing them into the eggs with a spatula. Press down on the tomatoes with the spatula, then cook for about 2 minutes, stirring occasionally, until the eggs are set and the tomatoes are hot. Season with salt and pepper to taste and stir one last time. Spoon out onto a large plate and serve.

Cantonese Egg Foo Yung
with Crabmeat, Asparagus, and Bean Sprouts

(⟳)

Egg foo yung, created in Chinese restaurants in this country, took the concept of a Western omelet and gave it a Chinese accent. The beaten eggs are often mixed with roast pork, shrimp, or chicken and a variety of fresh vegetables, such as bean sprouts, chives, sliced mushrooms, green beans, and julienned bamboo shoots. The omelet is pan-seared in hot oil until golden brown, and the high heat causes the vegetables to release their liquid, making the inside of the omelet soft and creamy, while the outside becomes crisp.

This is my favorite kind of omelet to serve for brunch, lunch, or even dinner, along with a salad or sliced fresh tomatoes and plain rice.

{ *Serves 4* }

6	large eggs
¼	cup chicken stock or Vegetable Stock (page 56)
¼	teaspoon kosher salt
¼	teaspoon freshly ground white pepper
3	medium asparagus spears
⅓	cup plus 1 tablespoon soybean oil, corn oil, or olive oil
4	large white button mushrooms, thinly sliced
3	scallions, white part only, sliced about ⅛ inch thick on the diagonal
½	cup bean sprouts, root ends removed
¼	cup chopped Chinese chives (see page 17) or regular chives
4	ounces jumbo lump crabmeat, picked over for any shells and cartilage
2	plum tomatoes, thinly sliced (optional)
2	tablespoons Honey Soy Glaze (page 7; optional)
	Fresh basil leaves or cilantro sprigs for garnish

In a medium bowl, with a small whisk or a fork, beat the eggs with the stock, salt, and white pepper. Pour half the eggs into another medium bowl.

Cut off the tough lower stems of the asparagus and discard. Cut the asparagus on the diagonal into thin slices about 1 inch long and ⅛ inch thick.

Heat 1 tablespoon of the oil in a large skillet or flat-bottomed wok over high heat. Add the mushrooms and cook, stirring, until they are just soft, about 1 minute. Add the asparagus and scallions and cook for another minute, just until heated through: do not overcook. Turn them out onto a plate and cool. Set the pan aside.

Divide the cooked vegetables into 2 portions and spoon into the bowls containing the eggs. Divide the bean sprouts, chives, and crabmeat evenly between the eggs and mix gently.

Wipe the skillet or wok clean, then heat half the remaining oil (a generous 2½ tablespoons) over high heat until very hot. Add one bowl of the egg mixture and swirl so the eggs spread around the pan. Turn the heat to medium-low and cook until the eggs are set and golden brown on the bottom, about 6 minutes. Turn the omelet over using a spatula and cook until the second side is well browned, about 6 minutes. Remove from the pan and keep warm. Wipe out the pan and repeat with the remaining oil and egg mixture.

Cut into quarters. Place 2 wedges of omelet on each plate, with the tomato slices, if desired. Spoon the soy glaze over the omelet, if using, and garnish with basil or cilantro.

Vegetables

Sautéed Artichoke Hearts

Artichokes remind me very much of the fresh bamboo shoots I enjoyed back in my country. No other vegetables compare to them in flavor and texture. Both are appealing year-round but are especially good in the spring. After the first frost, both develop a mature yet sweet flavor. Both have inedible tough outer leaves.

I like artichokes that have been cooked only briefly and are not overdone and mushy, so I thinly slice the tender inner hearts and sauté them for just a few minutes in extra-virgin olive oil and white wine.

{ Serves 4 }

¼ cup extra-virgin olive oil

2 garlic cloves, minced

2 shallots, thinly sliced

¼ cup dry white wine

2 extra-large artichokes, prepared as described on opposite page

Kosher salt and freshly ground pepper

Heat the oil in a medium saucepan over medium heat. Add the garlic and shallots and cook gently until softened, about 1 minute. Add the wine and turn the heat to high. Drain the artichokes well and add them to the pan. Cook, stirring, until just tender, about 2 minutes. Season to taste with salt and pepper.

Transfer to a bowl and cool, then serve or cover and refrigerate. *The artichokes keep well, refrigerated, for 3 days.* They can be served cold or rewarmed in a microwave oven or skillet.

To Prepare
Artichoke Hearts

This is the easiest way to prepare artichokes for any recipe in which you want to use just the hearts. I hate to let the leaves go to waste, though, and I often steam them for a few minutes and nibble on them, dipped in a little melted butter. Choose extra-large artichokes, which are tenderer than smaller ones. Their stems and leaves should be green, not brown or woody-looking. ❧ Fill a medium bowl with cold water and add the juice of 1 lemon. Working with 1 artichoke at a time, cut off the top inch of the artichoke with a serrated knife. Cut off the stem. Bend back the outer leaves close to the base until they snap off, then remove several more layers of leaves in the same way until you reach the pale yellow inner leaves. With a sharp paring knife, trim away any dark green fibrous parts remaining on the base of the artichoke. Cut the artichoke into quarters. Using a small dessert spoon or melon-ball cutter, remove and discard the fuzzy choke from each quarter. Cut each artichoke quarter into 3 wedges. Place the artichoke pieces in the bowl of lemon water to prevent them from browning. Repeat with the remaining artichokes.

Steaming Techniques

Steaming is as important a technique in China as baking is in the West. Almost every Chinese household has a steamer, with a large wok or pot as its base and a stack of tightly fitting bamboo (or stainless steel) steaming baskets on top. Vegetables, fish, chicken, pork, rice, and bread are all steamed. The moisture from the steam tenderizes the food, helps preserve the natural juices and color, and results in a subtle yet intense flavor. Steam can also help release fat, as does oven-roasting, but steamed foods have a much more delicate texture than roasted foods and never get dried out. ✿ When I came to this country in the late 1960s, it was very hard to find a steamer suitable for use in a home kitchen. The steamer baskets available were too unwieldy to use on top of a wok or pot and too bulky to store easily. But in recent years, several excellent versions have come on the market. A good steamer should have a tight-fitting lid, a deep wide bottom pot, and a snugly fitting basket. The fit is important because steam needs to build up within the steamer to a high enough temperature to cook the food sufficiently. ✿ In a traditional Chinese bamboo steamer, the droplets of liquid formed from the steaming are absorbed by the bamboo rather than falling onto the ingredients, and the bamboo adds flavor to what is cooked. However, bamboo steamers are very hard to keep clean. I prefer to use a high-quality double stainless steel steamer. On its own, the bottom pot is handy for sauces and soups or for braising and poaching. ✿ To steam, fill the bottom pot only halfway with water — the boiling water should never touch the steamer basket. To ensure that the food will cook quickly and retain its color, don't insert the basket into the steamer until after the water has come to a boil. When opening a steamer lid, keep a safe distance from the pot — the hot steam can easily burn your face and hands.

Chinese Steamed Artichoke Hearts

———————————————(☼)———————————————

Steamed artichoke hearts are more flavorful than boiled ones. But rather than simply steam them over water, I pour an aromatic mixture of cooked shallots and white wine over them; the wine keeps them from discoloring. Then, after they've cooked, I pour their juices into a saucepan and reduce them to a sauce. A dash of walnut oil added at the last minute enhances the naturally nutty flavor of the artichokes.

Serve warm or cold as a side dish or as part of a multicourse buffet.

———————————[*Serves 4 to 6*]———————————

1	tablespoon olive oil
2	shallots, thinly sliced
4	extra-large artichokes, prepared as described on page 239
½	cup dry white wine

Kosher salt and freshly ground pepper
1   tablespoon walnut oil
Fresh chervil sprigs (optional)

Heat the olive oil in a small skillet or saucepan over high heat. Sauté the shallots for 1 to 2 minutes, just until they are soft. Remove from the heat.

Drain the artichokes and place them in a shallow heat-proof bowl. Add the shallots and white wine. Fill the bottom of a steamer with water and bring to a boil. Place the bowl in the steamer basket, cover, and cook for about 5 minutes, just until the artichokes are slightly tender.

Carefully drain the liquid from the artichokes into a small saucepan. Arrange the artichokes on a large plate and sprinkle with salt and pepper to taste.

Cook the liquid over medium heat until it is reduced to approximately 3 tablespoons, about 5 minutes. Remove from the heat and whisk in the walnut oil. Add a pinch of salt and pour over the artichokes. Garnish with the chervil, if desired, and serve.

Stir-Fried Chinese Beans with Fennel and Basil

———————(✤)———————

The stir-frying technique in this recipe is traditional, but the combination of ingredients is not. Long beans are best here because they have more texture than ordinary beans and a sweeter flavor; green beans or haricots verts can be substituted if necessary. The fennel stays crisp, and the lime juice adds a citrusy counterpoint.

———————[*Serves 6*]———————

1	pound Chinese long beans
1	medium fennel bulb
1	cup soybean oil or light olive oil
1	small red bell pepper, cored, seeded, and julienned (about 1 cup)
2	shallots, thinly sliced
2	teaspoons dried shrimp, soaked, drained, and minced as described on page 75 (optional)
1	garlic clove, minced
½	cup chicken stock or Vegetable Stock (page 56)
1	tablespoon fresh lime juice
1	tablespoon soy sauce
1	cup fresh basil leaves, julienned
	Kosher salt and freshly ground pepper

Trim the ends of the beans and cut them into 2-inch lengths.

Cut the fennel bulb in half. Cut out the core and remove and discard any tough outer layers. Halve the bulb again so you have 4 pieces. Cut the sections lengthwise into ¼-inch-thick slices.

Heat the oil in a large skillet or flat-bottomed wok over high heat until it reaches 375 degrees. Add the beans, red pepper, and shallots and stir-fry for about 1 minute, until the beans and pepper are slightly softened. Drain in a colander set over a large bowl.

Return 1 tablespoon of the oil to the pan (you can save the extra oil for another use), add the dried shrimp, if using, and minced garlic and sauté over high heat for 30 seconds. Add the fennel and stock, turn the heat to low, and cook, stirring, for about 5 minutes, or until the fennel is tender.

Add the bean mixture, lime juice, and soy sauce and cook until the vegetables are firm-tender, about 2 minutes. Turn off the heat, mix in the basil, and season to taste with salt and pepper. Serve.

Chinese Long Beans

Take one taste of a Chinese long bean and you'll see why they're beloved. Now grown in this country, they are becoming much more common in Asian markets. They are members of the black-eyed pea family, and their flavor is somewhere between those of an ordinary string bean and an Italian pole bean. But it's their texture that sets them apart: when they're cooked, they become very tender yet also manage to retain some bite, never becoming too soft. They come in two colors, pale green and deep green. I prefer the deep green ones, which are sweeter than the lighter-colored beans. They can grow up to 3 feet long, but the best ones are about 18 inches — any longer and they lose their tenderness and flavor. Fresh long beans will keep in a plastic bag in the refrigerator for up to 5 days.

Sautéed Baby Bok Choy

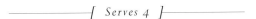

Don't pass this dish by because you think it's too simple: simplicity is the point. Its mild flavor is the ideal foil for more complicated dishes.

If you can't find very small bok choy (2 to 3 inches long), use larger ones. Trim off and discard the ends and any yellow or withered leaves. First cut each head in half lengthwise, then cut the leaves crosswise into 1-inch strips and proceed with the recipe.

[Serves 4]

1 pound baby bok choy, trimmed

2 tablespoons olive oil or corn oil

1 garlic clove, thinly sliced

2 shallots, thinly sliced

1/2 teaspoon kosher salt

1/4 cup chicken stock

Soak the bok choy in a large bowl of cold water for a few minutes to rid it of any dirt that may be trapped between the leaves. Lift out and drain well.

Heat the oil in a large skillet or flat-bottomed wok over high heat. And the garlic and shallots and cook until soft, about 1 minute. Add the bok choy, sprinkle with the salt, and stir-fry for 1 minute. Add the stock, cover, and turn the heat to low. Cook for 3 minutes, or until the bok choy is crisp-tender but still bright green. Using a slotted spoon, transfer the bok choy to a bowl and serve.

Baby Bok Choy

In recent years, several varieties of Chinese bok choy (also called pak choi) have become more readily available in this country. Baby bok choy, also known as Shanghai bok choy, is the most popular. It has a classical sculptured shape, beautiful jade green leaves, and juicy white stems. When buying bok choy, remember that smaller is better, because the heads are tenderer. Choose baby bok choy that are about 3 inches long if possible. If they are not available, then try to buy bok choy less than 7 inches long. They should have no brown spots. Discard any brown or yellow leaves and tough outer stems and cut large bok choy lengthwise in half. Submerge the bok choy in a large bowl or sink filled with ice water. Let sit for about 5 minutes to dislodge any sand hiding between the layers, then lift out of the water, leaving the grit behind, drain well, and pat dry. Stored in a zipper-lock bag in the refrigerator, bok choy will keep for up to a week.

Broccoli Rabe with Sun-Dried Tomatoes

The slightly bitter, mustardlike flavor of tender broccoli rabe is a good foil for the chewy sweetness of sun-dried tomatoes. Blanching the broccoli rabe stems and tops separately in boiling water keeps the tender tops from becoming overcooked. Then the rabe is sautéed briefly with garlic, white wine, and the sun-dried tomatoes to infuse it with flavor.

Serve with meat or fish or alongside sandwiches.

{ Serves 4 }

4	sun-dried tomato halves		2	garlic cloves, thinly sliced
1	bunch broccoli rabe		⅓	cup dry white wine
3	tablespoons olive oil			Kosher salt
1	shallot, minced			

Soak the sun-dried tomatoes in a small bowl of warm water until soft, about 10 minutes.

Meanwhile, strip off any large tough leaves from the broccoli rabe and discard. Cut off the tops and reserve. Peel the stems and cut into 2-inch lengths.

Cook the broccoli rabe tops in a large pot of boiling water for 1 minute. Remove with a slotted spoon and plunge into a large bowl of ice water to cool. Remove and drain. Add the stems to the boiling water and cook for 1 minute. Drain and plunge into the ice water, then drain again.

Drain the sun-dried tomatoes well and cut each tomato half into thin strips.

Heat the oil in a large skillet or flat-bottomed wok over high heat. Add the shallot and garlic and cook, stirring, for 1 minute. Add the broccoli rabe stems, sun-dried tomatoes, and white wine, turn the heat to low, and cook, stirring, for 2 minutes, or until the tomatoes are soft. Add the rabe tops and cook, stirring, until crisp-tender, about 2 to 3 minutes. Season to taste with salt and serve.

Brussels Sprouts and Portobello Mushrooms

(↻)

They may sound like an unlikely combination, but these two vegetables are made for each other. The meatiness of the portobellos complements the slight bitterness of the Brussels sprouts.

——————[*Serves 4*]——————

2	large portobello mushrooms
10	ounces Brussels sprouts (10–15)
3	tablespoons extra-virgin olive oil
2	garlic cloves, minced
1	small red onion, thinly sliced

¼	cup chicken stock, Vegetable Stock (page 56), or water
1	tablespoon soy sauce
1	teaspoon sherry wine vinegar or balsamic vinegar
	Kosher salt and freshly ground pepper

Remove the stems of the portobello mushrooms and save for another use, such as Mushroom Stock (page 56). With a teaspoon, scrape out the black gills from the underside of the caps and discard. (This will prevent the finished dish from turning an inky color.) Slice each mushroom cap crosswise into 3 pieces, then cut each piece into slivers about ⅛ inch thick.

Trim away the bottoms and tough outer leaves from the Brussels sprouts. Slice each sprout crosswise into 3 or 4 pieces (depending on size). Wash in cold water and drain.

Heat the oil in a large nonstick skillet over medium-high heat. Add the garlic and red onion and cook until soft, about 1 minute. Add the portobello slices and Brussels sprouts and stir until all the vegetables are coated with the oil. Add the stock or water, soy sauce, and vinegar and cook until the Brussels sprouts are softened, 2 to 3 minutes. Remove from the heat, season to taste with salt and pepper, and serve.

Portobello Mushrooms

Portobellos (or portabellas) are the largest of all cultivated mushrooms, with flat caps that can measure up to 6 inches in diameter. They are actually mature creminis, with a deeper flavor because of their longer growing period. They are a great substitute for meat, for when grilled, they taste a lot like steak. ✿ Unlike button mushrooms, which are usually best with the caps closed, portobello caps are wide open, with the gills clearly visible. Choose mushrooms with firm caps and dry, brownish gills. If the gills are very black and moist, the mushrooms are too old and will be too soft. The gills can discolor the other ingredients or sauces, so I scrape them out with a spoon after removing the stems. Wipe the outside of the caps with damp paper towels to clean; do not wash the mushrooms. ✿ Portobellos are sold in most supermarkets, either loose (with stems attached) or prepackaged whole or sliced caps. A pound of portobellos equals 3 to 4 medium-sized portobellos with their stems. ✿ Uncooked mushrooms don't freeze well, but cooked portobellos can be frozen for several months. Place in freezer containers or bags, pressing out as much air as possible.

Stir-Fried Brussels Sprouts, Chestnuts, and Chinese Sausage

(✿)

Crisp sprouts, smoky sausage, soft chestnuts: this is a recipe that I like to prepare in the fall, especially at Thanksgiving or during the Christmas holidays, and serve as a side dish with roasted duck, grilled venison, or pork.

[Serves 6 to 8]

8	ounces large Brussels sprouts
2	tablespoons soybean oil or olive oil
2	garlic cloves, thinly sliced
1	tablespoon grated peeled fresh ginger
2	Chinese sausage links, cut into 1/8-inch-thick rounds

1/4	cup dry white wine
	Braised Chestnuts (page 214) or 6 ounces drained canned or jarred chestnuts
2	tablespoons soy sauce

Trim the stem of each Brussels sprout and discard the tough outer leaves. Cut each sprout lengthwise into quarters. Wash in cold water; drain well.

Heat the oil in a large skillet or flat-bottomed wok over medium heat. Add the garlic and ginger and cook until fragrant, about 30 seconds. Add the sausage and cook until it turns color, about 1 minute.

Add the Brussels sprouts and white wine and cook, stirring, until the wine has evaporated and the sprouts are slightly softened, about 2 minutes. Add the chestnuts (along with any braising liquid) and cook, stirring, for 2 minutes, or until hot. Stir in the soy sauce and serve.

Chinese Sausages

Chinese sausages are quite different from the Western kind. Made from diced pork and pork fat, they are marinated in a mixture of spices, then air-dried in a cool, sunny place. The linked sausages are thin and hard, about 6 inches long, and well marbled, with a good flavor. In this country, most Chinese sausages are made by people from Canton who like to add sugar to them; consequently, they have a slight sweetness. ✿ Chinese sausages must be cooked before they are eaten. Steam them whole, then slice and serve, or slice them and sauté or cook along with rice. One pound generally equals 5 to 6 links. Stored in the refrigerator in a sealed bag, they will keep for a month. Or freeze for up to 3 months.

Sautéed Baby Carrots and Sugar Snap Peas

──────────────────(✿)──────────────────

For this dish, you really need the young carrots sold in bunches with the top leaves still attached, 3 to 6 inches in length. They're expensive compared with bagged carrots, but they're worth it. Prepackaged peeled "baby" carrots can pick up an off flavor from the plastic bags in which they are stored, and they don't have the natural fresh taste of real baby carrots. (They are actually not baby carrots at all but mature ones that have been trimmed to a uniform size by a machine.)

If you can't get the real thing, substitute ½ pound packaged baby carrots and doctor the flavor as follows: Cut them in half lengthwise. Fill a medium saucepan with water, bring to a boil, add ¼ cup sugar, and stir to dissolve. Add the carrots and boil for 4 minutes; drain well and proceed with the recipe.

─────────[*Serves 4*]─────────

½	bunch fresh baby carrots (about 10; see above)
8	ounces sugar snap peas
2	tablespoons olive oil

2	shallots, minced
¼	cup chicken stock or Vegetable Stock (page 56)
	Kosher salt and freshly ground pepper

Cut the tops and tips off the carrots, peel them, and cut each one lengthwise in half. Remove the strings from the sugar snap peas. Wash both vegetables in cold water and drain well.

Heat the oil in a medium skillet or flat-bottomed wok over high heat. Add the shallots, carrots, and sugar snap peas and cook, stirring, for 1 minute. Add the stock, turn the heat to low, and cook for 3 to 5 minutes, or until the vegetables are tender. Season to taste with salt and pepper and serve.

Spicy Cauliflower Curry

———————————— (✸) ————————————

The inspiration for this dish came from a spicy Indian version. I add zip by using lots of jalapeño peppers and fresh coriander seeds from plants that I grow in my garden every summer. The seeds taste nothing like cilantro (coriander) leaves but have a mild, almost orangelike flavor and aroma. Dried ground coriander can be substituted.

———————[*Serves 4 to 6*]———————

1	large head cauliflower
3	tablespoons olive oil
1	tablespoon grated peeled fresh ginger
3	jalapeño peppers, stemmed, seeded, and chopped
1	tablespoon fresh coriander seeds (see above)
	or 1 teaspoon ground coriander

1	teaspoon sugar
½	teaspoon garam masala
	Juice of 1 lemon
2	tablespoons finely chopped fresh cilantro

Trim the cauliflower and cut into 1-inch florets. (Save the tough bottom parts for stir-fries or for making soup.) Soak the cauliflower in a large bowl of cold water to crisp for 1 hour. Drain well.

Heat the oil in a medium saucepan over high heat. Add the ginger and jalapeños and cook, stirring, for 1 minute. Add the cauliflower, turn the heat to low, cover with a tight-fitting lid, and cook for 6 to 7 minutes, stirring occasionally. Add a tablespoon or two of water, if needed, to keep the vegetables from sticking.

Stir in the coriander, sugar, garam masala, and lemon juice, cover, and continue to simmer until the cauliflower is tender, 2 to 3 minutes. Sprinkle with the cilantro and serve.

Garam Masala

Garam masala is a blend of aromatic and hot spices traditionally used in Indian cooking. *Garam* means hot or warm, and *masala* means a spice mixture. It usually contains cinnamon, cumin, nutmeg, black pepper, coriander, cardamom, and/or cloves. The spices are first roasted, then ground. Garam masala blends are available in ethnic markets and some grocery stores; try out a few, then select the one you like the best. ✸ Sprinkle garam masala over cooked vegetables or add to curries or anything that needs a touch of warmth. Because the blend is so delicate, add it during the last few minutes of cooking or just before serving, or its flavor will dissipate.

Chinese Corn Cakes with Cilantro and Chives

I make these corn cakes when white corn is in season and serve them for breakfast, at lunch along with a salad, or at dinner with grilled meat, poultry, or fish. I make up a lot at one time and keep them in the freezer.

[Makes about 24 pancakes; serves 4 to 6]

1	cup all-purpose flour, or more as needed		1	large egg
1	teaspoon baking powder		1	tablespoon butter, melted and cooled
2	teaspoons sugar		¼	cup finely chopped fresh cilantro or flat-leaf parsley
½	teaspoon kosher salt		¼	cup chopped fresh chives
2½	cups fresh white corn (3 ears)		¼	cup corn oil, or more as needed
¼	cup milk, or more as needed			

Mix together the flour, baking powder, sugar, and salt in a medium bowl.

Place ½ cup of the corn in a food processor or blender, add the milk, egg, and melted butter, and puree. Add the dry ingredients and pulse just until blended. The batter should be the consistency of pancake batter. If it's too thick, mix in a little extra milk. If it is too thin, add a spoon or so more flour and pulse to blend.

Pour the batter into a medium bowl. Mix in the remaining 2 cups corn, the cilantro or parsley, and chives.

Preheat the oven to 325 degrees. Heat half the oil in a large nonstick skillet over medium heat. Drop rounded tablespoons of the batter into the hot oil, being careful not to overcrowd the pan. Cook until bubbles begin to appear on the tops and the cakes are lightly browned on the bottoms, about 2 minutes. Turn and continue to cook until browned on the second side, another 2 minutes. Place on a baking sheet and keep warm in the oven. Add the remaining oil and repeat until all the batter is used, using more oil if needed.

TO FREEZE THE CORN CAKES: Cool and spread them out on a flat tray or baking sheet lined with plastic wrap, cover loosely with plastic wrap, and freeze for 1 hour. Transfer to a heavy-duty zipper-lock bag, seal the bag, pressing out any excess air, and return to the freezer. To reheat, place the frozen cakes on a baking sheet and bake in a preheated 350-degree oven until hot, 10 to 15 minutes.

Broiled Chinese Eggplant

The soft, creamy eggplant contrasts with crunchy panko bread crumbs seasoned with fresh thyme and cilantro stems. This dish makes a convenient hors d'oeuvre or appetizer course, since you can prepare it ahead of time and heat it under the broiler just before serving.

Serves 4 as a side dish or a first course or 8 to 10 as an hors d'oeuvre

1	pound Chinese eggplant (see page 84)		2	tablespoons minced fresh thyme
3	tablespoons olive oil		1	tablespoon minced fresh cilantro stems
2	shallots, minced		¼	cup panko (Japanese bread crumbs; see page 28)
1	garlic clove, minced			Kosher salt and freshly ground pepper
1	tablespoon soy sauce		¼	cup soybean oil or corn oil

Remove the stems from the eggplant and cut off the bottom tips. Cut each eggplant crosswise into approximately 1-inch sections (about 5 pieces per eggplant). Soak the eggplant in a large bowl of cold salted water for about 20 minutes (you may have to put a plate on top of the eggplant to keep the pieces submerged). (Soaking the eggplant will prevent it from turning brown.)

Transfer the eggplant to paper towels to drain for about 10 minutes to remove most of the water.

Heat 2 tablespoons of the olive oil in a small saucepan over medium heat. Add the shallots and garlic and cook until soft, about 2 minutes. Add the soy sauce, then stir in the minced thyme, cilantro stems, and panko. Season to taste with salt and pepper. Remove from the heat.

Heat the soybean or corn oil in a large nonstick skillet over medium-high heat. Add the eggplant and cook, turning once, until lightly golden on both sides, about 3 minutes per side. Remove from the pan and drain on paper towels.

Preheat the broiler. Arrange the eggplant pieces on a nonstick baking sheet. Top with the herb mixture and drizzle with the remaining tablespoon of olive oil. *The dish can be prepared to this point up to 1 day ahead, covered loosely, and refrigerated. Remove from the refrigerator 1 hour before cooking.*

Broil the eggplant about 4 inches from the heat source for 3 to 5 minutes, until golden brown. Serve.

Braised Endive

—— (✿) ——

Braising Belgian endive makes it tender and mild. Served hot or at room temperature, it's an agreeable partner for dishes such as Pan-Seared Black Sea Bass with Caramelized Red Pepper Sauce (page 111), Salmon Braised with Soy and Ginger (page 98), or Panfried Skate with Orange Pernod Sauce (page 116).

——[*Serves 4*]——

4	Belgian endives		2	tablespoons sugar
4	tablespoons (½ stick) butter		1	tablespoon fresh lemon juice
	Kosher salt and freshly ground white pepper		½	cup chicken stock

Remove any wilted outer leaves from the endives. Slice lengthwise into quarters, then cut out and discard the small white core from each piece.

Melt the butter in a medium skillet over medium heat. Add the endives, season with salt and pepper to taste, and sprinkle with the sugar. Cook for 2 to 3 minutes, turning occasionally, just until the endives are glazed and very lightly browned.

Add the lemon juice and chicken stock. Bring to a boil, reduce the heat to low, and simmer until the endives are tender, about 5 minutes. Remove from the heat and serve.

Belgian Endive

Select Belgian endives that are small and compact, with leaf tips that are light yellow, not brown or green. Markets often store endives in boxes covered with tissue paper so they will retain their white color. When endive turns green, it becomes unpleasantly bitter.

Steamed Fennel

───────── (✿) ─────────

Steaming best captures fennel's flavor. I season it with garlic and hot red peppers to perk it up. Serve with Pan-Seared Black Sea Bass with Caramelized Red Pepper Sauce (page 111), Braised Red Snapper with Thai Curry Sauce (page 112), Salmon Braised with Soy and Ginger (page 98), or Pan-Seared Chicken Breasts with Morel Sauce (page 140).

──────── [*Serves 4*] ────────

2	fennel bulbs
2	tablespoons olive oil
1	garlic clove, thinly sliced
2	fresh hot red peppers, stemmed and thinly sliced
1	scallion, trimmed and cut into 1-inch lengths
½	teaspoon kosher salt
	Freshly ground pepper

Remove the tops from the fennel bulbs; save some of the feathery leaves for garnish. Trim the base of each bulb and remove and discard any tough outer layers. Halve the bulbs lengthwise, then slice in half again, and slice those pieces in half so you have 8 wedges per bulb. Place in a large bowl of ice water to crisp for about 10 minutes. Drain well.

Place the fennel in a shallow heatproof bowl that will fit in your steamer basket. Fill the bottom of the steamer with water and bring to a boil. Place the bowl of fennel in the steamer basket, cover, and steam for about 5 minutes, or until the fennel is tender. Arrange the fennel on a large serving plate and cover to keep warm. Drain the juices into a small bowl.

Heat the oil in a medium saucepan over high heat. Add the garlic and red peppers and cook until soft, about 1 minute. Add the reserved fennel juices, turn the heat to low and simmer for 2 minutes. Add the scallion, salt, and pepper to taste. Pour the sauce over the fennel, garnish with the reserved fennel leaves, and serve.

Baked Napa Cabbage Gratin

Although using cream and cheese shows a strong Western influence, this recipe has long been a very popular dish in Taiwan. Serve with Quick-Seared Sichuan Beef Tenderloin Stew (page 178), Braised Pork Belly (page 172), or Smoked Duck Breasts (page 160).

[Serves 8]

1	medium head napa cabbage (about 2 pounds)
3	tablespoons unsalted butter
¼	cup thinly sliced white onion
1	teaspoon kosher salt
½	cup heavy cream
½	cup chicken broth
⅓	cup freshly grated Parmesan cheese
⅓	cup grated mozzarella
1⅓	cups panko (Japanese bread crumbs; see page 28)

Discard the tough outer leaves of the napa cabbage, then remove any green leaves and trim the tips so that only the creamy white leaves remain. Shave any brown part off the root end but leave it intact. Cut the head lengthwise into quarters, then cut each piece lengthwise in half, for 8 pieces.

Add the butter and onion to a large heavy skillet that has a tight-fitting lid. Cook over medium heat, stirring, just until the butter melts, then add the salt, cream, and chicken broth. Add the cabbage, cut side down, in 2 layers. Cover the cabbage with a piece of buttered waxed or parchment paper, then with the lid. Bring the liquid to a boil, then turn the heat to low, and simmer until the cabbage is very tender, about 10 minutes.

Preheat the broiler until very hot. Butter a gratin dish just large enough to hold the cabbage in a single layer. Using a slotted spoon, transfer the cooked cabbage, cut side down, and onion to the gratin dish.

Mix the grated cheeses with the panko in a small bowl and sprinkle evenly over the cabbage. Broil 4 inches from the heating element for about 3 minutes, or until the topping is golden and the cheese melts. Serve hot.

French-Fried Parsnips

———————————— (✦) ————————————

In late fall and early winter, after the first frost has given them additional sweetness, parsnips are at their peak. Crisply fried, they are a good garnish for Korean-Style Grilled Sirloin in Pear Jalapeño Marinade (page 180) or any other grilled meat, fish, or poultry. Thet are even good with hamburgers instead of the usual fries.

——————————— [*Serves 4*] ———————————

3   medium parsnips (about 8 ounces)
    Soybean oil or corn oil for deep-frying
    Kosher salt

Cut off the tops and bottom tips of the parsnips. Peel with a sharp vegetable peeler; rinse and dry well. With the peeler, slice the parsnips lengthwise into long thin strips.

Add about 6 inches of oil to a deep pot and heat to 350 degrees. Deep-fry the parsnip strips in 2 or 3 batches, depending on the size of your pot, stirring frequently to sep-arate them, for about 2 minutes, or until they are golden and crisp. Be careful not to overcook, as they brown very quickly.

Using a slotted spoon, lift out the parsnips and place on a plate lined with paper towels to drain. Sprinkle with salt and serve immediately.

Parsnips

Small to medium parsnips are the tenderest. They should be firm, not limp or shriveled, with no brown spots. Large parsnips are often sweeter, but their center cores are very tough and stringy. If you buy large ones, remove the inner cores.

Sugar Snap Peas with Shiitake Mushrooms

(❀)

Here's a perfect example of contrast: crisp sugar snap peas and soft, meaty mushrooms. I prefer shiitakes here, but you can substitute creminis or even wild mushrooms.

[*Serves 6*]

1   pound sugar snap peas

8   ounces shiitake mushrooms

2   tablespoons soy sauce

1   teaspoon sherry wine vinegar or rice wine vinegar

1   tablespoon chicken stock, Vegetable Stock (page 56), or water

3   tablespoons extra-virgin olive oil

2   garlic cloves, thinly sliced

2   shallots, thinly sliced

2   tablespoons chopped fresh flat-leaf parsley
    Freshly ground pepper

Sugar Snap Peas

Snow peas have long been associated with Chinese cooking, but it has become increasingly hard to find small, tender snow peas in this country. However, sugar snaps — a cross between an English pea and a snow pea — are readily available. ❀ Buying good sugar snap peas is just as important as cooking them properly. Choose pods that are almost flat, with small peas inside; they're the tenderest. If you can, buy them with the tips still intact, as they are usually fresher, and string them yourself. ❀ I always taste a sugar snap pea before buying — it should be crisp, sweet, and tender. Avoid peas that have turned light green or that are very plump, with large peas inside.

Remove and discard the strings from the sugar snap peas. Remove the stems from the shiitake mushrooms and slice the caps into ¼-inch-wide strips.

Cook the peas in a medium saucepan of boiling water for 2 minutes, or until tender. Drain and plunge into a large bowl of ice water to stop the cooking. Drain again.

Mix the soy sauce, vinegar, and stock or water in a small bowl.

Heat the olive oil in a medium skillet or flat-bottomed wok over high heat. Add the garlic and shallots and cook for about 1 minute, until soft. Add the mushrooms and cook, stirring, for about 1 minute. Add the peas, stir, and cook for 1 minute, then pour in the soy sauce mixture and cook until all the liquid is absorbed, about 2 minutes. Turn off the heat, add the chopped parsley and pepper to taste, and serve.

Shiitake Mushrooms

Cooked shiitake mushrooms have a soft, slippery texture and a distinctive woody aroma. There are several varieties. To the Japanese, the most prized type is the *donko;* the Chinese call them flower mushrooms. These wild mushrooms have small, thick, dense dark brown caps with a pattern of whitish lines on the top. Nowadays, however, most shiitake mushrooms are cultivated; wild ones are a rarity.  Cultivated shiitakes are grown in many states today. They are usually 4 to 6 inches in diameter, and their texture is very different from that of the wild ones. Cultivated mushrooms generally have much thinner caps, and even when thick, they are usually puffy and soft, not at all like the meaty wild ones I knew as a child. Fresh shiitakes should have large, thick, plump caps with edges that curl under, without any bruises or signs of dryness on the edges.

Fingerling Potato and Green Bean Curry

———(✿)———

When I lived in Indiana, in the late 1970s, I organized an International Women's Club and we took turns cooking for each other in our homes. A friend from India often made a spicy curry with potatoes and green beans; I created this recipe from my memory of her dish.

Tiny baby fingerlings are particularly good for this recipe; if you can find them, use them whole. Fingerlings come in several varieties, and the skins may be brown, yellow, or even purple. They don't need to be peeled; just give them a good scrubbing. Serve this as a main course for lunch with rice or bread or as a side dish for dinner alongside grilled fish, chicken, or meat.

———[*Serves 4 to 6*]———

- 1 teaspoon cumin seeds
- 1 tablespoon coriander seeds
- 4 ounces haricots verts or thin green beans, cut into 1-inch lengths
- 2 tablespoons olive oil or corn oil
- 1 small onion, diced (about 1 cup)
- 1 tablespoon minced garlic
- 1 teaspoon minced peeled fresh ginger
- 2 jalapeño peppers, stemmed, halved, and thinly sliced

- ½ teaspoon ground turmeric
- 2 medium tomatoes, peeled (see page 123) and diced
- 1 pound fingerling potatoes, scrubbed and cut into 1-inch pieces
- 4 ounces fresh or frozen peas (½ cup)
- ½ teaspoon sugar
- 1 teaspoon kosher salt
- 2 tablespoons chopped fresh cilantro

Place the cumin and coriander seeds in a small dry skillet and toast over medium heat, shaking the pan, until the spices give off a pungent aroma, 1 to 2 minutes. Remove from the heat and cool.

Transfer the seeds to a spice grinder or coffee mill and grind to a fine powder.

Cook the green beans in a medium saucepan of salted boiling water for 2 minutes; the beans will still be firm. Drain and plunge into a bowl of ice water to stop the cooking. Drain again.

Heat the oil in a large skillet or flat-bottomed wok over medium heat. Add the onion, garlic, ginger, and jalapeños and cook for 1 to 2 minutes, until softened. Add the ground spices and the turmeric and cook for 3 minutes, stirring often, until fragrant. Stir in the onion and cook for 1 minute, or until softened, then add the tomatoes and cook for 3 minutes.

Add the potatoes, fresh peas (if using frozen peas, add during the last 5 minutes of cooking), green beans, sugar, salt, and ¼ cup water. Cover and cook until the potatoes are tender, stirring occasionally; add additional water if needed to keep the vegetables from sticking.

Mix in the cilantro, remove from the heat, and serve.

Steamed Curried Potatoes

Steaming brings out the natural sweetness of potatoes and helps retain their moisture. I prefer the buttery flavor of Yukon Gold potatoes here, but you can substitute Idahos. This dish is quite spicy — remove the seeds and veins from the jalapeños if you would prefer a milder version.

Brown mustard seeds can be found in specialty food stores and ethnic and Asian supermarkets.

[Serves 4]

1	pound Yukon Gold potatoes
2	tablespoons soybean oil or corn oil
1	small onion, finely chopped
1	teaspoon brown mustard seeds (see above)
1	teaspoon ground turmeric
1	jalapeño pepper, stemmed and minced
1	teaspoon kosher salt

Peel the potatoes and cut into approximately ½-inch cubes. Rinse under cold running water to remove some of the starch, and drain. (This will help prevent the potatoes from turning brown.)

Fill the bottom of a steamer with water and bring to a boil over high heat. Place the potatoes on the steamer rack, place in the steamer, cover, and steam just until they are tender, about 10 minutes. Transfer to a serving bowl.

Meanwhile, heat the oil in a small saucepan over medium heat. Add the onion and mustard seeds and cook until the onion is very soft, about 3 minutes. Add the turmeric and jalapeño pepper, mixing well, turn the heat to low, and simmer for 3 minutes. Stir in the salt.

Pour the onion mixture over the steamed potatoes, mix well, and serve.

Herbed Mashed Potatoes

Basil gives these potatoes a fresh herbal taste. Add it at the last minute so it keeps its bright color. You can substitute light cream or half-and-half for the heavy cream, if desired.

[Serves 6]

1½	pounds Yukon Gold potatoes, peeled and cut into chunks
⅓	cup heavy cream
2	tablespoons butter
½	teaspoon kosher salt, or more to taste
¼	teaspoon freshly ground white pepper, or more to taste
3	tablespoons basil puree (see page 41)

Cook the potatoes in a medium pot of boiling salted water until soft, about 15 minutes. Drain well and, while they are still hot, mash the potatoes with a potato ricer or masher. (Do not use a food processor.) Place the mashed potatoes in a medium bowl.

Microwave the cream and butter in a small glass bowl on high power just until the cream is hot and the butter is melted; do not boil. Or heat in a small saucepan over medium heat.

Add the hot cream, along with the remaining ingredients, to the potatoes and mix well. Taste to correct the seasonings, and serve immediately. *The potatoes can be made up to 6 hours ahead of time without the basil puree and set aside at room temperature, covered. Reheat in a microwave oven or a 325-degree oven just until warmed, then stir in the basil puree.*

Butternut Squash Goo Lai

Soft, sweet, and bursting with flavor, this is a family favorite. No one else I knew in China served this dish, but we ate it at least once a week while I was growing up. My grandmother made it with pumpkin, but since fresh pumpkin is not always available, I make it with butternut squash.

The shredded squash is coated with flour and steamed. The coating helps it retain its juiciness and changes the texture so it's almost reminiscent of pasta. Then the strands are separated and cooked in a little chicken stock with chives, scallions, and a scrambled egg. Serve as you would a pasta side dish, with roasted or grilled chicken or lamb chops, or with a salad.

[Serves 6]

1½	pounds butternut squash or pumpkin, peeled and coarsely grated
	Kosher salt
2	tablespoons all-purpose flour
2	tablespoons olive oil
2	shallots, thinly sliced

2	garlic cloves, minced
1	large egg, lightly beaten
2	scallions, thinly sliced
½	cup sliced (1-inch lengths) fresh chives
	Freshly ground pepper

Place the squash or pumpkin in a large strainer and rinse under cold water. Drain well, then sprinkle with 1 teaspoon salt, mix well, and let stand in the strainer, set over a bowl, for 20 minutes.

Using your hands, squeeze as much liquid from the squash as possible, and place it in a large bowl. Sprinkle the flour over the squash and mix well to coat evenly. Place the squash in a steamer rack, spreading it out to cover the entire area. (If the holes on your steamer rack are large, line it with a piece of cheesecloth to keep the squash from falling through.)

Fill the bottom of the steamer with water and bring to a boil. Add the squash, cover, and steam until tender but not mushy, about 3 to 4 minutes (begin to check for doneness after 2 minutes). Transfer the squash to a large bowl or baking sheet and use a fork to lift and separate the strands as they cool.

Heat the oil in a large nonstick skillet over medium heat. Add the shallots and garlic and cook until softened, about 2 minutes. Add the egg and cook, stirring with a fork, until the egg is set, using the fork to break it into small pieces. Add the scallions and stir for 1 minute. Add the squash, spreading it out evenly, cover, and cook until the squash is heated through, 2 to 3 minutes.

Remove from the heat and stir in the chives. Season to taste with salt and pepper and serve.

SIMPLE VARIATION

Red Bliss or Yukon Gold potatoes can be used instead of the squash.

Mashed Taro Root

Mashed taro root is richer and more flavorful than mashed potatoes, but on its own, it is heavy-tasting. Combining it with pureed mashed potatoes lightens it, bringing out the best in both vegetables.

[Serves 6 to 8]

2	tablespoons olive oil
½	cup finely chopped shallots
1	teaspoon kosher salt
½	teaspoon freshly ground white pepper

1	pound large taro root, peeled and cut into 1-inch-thick slices
1	pound Idaho (russet) potatoes, peeled and quartered
2	tablespoons butter, melted
½	cup heavy cream

Heat the oil in a medium saucepan over high heat. Add the shallots and cook, stirring, for 1 to 2 minutes, or until soft. Remove from the heat and season with the salt and pepper.

Fill the bottom of a steamer with water and bring to a boil. Place the taro root on the steamer rack, cover, and steam until just soft, approximately 15 minutes; do not overcook.

While the taro is steaming, cook the potatoes in a medium saucepan of boiling water until soft, about 15 minutes. Drain the potatoes well and mash while they are still hot, using a potato ricer or masher; do not use a food processor.

Place the mashed potatoes in a large bowl, add the butter and heavy cream, and mix well. Place the steamed taro root in a medium bowl and gently crush with a fork or spoon. Be careful not to overwork the taro; it should still have some lumps (if overworked, it becomes gluey and heavy). Add the shallot mixture to the taro and gently fold it in, incorporating well. Gently fold the taro mixture into the mashed potato mixture and serve.

SIMPLE VARIATION

Taro Pancakes

I often double this recipe so I have leftovers for pancakes. To make taro pancakes, cool the mashed taro-and-potato mixture and divide it in half. Place each half on a large piece of plastic wrap and form into a log about 2 inches wide. Wrap tightly and refrigerate until very cold. Cut into slices about 1 inch thick and sauté in a little olive oil or butter until hot and crisp.

Taro Root

Taro is a versatile root vegetable with a taste somewhere between those of a white potato, a sweet potato, and a chestnut. Its firm-textured flesh runs from creamy beige to pinkish violet, and it has a thin brown skin covered with shaggy hair. It is popular in southern China and throughout Southeast Asia as well as in Latin America, and it is sold under the name *malanga* in many supermarkets and Hispanic grocery stores. ❧ Coco malanga, the larger taro that I prefer, weighing from 1 to 3 pounds, has ivory flesh with reddish tints. Choose taro roots that have a uniformly brown skin with no scaly white spots. ❧ When julienned and fried, taro retains its crispness longer than a white potato. It can be sliced and stir-fried with other vegetables and meats, used as stuffing, or made into pancakes. It adds body and flavor to soups. Like other root vegetables, taro is great with braised meats or game. ❧ Because of its high starch content, the surface of taro root becomes slippery and sticky once it is peeled, so avoid washing peeled taro in water, which would make it too sticky. Never puree cooked taro in a food processor, or it will become gluey and heavy.

Chinese-Style Ratatouille

───── (✿) ─────

This dish was inspired by a ratatouille I first tasted in Nice. I prefer to stir-fry the eggplants separately and the other vegetables in stages to preserve their individual flavors and textures. Soy sauce, scallions, and cilantro in addition to the usual basil give it a Chinese twist. The tomatoes are added at the last minute so they remain firm and retain their freshness.

─────[*Serves 12*]─────

1¼   pounds Chinese eggplants (about 4 large; see page 84)
     Kosher salt
1   pound plum tomatoes, peeled (see page 123) and cored
1   cup extra-virgin olive oil
1   large or 2 small onions, quartered and thinly sliced crosswise
6   large garlic cloves, thinly sliced
4   jalapeño peppers, stemmed and thinly sliced
1   large red bell pepper, cored, seeds and veins removed, and cut into 1-inch pieces

1½   pounds small zucchini, trimmed, cut lengthwise in half, then sliced crosswise into ¼-inch-thick slices
     Freshly ground pepper
1   tablespoon sugar
1   tablespoon soy sauce
1   tablespoon red wine vinegar or sherry wine vinegar
1   bunch scallions, trimmed and cut into 1-inch pieces
½   cup fresh cilantro leaves, chopped
15   fresh basil leaves, julienned

Cut each eggplant lengthwise in half and then into ½-inch-thick slices. Soak the eggplant in a large bowl of salted water (1 tablespoon salt mixed with 4 cups water) for about 10 minutes. Drain the eggplant in a colander and dry on paper towels.

Meanwhile, cut each tomato crosswise in half, then cut into ½-inch-thick slices. Place in a bowl.

Heat ½ cup of the oil in a large skillet or flat-bottomed wok over high heat until hot. Add the eggplant, turn the heat to medium, and cook, stirring, until it is soft, 8 to 10 minutes. Using a slotted spoon, transfer the eggplant to a bowl.

Add the remaining ½ cup oil to the pan, then add the onion, garlic, jalapeños, and red pepper and cook over medium heat, stirring occasionally, until soft, 5 to 7 minutes.

Add the zucchini, sprinkle with 1 teaspoon salt, and cook for about 2 minutes, or until tender but not soft. Add pepper to taste. Return the eggplant to the pan, add the sugar, soy sauce, and vinegar, and mix well. Cook for about 2 minutes longer, until all the vegetables are tender and cooked through, stirring gently so as not to break them apart.

Add the tomatoes and scallions and cook for another minute; the tomatoes should retain their shape and not be too soft. Taste and correct the seasonings, adding more salt and pepper if necessary. Remove from the heat and stir in the cilantro and basil.

Spoon the ratatouille out onto a large platter and serve warm or at room temperature. *It will keep for a week, covered and refrigerated.*

Oven-Roasted Root Vegetables

A distinctive combination of root vegetables, this dish plays the mild flavor of celery root against caramelized sweet potato and carrots. However, almost any root vegetable will work well: turnips, butternut or kabocha squash, white potatoes, or beets. You'll need about 4 cups diced vegetables (preferably 1 cup each of four different kinds), but it doesn't matter if you use a little more or less. Plain olive oil can be substituted for the scallion oil.

Serves 4

1 small to medium celery root	1 medium sweet potato
2 medium parsnips	¼ cup Aromatic Scallion Oil (page 86)
1 large or 2 small carrots	Kosher salt and freshly ground pepper

Preheat the oven to 425 degrees. Peel the celery root, cut it into ½-inch dice, and place in a small bowl of cold water to keep it from turning brown.

Peel the parsnips, cut into ½-inch dice, and place in a large bowl. Peel the carrots and sweet potato, cut them into ½-inch dice, and add them to the parsnips.

Drain the celery root well, dry on paper towels, and mix with the other vegetables. Add the oil, season with salt and pepper, and toss well to coat.

Pour the vegetables, along with any extra oil, onto a large rimmed baking sheet and spread out evenly. Roast until the vegetables are tender and lightly browned, about 30 minutes; shake the pan and turn the vegetables every 10 minutes to prevent them from sticking. Serve hot.

Quick Sautéed Zucchini

———— (✿) ————

Most zucchini dishes are too soft for my taste. Stir-frying zucchini briefly keeps it much more flavorful, and it holds its shape. Here it gets an extra dimension from dried shrimp, but you can skip them if you like. This dish is equally good hot or cold. It will keep well overnight and can be served the next day.

———— [*Serves 6*] ————

1	pound young (4- to 6-inch-long) zucchini
2	large or 3 small scallions
2	tablespoons extra-virgin olive oil
2	garlic cloves, thinly sliced
2	tablespoons minced dried shrimp, prepared as described on page 75 (optional)

½	cup Vegetable Stock (page 56) or chicken stock
½	cup grape tomatoes, peeled (see page 123) and halved
2	tablespoons chopped fresh cilantro
	Kosher salt and freshly ground pepper

Trim the ends of each zucchini, cut it lengthwise in half, and then cut crosswise into ⅛-inch-thick slices. Trim the scallions; if they are large, cut them lengthwise in half. Cut the scallions into ½-inch lengths.

Heat the oil in a large skillet or flat-bottomed wok over high heat. Add the garlic and dried shrimp, if using, and stir-fry for about 30 seconds. Add the scallions and zucchini and cook, stirring, for 1 minute.

Add the stock and bring to a boil, then add the tomatoes and cilantro and cook until just heated through; the zucchini should remain firm. Remove from the heat, season to taste with salt and pepper, and serve. *The zucchini can be prepared 1 day ahead and refrigerated, covered. Serve cold or at room temperature.*

Condiments and Relishes

Pickled Baby Beets with Green Peppercorns

I got my first taste of beets in a dining hall at the University of Pittsburgh. The dark red slices were all the same size and cloyingly sweet. Later I found out that they were canned, cooked and processed with lots of sugar. What a difference from the fresh beets — golden, striped, and red — that I tasted many years later in California! They were firm, with a natural sweetness.

Most cooks wrap beets in foil and roast them in the oven. Steaming them with the skins on allows you to monitor the texture and degree of done-ness by inserting a knife into them. I prefer beets at the point when they are just cooked through but not too soft.

Baby beets have more flavor and are tenderer than the larger ones. They are usually available from spring until fall.

Serve with Poached Striped Bass with Balsamic Vinegar Sauce (page 108), Roast Chicken with Peppercorn Rub (page 135), or sandwiches.

[Serves 4]

- 1   pound small red, golden, or striped beets, trimmed and washed
- 1   tablespoon extra-virgin olive oil
- 1   teaspoon grated lime zest

- ¼   cup fresh lime juice, strained (about 2 limes)
- 2   tablespoons sugar
- ¼   teaspoon kosher salt
- 1   teaspoon green peppercorns

Fill the bottom of a steamer with water and bring to a boil over high heat. Set the beets on the steamer rack, insert the rack into the steamer, cover, lower the heat to medium, and steam for about 15 minutes, or until the beets are tender but firm, not soft. Remove them with tongs, place on a plate, and let sit until cool enough to handle.

Scrape the skins off with a small paring knife. Cut each beet into quarters, then slice into ⅛-inch-thick wedges. Place in a medium bowl and mix in the olive oil and lime zest.

Bring the lime juice, sugar, salt, and green peppercorns to a boil in a saucepan over medium heat and cook, stirring, for about 2 minutes. Turn off the heat, add the beets, and cool.

Refrigerate the beets overnight in a tightly covered container before serving. *The beets will keep, refrigerated, for a week.*

Spicy Broccoli Rabe Relish

———————————————————(✿)———————————————————

Broccoli rabe is slightly bitter, with just a hint of mustard flavor. Lightly cooked with garlic and hot peppers, it keeps its texture and sharp taste. Serve in sandwiches or as a side dish with rich main courses, such as Roasted Squab with Port Wine Sauce (page 151), Pan-Seared Chicken Breasts with Morel Sauce (page 140), or Braised Pork Belly (page 172).

——————————————[*Makes 3 cups*]——————————————

1   bunch tender young broccoli rabe
3   tablespoons extra-virgin olive oil
1   small red onion, cut into small dice
2   garlic cloves, minced

2   jalapeño peppers, stemmed and cut into $1/8$-inch-thick slices
Kosher salt and freshly ground pepper

Wash the broccoli rabe, drain in a colander, and trim off the bottom ends of the stems. Spread out on several layers of paper towels and dry for about 15 minutes.

Place 2 stalks of broccoli rabe side by side with the stem ends even on a cutting board and, with a sharp knife, cut into ¼- to ⅛-inch dice, starting with the stems and moving up to the tips. Repeat with the rest of the broccoli rabe. Place in a bowl.

Heat the oil in a large skillet or flat-bottomed wok over high heat. Add the onion, garlic, and jalapeños and cook, stirring, for about 2 minutes, until soft. Add the broccoli rabe and continue to cook, stirring, until it begins to wilt, about 2 minutes. Turn off the heat and sprinkle with salt and pepper to taste.

Spoon the broccoli rabe out onto a large plate and cool. Serve at room temperature or store in a tightly covered container in the refrigerator and serve cold. *The relish will keep, refrigerated, for about a week.*

Pickled Napa Cabbage

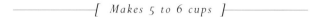

Because of the severely cold weather in Inner Mongolia and Manchuria, it's hard to grow fresh vegetables except during the brief summer season. Root vegetables are stored in cellars or preserved by sun-drying or pickling for use throughout the winter. One of the most famous pickled vegetables from this region is Manchurian sour cabbage. The women harvest Tientsin cabbage in the fall; this variety is from the same family as napa cabbage, but the leaves are much more loosely packed, and it is sweeter and crisper. The women cut the cabbages in half and layer them with salt, packing them tightly in huge urns. Then they fill the urns with cold water to eliminate air, which would cause the cabbage to rot, and weight it down with stones. After a couple of months, the cabbage ferments and becomes sour.

This quick and easy version is similar to the original in taste, but it is ready to eat in hours, not weeks.

{ Makes 5 to 6 cups }

2   pounds napa cabbage

2   tablespoons sugar

2   tablespoons plus 2 teaspoons kosher salt

1   cup white vinegar

Remove and discard the tough outer leaves of the cabbage. Slice off and discard the bottom of the stem. Cut the cabbage in half lengthwise and discard the core.

Rinse the cabbage well and drain. Slice crosswise into very thin strips and pack into a large container with a tight-fitting lid.

Place the remaining ingredients and 3 cups water in a medium saucepan and bring to a boil over high heat. Pour over the cabbage, pushing down on the cabbage to cover it with the hot liquid.

Cool to room temperature, then cover and refrigerate for at least 6 hours, or overnight, before serving. *The cabbage will keep for up to 3 days, covered and refrigerated.*

Napa Cabbage

Napa cabbage originated in northern China. It's a tender, large, tightly packed head of cabbage, with creamy yellow-white crinkled leaves and a mild yet distinct flavor. It is extremely versatile, for it can be eaten raw or cooked. Raw, it makes good coleslaw and can be used in salads or for pickling. When quickly stir-fried, it is even tenderer and sweeter. It's good added to soups and becomes meltingly soft when braised with meats or game. The wide leaves are also excellent for stuffing or wrapping around meat or vegetables to be braised or steamed. ✿ Although you can find napa cabbage year-round in most supermarkets, the best season for it is from fall to spring. ✿ Look for compact heads with white stems and firm, tightly closed creamy white leaves. Avoid napa cabbage with green leaves, which are usually bitter and tough. And never buy cabbage with black spots, as it will spoil quickly. Store, unwashed, in a plastic bag in the refrigerator; it will keep for 1 to 2 weeks.

Cucumber Mint Relish

Long, thin English cucumbers are best for this sweet-and-sour relish because they have fewer seeds than regular cucumbers and their skins are not coated with wax.

[*Makes about 2 cups*]

- 1   tablespoon white vinegar
- 1   tablespoon sugar
- 1   English cucumber
- 1   jalapeño pepper or Italian long hot pepper, stemmed and thinly sliced
- 1   teaspoon kosher salt
- ¼   cup fresh mint leaves, julienned

Put the vinegar and sugar in a small glass bowl and heat in a microwave oven at high power until the sugar is dissolved. Or heat in a small saucepan over low heat for about 1 minute. Cool.

Cut off both ends of the cucumber and discard; cut the cucumber in half crosswise, then in half lengthwise. Using a Japanese Benriner, mandoline, or sharp knife, thinly slice the cucumber crosswise. Place in a small bowl, along with the hot pepper and salt. Mix well and let sit for 10 minutes.

Pour the cucumber mixture into a strainer and gently press with your hands to drain off any liquid. Return to the bowl and mix in the cooled vinegar mixture and the mint.

Cover and refrigerate until ready to use. *The relish will keep overnight, but it is best the day it is made.*

Cucumbers

In 1968, when I was a newlywed living in Pittsburgh, I was thrilled to be doing my own cooking for the first time. I hunted in local supermarkets for the wonderful cucumbers that I grew up with but was disappointed to find nothing but large, seedy specimens with tough skins and little taste. I never bought them again. Luckily, English (hothouse) cucumbers, wrapped in plastic, can now be found in just about every supermarket. Although they are usually more expensive than the standard variety, they are much better, for their skins are thin and they are virtually seedless. During the summer, homegrown Kirbys (small pickling cucumbers) are available in farmers' markets. Kirbys are short and thick with greenish white skins; I peel these even though they are not coated with wax. The flesh is more pale green than white, and the cucumbers are pleasingly crisp.

Red Onion Relish

(❋)

These lightly caramelized onions coated in a soy-sugar glaze can be layered into a sandwich or mixed into almost any green salad. They are also great served alongside grilled meats or roast turkey.

[Makes about 1½ cups]

1	pound (1 large or 2 medium) red onions	½	teaspoon kosher salt
3	tablespoons dry white wine	2	tablespoons olive oil
1	tablespoon soy sauce	1	large garlic clove, thinly sliced
1	teaspoon sugar		

Cut the onions in half crosswise, then into thin slices, and separate the layers.

Combine the wine, soy sauce, sugar, and salt in a small bowl and stir until the sugar is dissolved.

Heat the oil in a large nonstick saucepan over high heat. Add the garlic and cook, stirring, for 1 minute. Add the onions and cook, stirring, for about 5 minutes, or until soft. Pour in the soy sauce mixture and cook for another minute, stirring constantly to coat the onions with the mixture. Remove from the heat and cool.

When cool, place in a container, cover, and refrigerate. Serve cold. *The relish will keep, refrigerated, for 1 to 2 weeks.*

Red Pepper Coulis

This coulis blends the smoky-sweet flavor of roasted red bell peppers with the heat of a hot chile pepper, creating a concentrated, colorful sauce for grilled fish or chicken, or even pasta. The coulis also makes a beautiful color and flavor contrast to White Corn Soup (page 38) when drizzled over the top.

Makes about 2½ cups

¼ cup olive oil

¼ cup chopped shallots

1 garlic clove, minced

1½ teaspoons tomato paste

1 fresh hot red pepper, stemmed

2 red bell peppers, roasted, peeled (see page 110), and cut into 1-inch chunks

3 cups chicken stock

Kosher salt

Heat the oil in a medium saucepan over medium heat. When it is hot, add the shallots and garlic and cook, stirring occasionally, for 30 seconds. Stir in the tomato paste and hot pepper and cook, stirring, for another minute. Add the roasted peppers, pour in the stock, and bring to a boil. Turn the heat to low and simmer, uncovered, for 20 minutes, or until all the vegetables are soft.

Cool slightly, then puree in a food processor or a blender. Season to taste with salt. Serve at room temperature. *The coulis can be refrigerated, covered, for 2 to 3 days or frozen in a tightly covered container for up to 2 months.*

Pan-Roasted Poblano Peppers

(✿)

In late summer, when poblanos are ripe, my mother-in-law pan-roasts them so they take on a rich flavor. I roast them with jalapeños to give them added heat, since poblanos are milder than most other hot peppers. Caramelizing them in a soy, vinegar, and sugar mixture brings out their smoky taste.

If you have difficulty finding fresh poblanos, substitute Italian long hot peppers. Serve with Smoked Duck Breasts (page 160), Simple Grilled Duck Breasts (page 159), or Braised Lion's Head Meatballs (page 164), or use as a sandwich filling.

{ Makes about 1 cup }

5	poblano chiles (about 1 pound), stemmed
2	jalapeño peppers, stemmed (optional)
2	tablespoons extra-virgin olive oil
2	garlic cloves, halved

1	tablespoon soy sauce
1	tablespoon balsamic vinegar
½	teaspoon sugar

Cut off and discard the tops of the poblanos and remove the seeds. Cut each chile lengthwise to make 6 long triangular pieces. If using jalapeños, cut them lengthwise in half and remove the seeds.

Heat the oil in a large skillet or flat-bottomed wok over high heat. Add the garlic and peppers, turn the heat to medium, and sear the peppers, turning frequently, until they are soft, 10 to 12 minutes.

Add the soy sauce, vinegar, and sugar. Remove from the heat and cool. Some of the skin may loosen and come off the peppers; if so, discard the skin.

Store in a tightly covered container, refrigerated. Serve cold or at room temperature. *The roasted peppers keep well for 1 to 2 weeks in the refrigerator.*

Poblano Chiles

Most commonly found in the market when they are dark green in color, poblanos are triangular, 2 to 3 inches wide at the top and 4 to 5 inches long. They have a mildly spicy taste and few seeds. Their season is summer to early fall. By late summer, ripe poblanos turn reddish brown and are at their peak of flavor.

Sun-Dried Tomato Chutney

This chutney pairs the contrasting textures and flavors of soft yet chewy sun-dried tomatoes, which have an intense, almost smoky flavor, with the clean, fresh taste of vine-ripened tomatoes.

Serve with Grilled Lamb Chops with Roasted Sesame Marinade (page 185), over a plain green salad, or with sandwiches.

Makes about 2 cups

3   tablespoons olive oil

1   shallot, minced

2   ounces sun-dried tomatoes halves (about 12 pieces), cut into ¼-inch dice

2   large firm vine-ripened tomatoes (about 1 pound), peeled (see page 123), seeded, and cut into ¼-inch dice

1   jalapeño pepper, stemmed, seeded, and finely chopped

1   tablespoon balsamic vinegar

1   teaspoon sugar

2   tablespoons chopped fresh cilantro
    Kosher salt and freshly ground pepper

Heat the oil in a medium saucepan over medium-low heat. Add the shallot and cook, stirring, until soft, about 1 minute. Add the sun-dried tomatoes and cook, stirring, until they are totally coated with oil and heated through, about 1 minute. Remove from the heat and spoon into a medium bowl.

Mix in the fresh tomatoes, jalapeño, balsamic vinegar, sugar, and cilantro. Season to taste with salt and pepper and cool. Serve at room temperature or cold. *The chutney will keep, refrigerated in a tightly sealed container, for up to 2 weeks.*

Cranberry-Ginger Relish

Made with raw cranberries that have been softened in a sugary, gingery mixture, this fresh, crunchy relish is lovely served with tea-smoked duck or lamb or with roast chicken, duck, lamb, or venison.

Makes about 2 ½ cups

1   12-ounce bag fresh cranberries

¼   cup honey

½   cup sugar

1   serrano or jalapeño pepper, stemmed and minced

2   tablespoons minced peeled fresh ginger
    Grated zest of 1 large orange

½   cup orange juice

1   tablespoon extra-virgin olive oil
    Kosher salt and freshly ground pepper

Place the cranberries in a food processor and pulse until they are coarsely chopped; pour into a large bowl. Stir in the honey, sugar, chile pepper, ginger, orange zest, and juice. Stir in the olive oil and add salt and pepper to taste.

Refrigerate the relish, covered, for at least 12 hours, or overnight, to mellow the flavors. Serve cold. *The relish can be stored in the refrigerator for up to 1 month.*

Mango-Kumquat Relish

The tart, citrus flavor of kumquats blends beautifully with the soft sweetness of raw mango. Serve this brilliant orange relish alongside duck, grilled chicken, or grilled lamb.

[*Makes 3 cups*]

8 ounces kumquats (about 2 cups)

1 tablespoon julienned peeled fresh ginger

¼ cup sugar

3 star anise

1 firm but ripe mango, peeled, pitted, and cut into ¼-inch dice (about 2 cups)

Rinse the kumquats well. Slice into ¼-inch-thick rounds and remove the seeds.

Soak the ginger in a small bowl of cold water for a few minutes, then drain.

Place the sugar, ¼ cup water, ginger, and star anise in a small saucepan, bring to a boil over high heat, and cook, stirring, for 2 minutes, to infuse the liquid with the spices.

Add the kumquats and cook, stirring, for 2 minutes, or until barely tender. Cool, and discard the star anise.

Add the diced mango to the relish and mix well. Refrigerate, covered, and serve cold. *The relish will keep for 1 week or longer in the refrigerator.*

Kumquat Conserve

Star anise and ginger punctuate this lightly cooked conserve of raisins, pineapple, and tart, citrusy kumquats. Serve with chicken dishes, such as Crisp Roasted Poussin with Leeks and Potatoes (page 149) or Oven-Roasted Shantung Chicken (page 132), or with roast turkey or pork.

Makes about 2 ½ cups

12	ounces kumquats (about 3 cups)
½	cup orange juice
½	cup sugar
2	tablespoons chopped shallots
1	tablespoon minced peeled fresh ginger
2	star anise
½	teaspoon ground cinnamon
	Pinch of ground cloves
	Pinch of kosher salt
¼	teaspoon freshly ground pepper
¼	cup chopped raisins
½	cup chopped fresh pineapple

Rinse the kumquats well. Cut them into very thin slices, about ⅛ inch thick, and remove the seeds.

Place the orange juice, sugar, shallots, ginger, star anise, cinnamon, cloves, salt, pepper, and raisins in a medium saucepan and mix well. Bring to a boil over medium heat and cook for 5 minutes, or until the raisins are soft and the liquid is syrupy.

Add the kumquats and pineapple and cook, stirring, for 2 minutes. Cool, then remove and discard the star anise.

Spoon the conserve into a glass jar and store, covered, in the refrigerator. Serve cold. *The conserve will keep, refrigerated, for up to 1 month.*

Kumquats

The kumquat is a tiny oval orange-yellow fruit native to eastern Asia. Its edible skin is sweet and the flesh is quite tart, with a bracing citrus flavor. Kumquats can be eaten raw but are most often candied, pickled, or used to make relishes, preserves, and marmalades.

🌀 Fresh kumquats are usually available from November to June. Look for firm fruit without blemishes. Refrigerated in a plastic bag, they will keep for 2 weeks or longer.

Forelle Pears

About the size of a Seckel pear, the Forelle is sweeter than all other varieties, with an intense perfume, a slightly crisp texture, and little of the graininess of a Seckel. It is available only from October through late winter. Like all pears, Forelles ripen well at room temperature. The green skin turns bright yellow, finally becoming a beautiful reddish gold. The ripening process can take several days. For best results, place them in a closed paper bag.

Ginger Pickled Pears

———————— (✿) ————————

These pears are served whole, so select the smallest ones you can find. If Forelle pears are not available, you can substitute Seckel pears. Serve alongside Wuxi-Style Braised Beef Short Ribs (page 177), Nanking Salt-Brined Duck (page 156), or Roast Chicken with Peppercorn Rub (page 135). They're also good for dessert.

———————[*Serves 4 to 6*]———————

Zest of 1 lime, removed with a small knife or peeler and cut into ⅛-inch-wide julienne

1 2-inch piece young or spring ginger or peeled regular fresh ginger, julienned

1 cup sugar

½ cup fresh lime juice

3 whole cloves

10 firm Forelle pears (see above), peeled

Bring a large saucepan of water to a boil over high heat, add the lime zest and ginger, and boil for 2 minutes.

Drain, and return the zest and ginger to the saucepan. Add the sugar, lime juice, and cloves, stir, and bring to a boil over medium heat. Cover and simmer until the sugar is dissolved, about 5 minutes, stirring once.

Add the pears. Using a spoon, gently toss the pears in the syrup for 1 minute, then add water to cover. Place a sheet of parchment paper on top of the pears and turn the heat to low. Return the liquid to a simmer and poach the pears until they are just tender, 5 to 30 minutes, depending on their size and ripeness. Test with a small knife after 5 minutes and continue to test them every 5 minutes or so, until they are tender.

Remove from the heat and cool in the syrup. Serve warm, at room temperature, or cold.

Store the pears in the syrup; they will keep, covered and refrigerated, for up to a week.

Pickled Rhubarb with Ginger

In the spring and early summer, you can find fresh young ginger in most Chinese grocery markets. The skin is translucent, and the fingers are pale brown with purplish tips. Fresh ginger is much more delicate than mature winter ginger, with very little fiber and a mildly spicy taste, and you don't need to peel it.

Grenadine enhances the beautiful red color of this relish, but you can omit it if you like.

Serve pickled rhubarb with roasted duck, chicken, pork, or venison.

[Makes 2 cups]

1   pound rhubarb, preferably strawberry rhubarb
1   2-inch piece young or spring ginger or peeled regular fresh ginger

½   cup sugar
½   teaspoon kosher salt
1   tablespoon grenadine (optional)

Cut off the leaves and both ends of the rhubarb stalks and discard. Wash well and pat dry. Using a sharp knife, thinly slice the rhubarb into half-circles about ⅛ inch thick. Place in a large bowl.

Using a Japanese Benriner, mandoline, or sharp knife, thinly slice the ginger. Soak in a small bowl of ice water for 5 minutes, then drain well.

Bring 6 quarts water to a boil in a large pot or kettle. Pour over the rhubarb and let sit for 1 minute, then pour it into a colander, shaking to drain well. Return the rhubarb to the large bowl.

Place ½ cup water, the sugar, salt, and ginger in a small saucepan and bring to a boil over high heat. Cover and cook over low heat for 5 minutes.

Pour the sugar syrup over the sliced rhubarb. Add the grenadine, if using, stir, and cool. Serve cold or at room temperature. *The relish will keep, stored in the refrigerator in a tightly closed container, for 2 weeks.*

Spicy Pickled Plumcots

———————————(✿)———————————

The plumcot, a new variety, is a cross between a plum and an apricot, with smooth, paper-thin, white-tinged burgundy skin and deep red, succulent flesh. I think it's better than either parent fruit, having an almost perfect sugar-to-acid balance. Because of its extraordinary flavor, the plumcot is becoming more popular in the marketplace.

———————[*Makes about 6 cups*]———————

- 2 cups sugar
- 3 star anise
- 1 3-inch piece fresh ginger, peeled and julienned
- 2 fresh hot red peppers
- 2 pounds ripe but very firm plumcots (see above)

Place 2 cups water, the sugar, star anise, ginger, and hot peppers in a 3-quart saucepan and bring to a boil over low heat, stirring until the sugar is dissolved. Simmer, uncovered, for 15 minutes. Remove from the heat and cool.

With a sharp paring knife, peel the plumcots and cut each into 8 wedges. Place in a container with a tight-fitting cover.

Pour the cooled syrup over the plumcots. Cover and refrigerate for at least 4 hours, or overnight. Serve cold. *The plumcots will keep, refrigerated, for up to a week.*

Desserts

Almond Cookies

(✿)

Light, flaky, crunchy, and fragrant, these are infinitely better than the traditional cookies served in many Chinese restaurants. Use blanched almond flour to keep them light in color. You can find it in specialty stores or order it by mail (see sources, page 321).

Makes about 24 cookies

1	cup all-purpose flour
½	cup almond flour
2	tablespoons sugar
8	tablespoons (1 stick) cold unsalted butter, cut into small pieces
½	teaspoon vanilla extract
1	tablespoon amaretto
½	cup confectioners' sugar

Preheat the oven to 325 degrees. Butter or spray two baking sheets.

Place the flours and sugar in a food processor and pulse to mix. Add the butter, pulsing until well blended. Add the vanilla and amaretto and pulse to blend. The dough will be loose and powdery-looking, but it will hold together when shaped. Transfer to a bowl.

With your hands, roll level tablespoon-sized portions of the dough into balls and place on the greased baking sheets about 2 inches apart. Bake until lightly golden, about 25 minutes, reversing the baking sheets, and switching positions halfway through to ensure even baking.

Meanwhile, sift the confectioners' sugar into a small bowl.

Let the cookies cool for a minute or so on the baking sheets, then remove and roll them in the confectioners' sugar and place on a rack to cool for 10 to 15 minutes.

Roll in the sugar again and return to the rack. *The cookies can be stored in an airtight container for up to 3 days or frozen for up to 3 months.*

Nut Flours

Made from the "cake" that remains after oils are pressed from nuts, nut flours add extra flavor to baked goods and are great for breading fish or chicken. Since they contain no gluten, they cannot be substituted for the entire portion of all-purpose flour in baked goods. Nut flours go bad quickly; store in sealed containers in the refrigerator for up to 3 months or in the freezer for up to 6 months. They are available in specialty food stores or can be obtained by mail (see sources, page 321). ✿ You can make your own version of nut flour by processing whole nuts until finely ground, then sifting them to remove any large particles. Be careful not to process the nuts for too long, or you will end up with nut butter.

Sesame Tuiles

———— (✦) ————

Terrific alone, these crunchy, crisp tuiles are even better when filled just before serving with Lychee and Lemon Thyme Sorbet (page 316) or any sorbet or ice cream.

For a fancy presentation, scatter a few fresh berries around them on the plate, garnish with a sprig of mint, and add a dollop of sweetened whipped cream.

Bake only one pan of cookies at a time, since they must be shaped while still warm.

———— [*Makes 12 tuiles*] ————

1½	cups confectioners' sugar
7	tablespoons unsalted butter, softened
¾	cup sesame seeds

½	cup cake flour
½	cup orange juice

Preheat the oven to 325 degrees. Line a baking sheet with parchment paper or a Silpat liner. If you don't have a cone-shaped metal mold to shape the cookies, crumple a ball of aluminum foil into a 6-inch-long cone, 3 inches at the widest part.

Combine all the ingredients in a medium bowl and mix together with an electric mixer on low speed just until smooth.

Using a narrow metal spatula, spread about a heaping tablespoon of batter into a 5-inch circle on the prepared baking sheet. Repeat to make a total of 3 cookies, spacing them at least 2 inches apart (the cookies will spread).

Bake for 8 minutes, or until lightly golden. Remove from the oven and let sit for 2 minutes on the baking sheet. One at a time, lift off the cookies while still warm and roll them around the mold or foil to shape into cones; leave them on for 1 to 2 minutes, until they harden a little, then slip off and place on a rack to cool. If the cookies become too brittle to shape, return the baking sheet to the oven for a few seconds to soften them. Repeat with the remaining batter, allowing the cookie sheet to cool between batches. *The cookies can be stored in an airtight container at room temperature for up to 3 days.*

SIMPLE VARIATION

The cookies can also be shaped into cups. Drape over inverted glasses or small bowls and gently mold the cookies around them.

Gianduja Mousse

—(✿)—

Gianduja is high-quality chocolate to which finely ground hazelnuts have been added. It is available in milk or dark chocolate form. I use milk chocolate for this recipe, since I prefer a lighter-flavored mousse. Callebaut and Cote d'Or both make gianduja milk chocolate. It can be found in specialty stores or ordered by mail (see sources, page 321).

—[*Serves 6*]—

5 ounces gianduja milk chocolate, chopped into pieces about the size of chocolate chips (¾ cup)	6 large egg yolks
2 cups heavy cream	¼ cup sugar

Melt the chocolate in a small bowl set over a pot of simmering water, stirring often, until completely smooth. Or melt in a microwave oven on the defrost cycle for 1 to 2 minutes.

Whip the cream in a large bowl until soft peaks form. Cover and refrigerate.

Place a heatproof bowl (or the bowl of an electric mixer) over a pot of simmering water. Place the egg yolks and sugar in the bowl and whisk until warm and slightly thickened, 2 to 3 minutes. Remove from the heat and beat with an electric mixer on medium speed until thick and cool, 5 to 10 minutes.

Fold the whipped cream into the cooled yolk mixture. Pour the warm melted chocolate into the bowl and fold in, using a rubber spatula.

Pour the mousse into six ramekins or wineglasses and refrigerate for 4 to 6 hours before serving.

SIMPLE VARIATION

If you can't locate gianduja chocolate, melt 1 tablespoon Nutella (found in supermarkets near the peanut butter) along with 5 ounces good-quality milk chocolate, such as Callebaut.

Lime Mascarpone Mousse

This refreshingly light mousse is the perfect ending to a hearty meal such as Star Anise Duck and Soybean Stew (page 161), Slow-Roasted Salmon and Israeli Couscous (page 100), or Braised Pork Belly (page 172). It is great for entertaining, as it must be made a day ahead of time.

[Serves 6 to 8]

1½ tablespoons powdered gelatin (from 2 envelopes)	6 large eggs, separated
6 tablespoons unsalted butter	¾ cup plus ⅓ cup sugar
Grated zest of 2 limes	½ cup mascarpone cheese
½ cup fresh lime juice	1 cup heavy cream

Sprinkle the gelatin over ⅓ cup water in a small glass bowl and soak for a few minutes, until softened. Stir, then heat for a few seconds in a microwave oven on medium power to dissolve the gelatin. Or warm in a small saucepan over very low heat, stirring, for a minute, just until the gelatin is dissolved (do not boil). Cool.

Place the butter, lime zest, and juice in a small saucepan and heat over low heat just until the butter melts; do not boil. Remove from the heat.

Place the egg yolks in a medium heatproof bowl, add the ¾ cup sugar, and beat with an electric mixer until thick. Pour in the hot lime juice mixture, beating constantly. Place the bowl over a pot of simmering water and continue to beat, using the mixer or a wire whisk, until thickened, 4 to 5 minutes. Add the gelatin mixture and stir until blended. Remove from the heat and beat until cool, 5 to 10 minutes.

In a large bowl, whip the mascarpone with the cream until soft peaks form. Fold in the cooled egg yolk–lime mixture.

Place the egg whites in a clean grease-free bowl and whip until soft peaks form. Gradually add the remaining ⅓ cup sugar and beat until the whites are stiff and glossy.

Fold the egg whites into the lime mixture. Divide the mousse among six to eight ramekins or serving dishes. Refrigerate overnight before serving.

Mascarpone

A fresh white Italian cheese, mascarpone is made from cow's milk and has a high butterfat content (often 75 percent or more), which makes it luxuriously soft, smooth, and creamy. Its texture is similar to that of stiff whipped cream. You can find it in upscale grocery stores and specialty food shops. Stored in the refrigerator, it will keep for up to a week.

Coconut Panna Cotta with Coconut Tapioca Sauce

———————(⟡)———————

This light, smooth Italian dessert takes on a Chinese accent with the addition of coconut milk and a coconut tapioca sauce, becoming even creamier and richer. Although wonderful when paired with the tapioca sauce, it is delicious with a simple topping of fresh diced or oven-roasted pineapple, sliced fresh strawberries, or any berries in season.

———————[*Serves 6*]———————

1	cup heavy cream
¼	cup sugar
1	envelope powdered gelatin
¾	cup plus 2 tablespoons whisked unsweetened coconut milk

Coconut Tapioca Sauce (recipe follows)
Oven-Roasted Pineapple (page 307) or ¾ cup diced fresh pineapple
Pineapple Granité (page 317; optional)

Place the heavy cream and sugar in a medium saucepan and heat over low heat just until the cream comes to a boil. Meanwhile, sprinkle the gelatin over 2 tablespoons water in a small bowl, stir, and let stand until softened.

Whisk the softened gelatin into the hot cream mixture, stirring until the gelatin dissolves completely. Remove from the heat and mix in the coconut milk; cool slightly, stirring occasionally.

When the panna cotta is lukewarm, pour about ½ cup of the mixture into each of six dessert dishes, wineglasses, plastic molds, or Styrofoam cups. Cover and refrigerate for at least 6 hours, or overnight.

If you used dessert dishes or wineglasses, spoon a little sauce over the top of each one. If you used plastic molds or Styrofoam cups, unmold the panna cotta into individual soup or dessert bowls and spoon the sauce around it.

Decorate with a few pieces of oven-roasted pineapple or 2 tablespoons of the diced, and top with a few spoonfuls of the granité, if using.

Coconut Tapioca Sauce

——————[Makes about 2 cups]——————

Served with a topping of mixed fresh berries, orange segments, sliced peaches, or nectarines, this sauce can stand on its own.

Be sure to use tiny tapioca pearls for this recipe, not larger pea-sized pearls or instant tapioca.

Parboiling the tapioca and then washing and draining it before cooking enables you to control the thickness of the sauce and keep it from becoming gummy and gluey, ensuring a much lighter and cleaner-tasting result.

2	tablespoons small tapioca pearls
¼	cup sugar
1	13.5-ounce can unsweetened coconut milk, whisked

Bring a medium saucepan of water to a boil over high heat. Add the tapioca, turn the heat to low, and simmer for about 15 minutes, or until the tapioca just begins to turn translucent; stir occasionally to keep it from sticking. Pour into a strainer to drain, rinse well under cold running water, and drain again. Immediately transfer to a small bowl (or the tapioca will stick to the strainer).

Combine the sugar and ¼ cup water in a medium saucepan and bring to a boil over medium heat, stirring until the sugar is dissolved. Stir in the coconut milk and tapioca and bring to a boil. Turn the heat to low and simmer for 10 to 12 minutes, stirring and scraping the bottom of the pan often to keep the tapioca from sticking, until the sauce begins to thicken and the tapioca is completely cooked.

Pour into a container and cool, then cover and store in the refrigerator. The sauce will thicken when cooled. *The sauce can be refrigerated, covered, for up to 3 days.*

Tapioca

Tapioca is a starch derived from the root of the cassava plant, native to the American tropics. The little white balls of pearl tapioca are made by forcing the moist starch from the root through special sieves. When cooked, the pearls become translucent, swelling and contributing body and a delightfully slippery texture, making for light desserts. ✿ Pearl tapioca comes in many different sizes; tiny pearls are the easiest and fastest to cook. (Although Pearl Milk Tea, sold in Asian markets all over the United States, is the most popular brand, its pea-sized pearls take longer to become tender and translucent, have a chewier texture, and do not absorb as much flavor from other ingredients.) Tapioca pearls are available in most supermarkets, health food stores, and Asian markets. Do not buy instant tapioca; it is not the same thing, and the results will be different.

Honeydew with Lime-Coconut Cream Sauce

Honeydew never tasted so good! The warm, creamy sauce with just a hint of coconut and lime enhances the fresh, crisp, cool green wedges. The sauce is also excellent with sliced ripe peaches.

[*Serves 6*]

½ cup whisked unsweetened coconut milk

½ cup half-and-half

Grated zest of 2 limes

2 large egg yolks

¼ cup sugar

1 teaspoon vanilla extract

1 tablespoon kirsch

½ honeydew melon, peeled, seeded, and cut into 12 thin wedges

Heat the coconut milk, half-and-half, and lime zest in a medium saucepan over low heat just until hot; be careful not to boil.

Meanwhile, beat the egg yolks and sugar in a medium bowl with an electric mixer until thick and light in color, 3 to 5 minutes. With the mixer on low speed, gradually pour the hot coconut milk into the egg mixture. Return the mixture to the saucepan and simmer, whisking constantly, until the mixture thickens slightly and coats the back of a spoon. Be careful not to overcook, or the eggs will curdle.

Strain the sauce into a bowl and stir in the vanilla and kirsch. Serve warm, at room temperature, or chilled. *The sauce can be made up to 2 days ahead and refrigerated, covered. Reheat in a double boiler or microwave oven, if desired.*

Spread a few spoonfuls of the sauce over the bottom of each of six dessert plates, top each with 2 wedges of honeydew, and serve.

Peach Crumble

This crumble is baked in individual portions. They unmold best when made in fleximolds, but any 3-inch molds or even muffin cups will work.

Serve the crumble with homemade peach ice cream or any premium peach or vanilla ice cream and some peach sauce and/or half a roasted peach if you like.

You can substitute nectarines for the peaches.

[Serves 6]

CRUST

½	cup plus 2 tablespoons all-purpose flour
3	tablespoons sugar
1	tablespoon firmly packed dark brown sugar
	Pinch of salt
4	tablespoons (½ stick) cold unsalted butter, cut into ½-inch pieces
1	large egg yolk
¼	teaspoon vanilla extract

CRUMBLE TOPPING

3	tablespoons all-purpose flour
3	tablespoons almond flour (see page 293)
3	tablespoons sugar
3	tablespoons firmly packed dark brown sugar
3	tablespoons cold unsalted butter, cut into ½-inch pieces
1	large peach, unpeeled, pitted and diced
	Peach Ice Cream (page 315)

OPTIONAL ACCOMPANIMENT

Peach Sauce (recipe follows), Oven-Roasted Donut Peaches (page 306)

TO MAKE THE CRUST: Place the flour, sugars, and salt in a food processor and pulse to mix. Add the butter and pulse until small crumbs are formed. Add the egg yolk, 1 teaspoon cold water, and the vanilla and pulse just until well blended.

Turn out onto a lightly floured surface and bring the dough together with your hands. Flatten into a round, wrap in plastic wrap, and refrigerate for at least 1 hour. *The dough can be made up to 2 days ahead.*

TO MAKE THE TOPPING: Place the flour, almond flour, and sugars in the food processor and pulse to mix. Add the butter and pulse until small crumbs are formed. *The crumble can be made up to 2 days ahead and refrigerated, well covered.*

TO ASSEMBLE THE CRUMBLE: Preheat the oven to 350 degrees. Cut the dough into 6 pieces. Shape into rounds, then flatten them with your hand and press 1 piece into the bottom of six 3-inch Silpat molds, nonstick muffin cups, or ramekins sprayed with vegetable spray. Top with the peaches and sprinkle each with about 2 tablespoons crumble.

Place the molds on a baking sheet and bake until golden brown, 35 to 40 minutes. Transfer to a rack.

The crumble can be baked ahead and unmolded once cool, wrapped well, and refrigerated for 2 to 3 days or frozen for up to 2 months. Thaw and/or reheat briefly in a 350-degree oven or warm in a microwave oven.

TO SERVE: Serve the crumble warm or at room temperature. Unmold onto individual plates or into soup bowls, then turn right side up. Serve with a scoop of ice cream. If desired, pour about ¼ cup sauce around each crumble and top with half a roasted peach.

SIMPLE VARIATION

The crumble can also be baked in a 7- or 8-inch springform pan and cut into pie-shaped wedges to serve. The baking time will be the same as for the individual crumbles.

Peach Sauce

Makes about 2 cups

For a quick and easy dessert, serve this over peach or vanilla ice cream or with pound cake, a few slices of ripe fresh peaches, and sweetened whipped cream.

2	medium peaches, unpeeled, halved and pitted
¼	cup Champagne or dry white wine
2	tablespoons sugar
½	vanilla bean, split and seeds scraped out
1	small cinnamon stick
	Pinch of salt

Place all the ingredients in a large saucepan, add 1½ cups water, and bring to a boil over high heat. Turn the heat to low and simmer for 20 to 30 minutes, or until the peaches are very soft.

Cool, remove the cinnamon stick and vanilla bean, then puree in a blender or food processor. Strain through a fine sieve. Cover and refrigerate for a few hours, or overnight, before serving.

Vanilla and Vanilla Beans

Vanilla beans have a richer, fuller flavor than vanilla extract. Grown in Madagascar, Indonesia, Mexico, and Tahiti, the different types vary slightly in flavor and fragrance. The best beans are oily to the touch, look sleek, and have a rich aroma. Avoid beans that have little scent or are brittle, dry, or mildewed. ✿ To cut open a bean, lay it flat on a cutting surface. Holding one end of the bean down, carefully slice it open lengthwise to expose its thousands of tiny seeds. Scrape the seeds from the pod, using the tip of your knife or a teaspoon. Depending on the recipe, you can use just the seeds or both seeds and pods. ✿ You can rinse and dry the pods after one use and save them to make vanilla sugar: store the dried pods in a jar of sugar (allotting 2 beans per pound of sugar) for a week or so before using the sugar. You can also grind the beans in a food processor along with some of the sugar called for in the recipe to add to baked goods. ✿ Stored in an airtight container in a cool, dark place, vanilla beans will keep for up to 2 years. Don't refrigerate them, as this can cause them to harden and crystallize. ✿ If using vanilla extract, do not add it to very hot cooked foods; allow them to cool a little first, or the flavor will evaporate. Never buy imitation vanilla; it is made from wood pulp by-products and has a harsh, chemical taste.

Oven-Roasted Donut Peaches

Glazing the peaches in the oven gives them a lovely golden color and a sweeter flavor. You can also serve the glazed peaches as a garnish alongside roasted meats or poultry.

[*Serves 3*]

3   donut peaches

2   tablespoons superfine sugar

Preheat the oven to 375 degrees. Wash the peaches well and dry. Do not peel. Cut them horizontally in half and remove the pits. Place on a baking sheet cut sides up and sprinkle with the sugar.

Bake for 5 minutes, or until tender and lightly glazed. Remove and cool before serving. Use the same day they are made, or the peaches will darken.

SIMPLE VARIATION

Ordinary small, firm peaches can be substituted for the donut peaches. Bake for 8 to 10 minutes.

Donut Peaches

Although fairly new to this country, the donut peach had its beginnings in China thousands of years ago. A variety of white peach, it is flat and doughnut-shaped (but with no hole), with a small, freestone pit about the size of a pistachio. Donut peaches are extremely juicy and sweeter than ordinary peaches. They are so unusual-looking that Chinese women often put a bowl of them on their dining room table as a centerpiece. Select brightly colored fruit without any traces of green, with no bruises, and with plump, smooth skins. A ripe donut peach will be very fragrant. Donut peaches are usually picked while still hard and will ripen best if left out on the counter for a few days or put in a brown paper bag to hasten the process. Don't refrigerate until they are fully ripe, and don't keep them in the refrigerator for more than a day or two. Like nectarines, they will lose juice and flavor if refrigerated too long. Like most other peaches, donut peaches are available in the summer months, from July through mid-August.

Oven-Roasted Pineapple

Roasting pineapple mellows its acid taste, and the butter-and-rum topping elevates it to greatness. Serve with Coconut Panna Cotta with Coconut Tapioca Sauce (page 298), Pineapple Sorbet (page 317), or Pineapple Granité (page 317). Or serve alongside grilled poultry.

[Serves 4 to 6]

1	2-inch section fresh pineapple, preferably Golden Pineapple
2	tablespoons butter
1	tablespoon dark rum

Preheat the oven to 350 degrees. Line a baking sheet with parchment paper. Peel the pineapple and slice into four ½-inch-thick rings. Slice the rings into quarters, remove and discard the core, and place on the baking sheet.

Melt the butter in a small saucepan over low heat. Or place in a small glass bowl and melt in a microwave oven. Mix in the rum.

Brush both sides of the pineapple generously with the rum-butter mixture. Bake for about 15 minutes, or until light golden brown, turning once. Serve warm or at room temperature.

Asian Pears

Also known as Chinese, Japanese, Oriental, sand, or apple pears, Asian pears are round and look more like apples than pears. Their skin is greenish yellow or russet, depending on the variety, and they are very juicy, with a crisp, crunchy, pleasantly gritty texture; they retain some of this texture when cooked. Unlike European pears, which are usually harvested green and allowed to ripen at room temperature, Asian pears are best if left to ripen on the tree, like apples and peaches. Since they are still hard when ripe, smell the fruit and choose the ones that are most aromatic. ⟳ Store ripe Asian pears in paper bags in the produce bin of your refrigerator. They will keep for several weeks.

Asian Pear Tatin

For these caramel-brushed inverted pear tarts, use small, firm Asian pears that are about 3 inches in diameter. Store-bought frozen puff pastry works very well for this recipe; thaw according to the instructions on the package. See page 319 for more details on making caramel.

[Serves 4]

¾ cup sugar

4 Asian pears

4 tablespoons (½ stick) unsalted butter, melted

8 ounces puff pastry

Vanilla ice cream, whipped cream, or crème fraîche for serving (optional)

Preheat the oven to 375 degrees. Place the sugar and ¼ cup water in a medium saucepan and stir. Heat over medium heat for 7 to 8 minutes until the sugar dissolves and the mixture caramelizes and turns a light amber color (320 degrees on a candy thermometer). Immediately pour the caramel into four 6-ounce ramekins.

Peel the pears. Check to see that they will fit into the ramekins; if they are too large, shave them down with a vegetable peeler or small paring knife. Core, using an apple corer to keep them whole.

Brush the pears all over with some of the melted butter and place each pear in a caramel-coated ramekin. Set the ramekins on a baking sheet and bake for 30 minutes.

Meanwhile, on a lightly floured surface, roll out the puff pastry to ¼ inch thick. Using a fork, prick the dough all over. Cut out 4 circles using a 3-inch cookie cutter. Or, using the bottom of a ramekin as a guide, cut out the circles with a small sharp knife.

Carefully remove the baking sheet from the oven, and brush the remaining butter on the exposed surfaces of the pears. Place 1 pastry circle on top of each pear and press down around the pear (be careful — the pears are hot). Return to the oven and bake for 35 to 40 minutes, rotating the pan, until the pears are soft when tested with a small knife and the crust is browned.

Place a cooling rack over a shallow baking pan. Remove the tarts from the oven and let sit for a few minutes. Then, very carefully, using a towel or pot holder and spatula, flip each tart out of the ramekin and onto the rack. Some of the caramel will drain into the bottom pan; pour into a small container and reserve.

Cool the tarts for 10 minutes, then brush the exposed surface of the pears with the reserved caramel. Serve warm, topped with vanilla ice cream, whipped cream, or a generous spoonful of crème fraîche, if desired.

(If the pears have cooled when you are ready to serve them, rewarm in a preheated 375-degree oven for a few minutes. Heat the reserved caramel in a microwave oven or a small saucepan until liquid and brush the exposed surface of the pears with a little of it to give them a shiny glaze.) The pears are best served the day they are made.

Almond Financiers with Kumquat–Fuyu Persimmon Sauce

These tiny French tea cakes, with slightly domed tops and lovely golden brown crusts, are soft and springy, fragrant with browned butter and almonds. They freeze beautifully and make a fabulous last-minute dessert, even without the sauce.

[Serves 10]

12	tablespoons (1½ sticks) unsalted butter, plus 1 tablespoon for greasing molds
½	cup all-purpose flour
½	cup almond flour (see page 293)

1¼	cups confectioners' sugar, plus more for dusting cakes
5	large egg whites
	Kumquat–Fuyu Persimmon Sauce (recipe follows)
	Crème fraîche or whipped cream (optional)

Preheat the oven to 325 degrees. Melt the 1 tablespoon butter. Using a pastry brush, lightly butter ten 3-inch (4-ounce) ring molds and dust them with flour.

Melt the remaining 12 tablespoons butter in a small saucepan over low heat and cook, shaking the pan occasionally, until light brown, about 5 minutes. Remove from the heat.

Sift the flours and confectioners' sugar together into a large bowl. With an electric mixer on low speed, gradually beat in the warm browned butter, scraping down the sides of the bowl to mix well. Slowly beat in the egg whites, beating until well combined.

Place the ring molds on a baking sheet lined with a Silpat liner or parchment paper and spoon the batter into them, filling them about three-quarters full. Bake for about 20 minutes, or until golden brown.

Loosen the cakes from the baking sheet by slipping a spatula under each mold, and transfer to a clean work surface. Run a small knife around the sides of each cake and slip off the ring molds.

The cooled cakes can be wrapped and refrigerated for 2 to 3 days or frozen for up to 3 months. Warm in a 325-degree oven before serving.

Dust each cake with a little confectioners' sugar and place on individual dessert plates. Spoon the sauce around the cakes and top with a small spoonful of crème fraîche or whipped cream, if desired.

SIMPLE VARIATION

If you don't have ring molds, you can use 4-ounce (3-inch) soufflé molds, baking or custard cups, or ramekins for the financiers. Butter the bottoms of the molds, line with circles of parchment paper, and then butter and flour the molds.

Kumquat–Fuyu Persimmon Sauce

———[Makes 2 cups]———

This bright-tasting, marmalade-like sweet-sour sauce of candied kumquats and lightly cooked crunchy persimmons is sensational over ice cream.

2	medium Fuyu persimmons (see page 155)
8	ounces kumquats
½	cup sugar
½	cup dry white wine
3	tablespoons light rum
½	teaspoon almond extract

Peel, quarter, and core the persimmons. Cut them into lengthwise slices, about 3 slices per quarter (you will have about 24 sections). Place in a bowl.

With a small sharp knife, quarter each kumquat. Remove the flesh from each section of the rind with your knife; reserve both separately.

Place the sugar, ¼ cup water, and the kumquat flesh in a small saucepan, bring to a boil over medium heat, and cook for about 5 minutes, stirring occasionally. Strain through a fine sieve, pressing down hard to remove all of the liquid. Return the liquid to the saucepan; discard the solids.

Return the saucepan to the heat, add the reserved rinds, and cook over low heat until they are tender, about 10 minutes. Add the white wine, rum, and persimmon slices and bring to a boil. Turn off the heat, add the almond extract, and cool.

Serve chilled or at room temperature. *The sauce can be refrigerated, covered, for up to 2 days.*

Apple Brioche Bread Pudding

—————————— (✿) ——————————

This lightly sweetened bread pudding, with a hint of five-spice powder, is moist and airy and melts
in your mouth. You can use any egg bread — I like brioche, but challah will also work well.

————————— [*Serves 6*] —————————

Sugar for dusting

1   brioche loaf (about 1 pound)

APPLE FILLING

1   large Granny Smith apple, peeled, cored, and cut into
¼-inch dice

1½–2 teaspoons sugar

¼   teaspoon five-spice powder

1   tablespoon unsalted butter

CUSTARD

⅓   cup sugar

½   teaspoon five-spice powder

3   large eggs

1⅔   cups whole milk

Caramelized Apple Puree (page 314; optional)

Sweetened whipped cream or vanilla or butterscotch ice
cream (optional)

Butter six large (½-cup) muffin cups or ramekins or an 8-inch round cake pan, and dust with sugar.

Slice off the brioche crusts. If using individual molds, cut six 3-inch rounds approximately ¼ inch thick. If using a cake pan, fit together enough pieces of crust to cover the bottom. Line the molds or pan with the crusts and set aside. (The crusts will make unmolding easier.) Dice the remaining bread into ¼-inch cubes; you should have 5 to 5½ cups.

TO MAKE THE APPLE FILLING: Toss the apple with the sugar and five-spice powder in a medium bowl. Melt the butter in a medium skillet over high heat. Add the apple and sauté for 1 to 2 minutes. Remove from the heat.

TO MAKE THE CUSTARD: In another medium bowl, mix the sugar and five-spice powder together, then whisk in the eggs and milk.

Layer the lined molds or cake pan alternately with the apple filling and the brioche cubes, making about 3 layers of each and ending with the bread cubes. Press down well with

your hand. Pour in the custard mixture and press down again with your hand or a large spoon. Let sit for about 20 minutes so the bread absorbs the custard.

Preheat the oven to 325 degrees. Place the muffin pan, ramekins, or cake pan in a baking pan. Fill with enough boiling water to reach halfway up the sides of the molds or pan and cover with a sheet of aluminum foil. Bake for 25 minutes. Uncover and bake for 10 to 15 minutes longer, until the custard is set and the tops are a light golden brown. Remove from the water bath and cool for about 10 minutes.

Invert individual puddings again onto the plates, crust side down. Invert the large pudding onto a platter, cut into wedges, and place on serving plates. Serve warm with, if you wish, a dollop of apple puree or whipped cream or a scoop of ice cream.

The cooled pudding can be wrapped well and refrigerated for 1 to 2 days; it can also be frozen for 3 months. Warm while still frozen in a 325-degree oven until hot.

Caramelized Apple Puree

———————(✿)———————

This caramelized puree accentuates the flavor of Apple Brioche Bread Pudding (page 313), and it makes a good light dessert on its own, served plain or with a dollop of sweetened whipped cream, crème fraîche, or sour cream. It also is an excellent accompaniment to pork and other savory dishes; I especially like it with sautéed foie gras.

———————[*Makes 1 ½ cups; serves 4*]———————

6 Granny Smith apples, peeled, cored, and chopped

2 tablespoons sugar

3 tablespoons unsalted butter

1 teaspoon minced peeled fresh ginger

2 tablespoons Calvados or applejack

Combine the apples, sugar, butter, and ginger in a large sauté pan or a deep skillet and cook over high heat, stirring often, until the apples begin to turn brown, 10 to 15 minutes.

Add ½ cup water, reduce the heat to medium-low, and simmer for another 20 minutes, stirring often to keep the apples from sticking and burning. The apples should be well browned and caramelized. Remove from the heat, add the Calvados or applejack, and cool for just a few minutes.

Puree the hot apples by passing them through a fine sieve into a small bowl; you can also pass them through a food mill fitted with a fine blade. Cool, then cover and refrigerate. *The puree will keep, refrigerated, for up to a week. Or freeze for up to 3 months.*

Peach Ice Cream

(❋)

If you've never made your own ice cream, you are in for a treat! You can find both manual and electric ice cream makers everywhere, and some of them are quite reasonable in price. It goes without saying that electric ones are much easier to use.

—[*Makes about 3 pints*]—

2	cups sugar		2	cups milk
1	tablespoon fresh lemon juice		2	cups heavy cream
1	1½-inch slice fresh ginger, crushed		1	vanilla bean
1	2-inch piece cinnamon stick		10	large egg yolks
4	ripe but firm large peaches, preferably yellow freestone			

To poach the peaches, place 2 cups water, 1 cup of the sugar, the lemon juice, ginger, and cinnamon stick in a saucepan just large enough to hold all the peaches. Bring to a boil over high heat, turn the heat to low, and simmer for 5 minutes to blend the flavors. Meanwhile, peel the peaches, leaving them whole.

Place the peaches in the simmering liquid, cover, and cook until tender, 10 to 12 minutes. Cool in the syrup. *The peaches can be poached up to 3 days ahead and refrigerated, covered, in the poaching liquid.*

Halve the peaches and discard the pits. Puree 2 of the peaches in a food processor or blender. Chop the remaining 2 peaches into small dice.

Pour the milk and cream into a large saucepan. Split the vanilla bean and scrape the seeds from it; add the bean and seeds to the pan. Slowly bring to a boil over low heat.

Meanwhile, in a large bowl, whip the egg yolks and the remaining 1 cup sugar with an electric mixer until thick and light in color and the mixture forms a ribbon when the beaters are lifted.

When the vanilla cream mixture comes to a boil, remove from the heat and whisk ½ cup into the egg mixture. Pour all the yolk mixture back into the hot cream, whisking constantly. Cook over low heat, stirring constantly with a wooden spoon, until the mixture coats the back of the spoon and holds a line drawn down the middle with your finger or the tip of a spoon (it should reach 185 degrees on an instant-read thermometer). Strain the custard through a fine sieve into a large clean bowl and cool, stirring occasionally, over a bowl filled with ice water. Discard the solids.

When the custard is cold, mix in the peach puree and the diced peaches. Freeze in an ice cream maker according to the manufacturer's directions.

The ice cream can be frozen for up to 2 weeks.

Lychee and Lemon Thyme Sorbet

(✿)

Lemon tempers the sweetness of the lychees, and lemon thyme adds an unusual, elusive touch. If
lemon thyme is not available, regular thyme can be substituted.

[*Makes 1 pint*]

1   15-ounce can whole pitted lychees in syrup

2   teaspoons honey

3   sprigs fresh lemon thyme

1   tablespoon fresh lemon juice

8   ounces fresh lychees, peeled and pitted (optional)

Fresh mint sprigs for garnish (optional)

Puree the canned lychees, with their syrup, in a food processor or a blender until smooth. Transfer to a 2-quart heavy saucepan, add the honey, lemon thyme, and lemon juice, and bring to a boil over high heat, stirring constantly. Boil for 1 minute, then remove from the heat and cool.

Pour the lychee mixture into a bowl, cover, and refrigerate overnight to infuse the mixture with the lemon thyme.

Strain the mixture through a sieve into a bowl, pressing well to extract all the liquid. Discard the solids. Freeze the mixture in an ice cream maker according to the manufacturer's instructions. *The sorbet can be stored, tightly covered, in the freezer for up to 3 days.*

Spoon the sorbet into a glass bowl and garnish with chilled fresh lychees and sprigs of fresh mint, if desired.

Lychees

Lychees have been grown in China for more than a thousand years. Sometimes spelled *litchee, lichi,* or *lichee,* this delicately sweet fruit is creamy white and slightly crisp. It is about the size of a walnut, with a thin reddish brown or purple rough shell that is easily removed: just tear it open at the stem end and pop out the fruit. Split the flesh in half and remove the inedible hard brown seed; it will slip out easily. ✿ Fresh lychees are available in summer in Asian markets and large supermarkets. Select bright, evenly colored fruit with moist-looking, undamaged skin. When the lychee is fully ripe, the skin turns a dull red-brown and its scaly texture flattens. Store in the crisper of the refrigerator for up to 3 weeks.

Pineapple Sorbet

This sorbet has an intense pineapple flavor, since the fruit is neither cooked nor strained out. Try to find Golden Pineapples, which are much sweeter than other varieties and fully ripened. (Pineapples do not continue to ripen once they are picked.) This variety, easily identified by its attached tag, has been trademarked by Del Monte and is grown in Hawaii.

Serve the sorbet with Sesame Tuiles (page 295), on top of Coconut Panna Cotta with Coconut Tapioca Sauce (page 298), or with fresh berries.

[Makes 2½ to 3 pints]

½ cup sugar

1 pineapple, preferably a Golden Pineapple (see above), about 3½ pounds

Bring ½ cup water and the sugar to a boil in a small saucepan over high heat, stirring to dissolve the sugar, and boil for 1 minute. Cool.

Peel, core, and slice the pineapple into chunks. Place in a food processor or a blender along with the cooled sugar syrup and process until smooth. (Depending on the size of your machine, you may have to do this in 2 batches.) Place in a covered container and refrigerate until well chilled.

Freeze in an ice cream maker according to the manufacturer's instructions. *The sorbet will keep for up to a week in the freezer, tightly covered.*

Pineapple Granité

[Makes about 1½ pints]

Halve the recipe. Instead of refrigerating the sorbet base, pour the mixture into a small rectangular pan, cover with aluminum foil or plastic wrap, and freeze for several hours, or until very firm.

To serve, scrape across the top of the mixture with a fork, gather the granité on a spoon, and transfer to small individual dessert bowls or wineglasses. Or use as a topping for Coconut Panna Cotta with Coconut Tapioca Sauce (page 298).

Pear Sorbet with Caramelized Pears and Poire William

Think of this dessert as pear with pear and more pear. Adding Poire William, a pear brandy, to the sorbet keeps it from freezing too hard and gives it a more pleasing texture.

─────── [*Serves 8*] ───────

POACHING SYRUP

1¹/₂ cups sugar

Grated zest and juice of 2 lemons

PEAR SORBET

9 large ripe but firm Anjou or Bartlett pears

1 cup sugar

3 tablespoons fresh lemon juice, or more to taste

2 tablespoons Poire William

CARAMEL SAUCE

1¹/₂ cups sugar

2–3 drops fresh lemon juice

Poire William for serving (optional)

TO MAKE THE POACHING SYRUP: Place 6 cups water, the sugar, and lemon zest and juice in a saucepan large enough to hold the pears. Bring to a boil over high heat, then turn the heat to low and simmer for about 20 minutes.

Meanwhile, peel the pears, cut them in half, and core them. Add the pears to the hot syrup and simmer just until tender. The amount of time will depend on the ripeness of the pears; begin to check after 10 minutes by piercing them with the tip of a sharp knife. As soon as they are tender, remove from the hot liquid with a slotted spoon. Reserve the syrup and cool. Set aside 5 of the pears for the puree.

Transfer the remaining 4 pears to a bowl, pour over the cooled syrup, cover, and refrigerate. *The poached pears can be prepared 1 to 2 days ahead and refrigerated. The poaching syrup can be saved to use again; freeze, covered, for up to 6 months.*

TO MAKE THE SORBET: Puree the reserved 5 pears in a food processor. Measure the puree; you will need 4 cups. If you don't have enough, add enough of the cool poaching syrup to make up the difference. Add the sugar, lemon juice, and the Poire William and pulse to blend. Pour into a bowl, cover, and refrigerate.

When the pureed pear is cold, place in an ice cream maker and freeze according to the manufacturer's instructions. *The sorbet can be stored, tightly covered, in the freezer for up to 2 weeks.*

TO MAKE THE CARAMEL SAUCE: Place the sugar and ½ cup water in a medium saucepan and stir to dissolve the sugar. Heat over medium heat until the mixture caramelizes and turns a light amber color. Remove from the heat and add the lemon juice. Cool, then pour into a small jar, cover, and refrigerate. *The caramel keeps well; any leftover caramel can be stored in the refrigerator for up to 1 month and used for other desserts.*

Foolproof Caramel

Traditional recipes for caramel call for washing down the sides of the saucepan with a pastry brush dipped in water to dissolve any sugar crystals, which can cause the caramel to crystallize. Instead, simply cover the caramel as it begins to cook. The steam that rises will dissolve any crystals clinging to the sides. ✿ Place the sugar and water in a saucepan and stir to dissolve the sugar. Cover with a lid. Heat, without stirring, over medium heat, lifting the lid occasionally to check, until the mixture just begins to turn color. Remove the lid and, shaking the pan frequently, watch the caramel like a hawk: once it starts to change color, the process will go very quickly and it can easily burn. When the caramel is ready (320 degrees on a candy thermometer), immediately remove the pan from the heat and use as directed.

TO SERVE: Drain the refrigerated pears well. Slice each half very thinly lengthwise, keeping the slices together.

Using a spatula, carefully place a sliced pear half on each of eight plates. Drizzle a little of the cold caramel sauce over the pears. Place a large scoop of sorbet next to the pears, pour 1 teaspoon Poire William over each portion of sorbet, if desired, and serve immediately.

Mail-Order Sources

ARC Greenhouses

P.O. Box 191
Shiloh, NJ 08353
(856) 451-3561
Fax: (856) 451-5129
www.arcgreenhouses.com
Micro-greens, baby greens, and herbs

Blue Moon Acres

P.O. Box 201
Buckingham, PA 18912
(215) 794-3093
Fax: (215) 794-2406
Micro-greens and baby greens

Bridge Kitchenware

214 East 52nd Street
New York, NY 10022
(212) 688-4220
Fax: (212) 758-5387
www.bridgekitchenware.com
All types of kitchen equipment

D'Artagnan

280 Wilson Avenue
Newark, NJ 07105
(800) 327-8246
Fax: (973) 465-1870
www.dartagnan.com
Game birds, Kobe beef, truffle oil

Earthy Delights

1161 East Clark Road, Suite 260
DeWitt, MI 48820
(800) 367-4709
Fax: (517) 668-1213
http://earthy.com
Imported Italian pasta, including artichoke pasta

Jamison Farm

171 Jamison Lane
Latrobe, PA 15650
(800) 237-5262
Fax: (724) 837-2287
www.jamisonfarm.com
Lamb

Kalustyan's

123 Lexington Avenue

New York, NY 10016

(212) 685-3451; (800) 352-3451

Fax: (212) 683-8458

www.kalustyans.com

Grains, rice, condiments, spices, nut flours

Nuts4U

P.O. Box 1864

Sugar Land, TX 77487

(800) 688-7482

Fax: (281) 277-2924

www.nuts4u.com

Nut flours

The Oriental Pantry

423 Great Road

Acton, MA 01720

(978) 264-4576

Fax: (781) 275-4506

www.orientalpantry.com

Sauces, seasonings, teas

Penzeys Spices

W19362 Apollo Drive

Muskego, WI 53150

(800) 741-7787

Fax: (262) 785-7678

www.penzeys.com

Spices and seasonings

Phillips Mushroom Farms

1011 Kaolin Road

Kennett Square, PA 19348

(610) 925-0520

Fax: (610) 925-0527

www.phillipsmushroomfarms.com

Specialty mushrooms

Sid Wainer & Son

2301 Purchase Street

New Bedford, MA 02746

(800) 423-8333

(508) 999-6408

Fax: (508) 999-6795

email: sales@sidwainer.com

www.sidwainer.com

Fresh vegetables and wild mushrooms

World Spice Merchants

1509 Western Avenue

Seattle, WA 98101

(206) 682-7274

Fax: (206) 622-7564

www.worldspice.com

Spices, herbs, and teas

World Wide Chocolate

P.O. Box 77, 116 Range Road

Center Strafford, NH 03815

(800) 664-9410

Fax: (800) 664-9410

www.worldwidechocolate.com

Specialty chocolates, including gianduja

Index

Note: page numbers in *italics* refer to recipe photographs.

beef
    carpaccio with Vietnamese vinai-
        grette, 31
    Korean-style grilled sirloin in pear
        jalapeño marinade, 180–81
    shaking filet mignon with sea scal-
        lops, 129
    short ribs, Wuxi-style braised, 177
    soup with somen noodles, 54, 55
    tenderloin, grilled, with rosemary
        soy marinade, 182
    tenderloin stew, quick-seared
        Sichuan, 178, 179
beet(s)
    golden, and arugula salad with cit-
        rus vinaigrette, 66, 67
    pickled baby, with green pepper-
        corns, 274
    rhubarb, and grapefruit salad, 78,
        79
Benriner, xiii
black sea bass, pan-seared, with
        caramelized red pepper sauce,
        110, 111
bok choy, baby
    about, 245
    crispy jumbo shrimp with
        caramelized orange sauce,
        119, 120
    sautéed, 244, 245
braising techniques, 170–71
brandy-infused hoisin sauce, 169
bread crumbs, Japanese-style, about,
        28
bread pudding, apple brioche, 313

bread pudding, chestnut, 215
brine, sake ginger, 102
brines, Chinese, 137
brioche bread pudding, apple, 313
broccoli rabe
    relish, spicy, 275
    and shiitakes, vegetable rice with,
        209
    with sun-dried tomatoes, 246, 247
    tomatoes, and artichokes, artichoke
        pasta with, 200
Brussels sprouts
    about, 92
    chestnuts, and Chinese sausage,
        stir-fried, 250, 251
    and portobello mushrooms, 248
    shaking filet mignon with sea scal-
        lops, 129
    Sichuan pickled, 91
buckwheat noodles, homemade, 201
butternut squash
    goo lai, 265
    roasted, soup, 40

C

cabbage
    braised lion's head meatballs,
        164–65
    cured ham, and roasted Fuyu per-
        simmons, stuffed quail with,
        152–54, 153
    napa, about, 277
    napa, gratin, baked, 258
    napa, pickled, 276

    napa, and sun-dried tomato salad,
        73
    red, and jicama salad with spicy
        dried shrimp vinaigrette, 74,
        75
Cantonese egg foo yung with crab-
        meat, asparagus, and bean
        sprouts, 234, 235
Cantonese salt-water chicken with soy
        ginger vinaigrette, 136
caramel, preparing, 319
caramel sauce, 318–19
carpaccio, beef, with Vietnamese
        vinaigrette, 31
carrots
    baby, and sugar snap peas, sautéed,
        252
    oven-roasted root vegetables, 270
    ten-vegetable vegetarian hot-and-
        sour soup, 36
cauliflower curry, spicy, 253
cauliflower risotto with wild mush-
        rooms, 212, 213
celery root
    about, 37
    oven-roasted root vegetables, 270
    roast chicken with peppercorn rub,
        135
    ten-vegetable vegetarian hot-and-
        sour soup, 36
cellophane noodles
    about, 90
    Chinese chive pancakes, 16
    Mandarin potato salad with,
        88, 89

peanut(s)
    cilantro pesto, 195
    and cilantro pesto, orzo with, 198
    pad Thai, 206–7
    sauce, spicy, warm crisp-fried tofu
        salad with fresh spinach and,
        222, 223
pear(s)
    Asian, about, 308
    Asian, Tatin, 308, 309
    Forelle, about, 286
    ginger pickled, 287
    jalapeño marinade, Korean-style
        grilled sirloin in, 180–81
    sorbet with caramelized pears and
        Poire William, 318–19
peas
    fingerling potato and green bean
        curry, 262, 263
    pressed tofu, and tomatoes, white
        corn with, 230, 231
    shrimp with lobster sauce, 122,
        123
    silken tofu and bay scallop soup, 49
    slow-roasted salmon and Israeli
        couscous, 99, 100–101
    soba noodles with ginger, scallions,
        and shrimp, 193
    sugar snap, about, 260
    sugar snap, and baby carrots,
        sautéed, 252
    sugar snap, with shiitake mush-
        rooms, 260
    wok-braised tofu with tomatoes
        and mushrooms, 221

pea shoots
    about, 52
    beef soup with somen noodles, 54,
        55
    duck wonton soup, 50, 51–53
    panfried skate with orange Pernod
        sauce, 116–18, 117
peppercorn, Sichuan, oil, 93
peppercorns, Sichuan, about, 93
pepper(s)
    bell, how to julienne, 187
    Chinese-style ratatouille, 268, 269
    Korean-style grilled sirloin in pear
        jalapeño marinade, 180–81
    poblano, about, 281
    poblano, pan-roasted, 281
    red, caramelized, sauce, pan-seared
        black sea bass with, 110, 111
    red, coulis, 280
    roasting and peeling, 110
    spicy pork tenderloin with
        poblanos and plums, 176
persimmons. See Fuyu persimmon(s)
pesto, cilantro, 195
pickled baby beets with green pepper-
        corns, 274
pickled Brussels sprouts, Sichuan, 91
pickled daikon salad with oranges, 80
pickled napa cabbage, 276
pickled pears, ginger, 287
pickled plumcots, spicy, 289
pickled rhubarb with ginger, 288
pineapple
    granité, 317
    kumquat conserve, 284, 285

    oven-roasted, 307
    sorbet, 317
pine nuts, toasted, and diced vegeta-
        bles, braised orzo with, 196,
        197
plumcots, spicy pickled, 289
plums and poblanos, spicy pork ten-
        derloin with, 176
poblano(s)
    about, 281
    peppers, pan-roasted, 281
    and plums, spicy pork tenderloin
        with, 176
polenta, creamy coconut, 216, 217
pompano, baked, with slow-roasted
        tomatoes, 114
pork
    belly, about, 173
    belly, braised, 172, 173
    braised lion's head meatballs,
        164–65
    butt, about, 165
    Chinese sausage, about, 250
    chops with spicy tomato sauce,
        166, 167
    lo mein with tomatoes and fresh
        herbs, 204, 205
    moo-shu, with fresh mushrooms,
        168
    stir-fried Brussels sprouts, chest-
        nuts, and Chinese sausage,
        250, 251
    stuffed quail with cabbage, cured
        ham, and roasted Fuyu per-
        simmons, 152–54, 153

sesame (seeds) (*cont.*)

tuiles, *294, 295*

Shanghai-style spring roll wrappers, about, *5*

Shantung chicken, oven-roasted, *132–34, 133*

shellfish. *See also* shrimp

Cantonese egg foo yung with crab-meat, asparagus, and bean sprouts, *234, 235*

coconut lobster sauce, *11*

lobster ravioli with soybean puree and coconut lobster sauce, *8–9, 9*

lobster stock, *57*

scallops, buying, *128*

seared scallops with mushrooms and creamy mushroom sauce, *125, 126–27*

shaking filet mignon with sea scallops, *129*

shrimp with lobster sauce, *122, 123*

silken tofu and bay scallop soup, *49*

warm asparagus, scallop, and arugula salad, *24*

shrimp

dried, about, *75*

dried, vinaigrette, spicy, red cabbage and jicama salad with, *74, 75*

ginger, and scallions, soba noodles with, *193*

grilled, with avocado and spicy papaya vinaigrette, *22*

jumbo, crispy, with caramelized orange sauce, *119, 120*

lobster ravioli with soybean puree and coconut lobster sauce, *8–9, 9*

with lobster sauce, *122, 123*

pad Thai, *206–7*

Sichuan, *124*

spicy seafood rice soup, *44*

wok-shaking, with pink peppercorns, *20, 21*

Sichuan beef tenderloin stew, quick-seared, *178, 179*

Sichuan peppercorn oil, *93*

Sichuan peppercorns, about, *93*

Sichuan pickled Brussels sprouts, *91*

Sichuan shrimp, *124*

soba noodles

about, *190*

cold, with lime coriander vinaigrette, *190, 191*

with ginger, scallions, and shrimp, *193*

somen noodles, about, *55*

somen noodles, beef soup with, *54, 55*

sorbet

lychee and lemon thyme, *316*

pear, with caramelized pears and Poire William, *318–19*

pineapple, *317*

soups. *See also* stocks

beef, with somen noodles, *54, 55*

chicken pumpkin, velvety, *46, 47*

coconut, with leeks and mushrooms, *42*

duck wonton, *50, 51–53*

roasted butternut squash, *40*

seafood rice, spicy, *44*

silken tofu and bay scallop, *49*

ten-vegetable vegetarian hot-and-sour, *36*

white corn, *38, 39*

soybean oil, about, *118*

soybean(s)

dried yellow, about, *232*

fresh green, about, *10*

milk, homemade, *232*

pressed tofu, and shiitake mushrooms, braised, *229*

puree, *10*

sesame-crusted halibut with mixed beans and Thai lemongrass sauce, *103, 104–5*

slow-roasted salmon and Israeli couscous, *99, 100–101*

and star anise duck stew, *160*

warm crisp-fried tofu salad with fresh spinach and spicy peanut sauce, *222, 223*

soy (sauce)

about, *138*

and ginger, salmon braised with, *98*

ginger vinaigrette, *138*

glaze, honey, *7*

rosemary marinade, grilled beef tenderloin with, *182*

spinach

crispy tuna spring rolls with fresh herb salad, *4, 5*

fresh, and spicy peanut sauce, warm crisp-fried tofu salad with, *222, 223*

panfried skate with orange Pernod
sauce, 116–18, *117*

shaking filet mignon with sea scallops, 129

soba noodles with ginger, scallions,
and shrimp, 193

spring rolls, crispy tuna, with fresh
herb salad, 4, *5*

spring roll wrappers, Shanghai-style,
about, 5

squab, roast, with port wine sauce,
151

squash. *See also* zucchini

butternut, goo lai, 265

butternut, roasted, soup, 40

kabocha, about, 48

velvety chicken pumpkin soup, 46,
47

squid, grilled, with endive and mango
salad, *29, 30*

star anise duck and soybean stew,
160

steaming techniques, 240

stew, quick-seared Sichuan beef tenderloin, *178, 179*

stew, star anise duck and soybean, 160

stir-frying principles, xv

stocks

duck, 58

lamb, 59

lobster, 57

mushroom, 56

vegetable, 56

striped bass, poached, with balsamic
vinegar sauce, 108–9

sugar, rock, about, 102

sweet potatoes

oven-roasted root vegetables, 270

roast chicken with peppercorn rub,
135

T

tamarind, about, 208

tamarind puree, 208

tapioca, about, 301

tapioca sauce, coconut, 300

taro root

about, 267

mashed, 266

pancakes, 266

tartare, salmon, 15

tempura batter, 121

terrine, jellied lamb, with cucumber
mint relish, *32, 33*

Thai curry paste, about, 107

Thai curry sauce, 113

Thai curry sauce, braised chicken
with, 144

Thai lemongrass sauce, 106

tofu

braised lion's head meatballs,
164–65

chili, 224

firm, about, 220

moo-shu pork with fresh mushrooms, 168

pad Thai, 206–7

pressed, about, 229

pressed, peas, and tomatoes, white
corn with, *230, 231*

pressed, shiitake mushrooms, and
soybeans, braised, 229

silken, about, 227

silken, and bay scallop soup, 49

silken, crispy panfried, with creamy
sun-dried tomato sauce, 225,
226

ten-vegetable vegetarian hot-and-
sour soup, 36

warm crisp-fried, salad with fresh
spinach and spicy peanut
sauce, 222, *223*

wok-braised, with tomatoes and
mushrooms, 221

tomato(es)

artichokes, and broccoli rabe, artichoke pasta with, 200

and asparagus salad, panko-crusted
goat cheese with, *26, 27*

braised red snapper with Thai curry
sauce, 112

Chinese long beans with toasted
almonds, 82, *83*

Chinese-style ratatouille, *268, 269*

cilantro pesto, and zucchini, pasta
with, 194

fingerling potato and green bean
curry, 262, *263*

and fresh herbs, pork lo mein with,
204, 205

grilled beef tenderloin with rosemary soy marinade, 182

and mushrooms, wok-braised tofu
with, 221

and parsnips, braised lamb blade
chops with, 183